MEGA MACHINES

MEGA MACHINES

THE BIGGEST MACHINES EVER BUILT
SHIPS • PLANES • TRAINS • CARS • ROCKETS • DIGGERS • CRANES • TRUCKS

Richard Gunn

Bath · New York · Singapore · Hong Kong · Cologne · Delhi · Melbourne

First published in 2007
Parragon
Queen Street House
4 Queen Street
Bath BA1 1HE, UK

Copyright © Parragon Books Ltd 2007

ISBN 978-1-4054-8655-2

Editorial and design by
Amber Books Ltd
Bradley's Close
74–77 White Lion Street
London N1 9PF
www.amberbooks.co.uk

Project Editor: Sarah Uttridge
Design: Zoë Mellors and Hawes Design
Picture Research: Kate Green

Printed in China

Contents

INTRODUCTION

ABOVE: Traditionally, electric cars have been small to help conserve power, but the developmental eight-wheeled Eliica electric car is practically the mass of a small truck. Is this the size of things to come?

CLOCKWISE FROM TOP LEFT: Shanghai Maglev train; Liebherr A974 B log loader; Mil Mi-24 Hind helicopter; Space Shuttle crawler; Cutty Sark.

Machines are everywhere these days. They characterize the modern world in fact, and have been largely responsible for creating our civilization as it is at the moment. Imagine life without all the various devices that we rely on these days—television, DVD players, home computers, washing machines, cars—and suddenly, the word "modern" seems no longer applicable. To lose the machines we now take so for granted is to take a giant leap back in time ... further back even than the nineteenth century, when mechanization first started to make its presence felt in everyday life.

But such is the quickening march of technology that most machines around us are getting smaller and smaller. The trend is towards more and more miniaturization: If something can be made tinier, easier to use, more compact to carry around, then somebody somewhere will be working on doing so. The recent electronic era has seen some equipment shrink to the point of the barely credible. Want to store several thousand songs on something the size of a small stock cube? No problem. Fancy taking photos with a digital camera much smaller than a conventional film canister? Easy these days. Want to put the complete works of Shakespeare on a small memory card? Simple enough ... and there'll still be lots of room to spare for several encyclopedia volumes as well.

Pocket-sized versus mega

But such pocket-sized equipment, as handy and intricate as it may be, isn't actually that awe-inspiring. A collection of plastic and wires doesn't have too much soul or charisma. For a machine to truly impress, it has to be big. Actually, bigger than big. Massive in fact—a genuine mega machine. And it has to do incredible things as well, in a manner that demonstrates how much raw power and brute strength lies beneath its imposing surface. And that's why this book has been written, as a celebration of some of the most epic machines and vehicles ever to have been built. There isn't much inside these pages that could be characterized as small, but a great deal that ticks the box marked "levanthian." From the fields of land, sea, air, and space, we've picked the greatest, most astonishing machines from history, enormous feats of engineering, both mobile and static, capable of performing spectacular tasks. In short, giants for which the usual reaction is usually nothing less than "Wow!" And deservedly so.

The world's largest

It's not enough for a machine to just be the second or third biggest of its type to be included in this book. We've searched out the absolute superlatives of their kind. It hasn't actually been that simple a task, gathering up hundreds of the planet's most awesome engineering creations. Finding out the largest ship, the largest airplane, the largest land vehicle, or the largest spacecraft is straightforward enough—such creations are justifiably famous and well-publicized. But try to come up with a long list of less obvious machines, and things start to get a bit more difficult. Where exactly is the world's biggest particle accelerator? How much grass can the planet's widest mower cut? All construction cranes are tall, but which one in particular stands head and shoulders above the rest? The answers aren't always obvious. In addition, many manufacturers lay claim to one of their products being the largest of its type, practically all will claim that theirs is also the best of course. Then there are the enthusiasts who love a particular machine, and make bold—and sometimes not strictly true—claims about just how remarkable it is. Sorting out the gargantuan from the merely huge has been a job

ABOVE: Air Force One is the President of the United States' Boeing 747 flying office, and is so large and well-equipped that the US Government can almost be run from the air.

LEFT AND FAR LEFT: AL Jon Inc Vantage Compactor and Spaceshipone.

almost as complicated as many of the machines in here.

But, hopefully, what you'll find within these pages is, as near as possible, a definitive tour of the past, present, and, in some cases, future, of mankind's greatest machines. Not all exist any more. And many of those that still do carry out their tasks well out of the view of the public, rarely glimpsed by anybody not directly involved with them. If you do get the chance to see the real things then seize it, because these revolutionary mega machines are little short of fascinating and awe-inspiring in the actual metal.

Even from a distance, most have the ability to astonish by how much they dominate the surrounding landscape, while up close, where their true scale becomes apparent, they're often little short of breathtaking. Those that do shy away from the limelight and are rarely glimpsed in action can at least be enjoyed here, from the comfort of your favorite chair, in words and pictures. Even in 2D form, they're still something to behold.

You'll never be quite as impressed by a small machine ever again…

ABOVE: Despite its size, this Mammoet crane, is a mobile unit, moved around the world to where it is needed, to lift the world's heaviest items.

TOP RIGHT AND RIGHT: The Hummer H1 and "Freedom of the Seas."

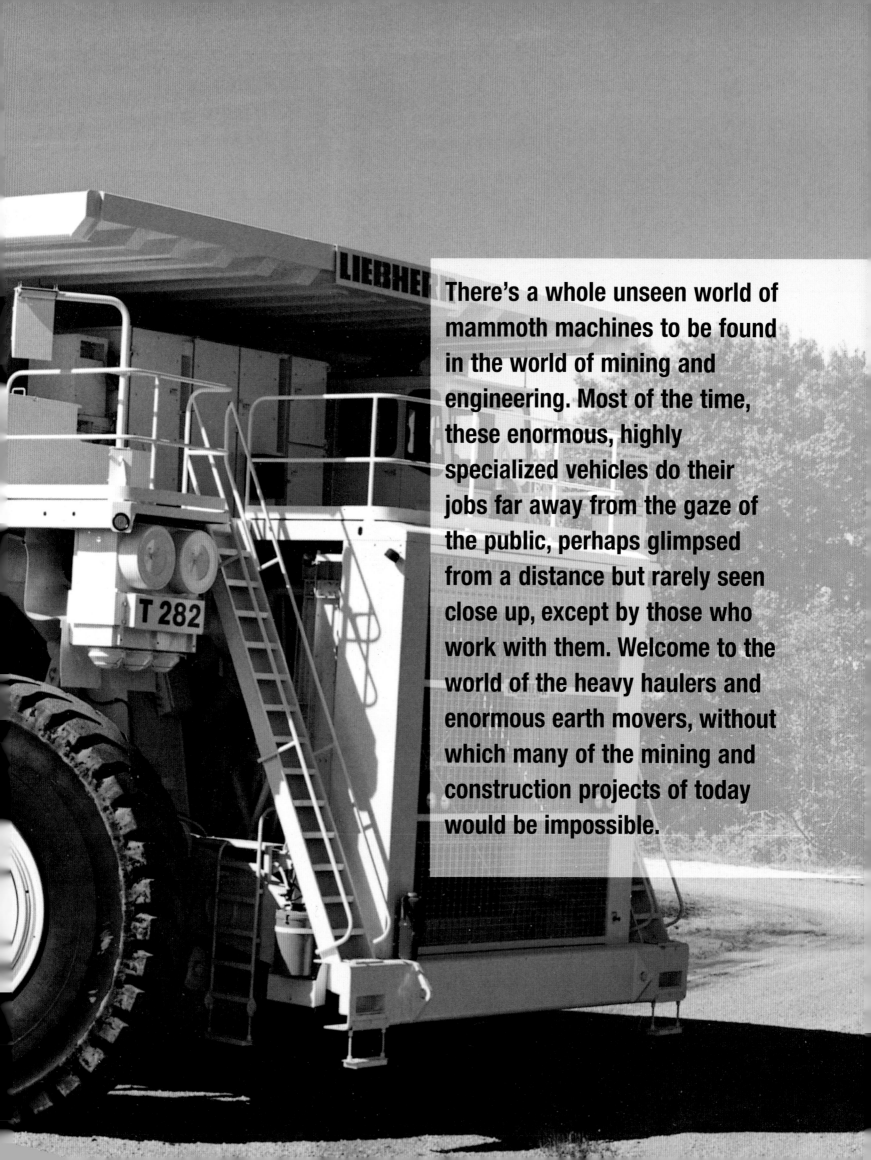

There's a whole unseen world of mammoth machines to be found in the world of mining and engineering. Most of the time, these enormous, highly specialized vehicles do their jobs far away from the gaze of the public, perhaps glimpsed from a distance but rarely seen close up, except by those who work with them. Welcome to the world of the heavy haulers and enormous earth movers, without which many of the mining and construction projects of today would be impossible.

The Terex Titan. You may never have heard of it, but if you were ever to see it in the metal, it's something you probably wouldn't forget. The aptly named Titan, only one of which was ever built, is the largest earth-moving truck of all time. Constructed in 1974, it spent most of its life working at a mine in Canada until retirement in 1990—at which point, its fame gave it a second life as a tourist attraction. Measuring 66ft (20m) long and 22.6ft (6.9m) tall, not even the monster trucks of today can surpass its proportions, even if they can now, just about, pip its 317.5 ton (317,515kg) capacity.

BELOW: The wide, long tunnels of today are made easier by giant tunnel boring machines like "Big Becky" here.

But the Titan is just one example of the many larger-than-life, but virtually unknown, machines found in modern mining and engineering operations. Fulfilling very different roles but comparable in their own scale to the Titan are vehicles such as Gomaco GP-5000 paver, capable of laying concrete surfaces up to 50ft (15.2m) in width. Then there's the ACCO crawler bulldozer of 1980, as high as a two-storey building, looking tougher than a tank, and another unique, one-off machine. The same Italian company also built the world's largest grader, with a 33ft (10m) blade to flatten rough surfaces, created for a project in Libya that had also required its bulldozer. It must have been quite some undertaking.

But even these were dwarfed by leviathans such the LeTourneau LT-360, a scraper—which cuts into the ground and then "scrapes" up the material into hoppers—featuring eight 635hp (473.5kW) engines and the ability to self-load 326.5 tons (326,586kg) into itself. It wasn't just the largest of its type ever, but also one of the biggest rubber-tired vehicles of all time. And in turn, the LT-360 was a mere toy compared to something like the Marion 6360 stripping shovel. Another single machine, and nicknamed the Captain, this 1965 electrically powered landscape chomper is still the largest vehicle to move under its own power on land. It would probably still be working today, had not fire claimed it in 1991. At 13,608 tons (13,607,771kg), it weighed the same as the

just-as-intimidating Bucyrus-Erie 4250-W dragline of 1969 named Big Muskie, another gargantuan excavator, but one that "walked" using huge metal feet rather than rolling on caterpillar tracks like the Captain.

But not every colossal engineering machine works above the surface. Next time you're in a long, recently built tunnel, consider what went into building it. More likely than not, it was excavated by a TBM—tunnel boring machine—which chews its way through the earth. At the time of writing, the largest hard rock TBM of all time—built by Robbins, the same company that made the TBMs for the Channel Tunnel between England and France— had just started work on a tunnel under the city of Niagara Falls in Canada. Its height: 47.2ft (14.4m). Its speed: 49.2ft (15m) per day. Its cost: $35 million. And its name: Big Becky.

ABOVE: The unique and enormous Terex Titan gave new meaning to the phrase "Monster Truck."

ABOVE: Once the job of
hundreds of workmen,
building canals these
days has been much
simplified by complicated
machines such as this.

RIGHT: Big Muskie
may have been massive,
but that didn't stop this
dragline being able
to "walk"—albeit
rather slowly!

You're looking at the biggest manmade vehicle on the planet. Nothing is larger than the Man Takraf RB293 bucket-wheel excavator—a huge engineering machine that's practically capable of eating mountains.

THE LARGEST LAND VEHICLE

MAN TAKRAF RB293 BUCKET-WHEEL EXCAVATOR

SPECIFICATIONS

Country: Germany

Year built: N/A

Dimensions: 722ft (220m) long; 310ft (94.5m) high

Capacity: Up to 65,616ft^3 (20,000m^3) per hour

Weight: 15,650 tons (14,196,000kg)

Maximum speed: 0.0012–0.006 miles (2–10m) per second

Cost: Upwards of $100 million

We'll get the specifications out of the way first, because the RB293 bucket-wheel excavator is a truly extraordinary mega machine. It weighs 15,650 tons (14,196,000kg). It is 722ft (220m) long and 310ft (94.5m) tall at its highest point. It is capable of shifting 8.475 million ft^3 (240,000m^3) of earth a day, and can dig up to a height of 164ft (50m). It's not the sort of vehicle you want to get in the way of!

Digging wheel

Used for opencast coal mining in Westphalia, Germany, the RB293's main task is to remove surplus material prior to coalmining operations. It does this via the large rotating 69ft (21m) wheel mounted on its front boom, which is equipped around its circumference with scoops. The over-burden falls onto a conveyer belt, which then carries it back, via a series of following tracked belts, behind the machine. To put how much soil and rock the RB293 can chomp through into perspective, its daily rate of clearance is the same as a football field dug down to a depth of 98ft (30m).

Such a vast feat of mobile engineering is beyond being moved by a conventional fuel-powered engine, so the machine is supplied externally by electricity, approximately 16,500 kilowatts being required for this task (or the power of 165,000 100-watt lightbulbs). Despite this immense strength, it covers distances very slowly indeed. In 2001, a similar machine made a 14 mile (22,5km) trip to another mine. It took the machine three weeks to get there.

ABOVE AND TOP: Pictures can't do the incredible size of the RB293 proper justice, although some idea of its 69ft (21m) cutting wheel and the lengthy conveyer belt that carries the waste material can be gauged from these shots.

THE LARGEST DUMP TRUCK (DIESEL ELECTRICAL)

LIEBHERR T 282B

Liebherr's massive T 282B dumper just edges out Caterpillar's 797 for the title of the largest truck in the world.

So huge it can't be driven on roads, these trucks are confined to the world's great mining and engineering sites.

RIGHT: The four enormous tires on the rear axle of the Lierbherr T 282B help distribute the dumper body's payload weight, as well as provide good grip on rough surfaces.

SPECIFICATIONS

Country: Germany

Year built: 2004

Dimensions:
47ft 6in (14.5m) long;
24ft (7.3m) wide

Capacity: 440 tons
(400,000kg)

Maximum speed:
40mph (65km/h)

Power: 3650bhp
(2.7mW)

Cost: $3.5 million

The Liebherr T 282 truck appeared in 1998 as a German contender to the enormous material-carrying vehicles built by the likes of US manufacturers such as Caterpillar. However, it wasn't until 2004 that the range was refined and made larger still, with the resultant T 282B finally becoming the biggest truck on the planet.

As tall as three storeys

The sheer size is staggering. As tall as a three-storey building, only a few dozen are sold each year. They are made in a dedicated factory that covers the area of more than seven football fields, yet can only work on four trucks at one time. The vehicles aren't completed here,

but have to be finished off at the worksite. And if they subsequently move anywhere else for another job, they have to be disassembled again.

Aside from its sheer stature, what makes the T 282B stand out from the rest of the dump-truck crowd is that instead of a diesel-mechanical drive system, its Detroit Diesel/MTU engine powers two electric motors on the rear axles, making it an AC diesel-electric truck—the first of its type to employ this supposedly more refined drive system. However, despite the multimillion dollar price tag of each T 282B, you still don't get a CD player or air-conditioning as standard. They're classed as optional extras!

THE LARGEST DUMP TRUCK (DIESEL MECHANICAL)

CATERPILLAR 797B

The gigantic 797B has only recently been surpassed as the world's largest truck. However, it is still officially the biggest diesel-mechanical drive dumper around, and more than capable of taking on the toughest mining and engineering tasks.

U p until 2004 (and the advent of the Liebherr T 282B) Caterpillar's 797B off-road dumper was the hugest and most impressive of them all. However, when Liebherr's new behemoth came on the scene, it managed to surpass the 797B's load ability by 22 tons (20,000kg).

But never mind, because Caterpillar can still call the 797B the world's biggest diesel-mechanical drive dumper truck, where the diesel engine directly powers the axles via a seven-speed transmission. Used primarily for open-pit mining, a full load in the dumper body is 418 tons (380,000kg), which happens to be 112 tons (102,000kg) more than the vehicle's own bodyweight. What really limits the 797B being capable of carrying more is simply tire technology. Despite each tire on the 797B weighing 4.5 tons (4000kg) and standing 13ft (9.7m) tall, they still have to be replaced every 35,000 miles (56,327km). Bigger weights would significantly reduce this interval.

A big power source is needed to move all this weight around, even if top speed is a mere 42mph (68km/h). In fact, the Cat 3524B engine is actually made up of two 12-cylinder engines coupled together. This creates a 7146in^3 (117.1 liter) 24-cylinder turbocharged diesel unit, with a power output of 3550bhp (2647kW), fed by a tank with a capacity of 1800 gallons (6814 liters) of fuel. Such features make it almost as much an impressive mega machine as the 797B it actually powers!

SPECIFICATIONS

Country: USA
Year built from: 2002
Dimensions:
25ft (7.6m) long;
47ft 6in (14.5m) wide
Capacity: 380 tons
(345,000kg)
Weight: 278 tons
(252,000kg)
Maximum speed:
42mph (68km/h)
Cost: $5–6 million

BELOW AND RIGHT: The Caterpillar off-highway truck is a gigantic vehicle. Comparison of two workers standing beside the 797B graphically illustrates this.

THE LARGEST ARTICULATED TRUCK

BELL B50D

One problem with rigid-body mining trucks is that they're not very maneuverable and don't handle rough ground very well. Articulated dump trucks get around that problem by being pivoted behind the cab and offering all-wheel drive. The leader of the pack is the Bell B50D.

SPECIFICATIONS

Country: South Africa
Year built: 2005
Dimensions:
35ft (10.75m) long;
12ft 6in (3.8m) wide
Capacity: 50 tons
(45,400kg)
Weight: 79,704lb
(36,153kg)
Maximum speed:
32.5mph (52km/h)
Power: 510bhp
(380kW)
Cost: N/A

BELOW: A Bell B50D in its natural environment. The articulated swivel joint is behind the cab and gives the truck excellent maneuverability for its size.

While an articulated dump truck (ADT) will never match the sheer size of its rigid-bodied rivals, they are far more versatile than their bigger brothers. As rugged as the monster dumpers are, they do need smooth surfaces to work on. And there aren't always a lot of those around mining sites. However, thanks to having an articulated chassis and all their wheels powered, an ADT can handle most conditions (surface and weather) and keep going no matter what.

Versatile and innovative

One of the most recent vehicles to enter this field has been Bell's B50D, which immediately made a mark for itself simply by being larger than its rivals. The six-wheeled creation, powered by a Mercedes-Benz V8 turbocharged engine, also introduced a couple of firsts into the sector, neither of which would be out of place in a much more sophisticated road vehicle.

To make the B50D even more of a practical tool, the truck is fitted with an active suspension system, which alters itself depending on whether a load is being carried or not. And it has a vehicle "machine production and condition measuring" system, known as Fleetm@tic, which records all key operational data, including where the truck is, what it is doing, and how much it is carrying. This is transmitted to a satellite, which then passes the data on by email or via a website. Highly technical indeed for a humble dump truck.

CATERPILLAR AD55

You would expect trucks that have to work underground to be compact and easily maneuverable. Not so. Today's mines are so large that even monsters like the Caterpillar AD55 can cope well within their wide tunnels.

BELOW: The AD55 is a rarely glimpsed mining machine, spending most of its time underground. The low-profile shape is dictated by the confined tunnels the truck has to work in.

SPECIFICATIONS

Country: Australia

Year built from: 2000

Dimensions:
38ft (11.5m) long;
11ft (3.3m) wide

Weight: 52 tons
(47,000kg)

Load capacity: 60 tons
(55,000kg)

Cost: Approximately
$1.4 million

Admittedly, underground trucks aren't quite the size of their siblings above ground. However, modern vehicles like Caterpillar's AD55—introduced in 2000, and still the world's biggest below-surface dump truck—are impressive by any standards.

Loaded by chutes

Capable of working in a space of just 16ft 6in x 16ft 6in (5 x 5m), the articulated AD55 can carry 5.5 tons (5000kg) more than its nearest rival, giving it a total capacity of 60.6 tons (55,000kg). Its very squat bodywork and low-profile tires help it to achieve this—although with its back hopper raised, the AD55's overall height goes up from 12ft 6in (3.8m) to almost 23ft (7m). This isn't usually an issue within

a mine, as the purpose of vehicles like the AD55 is to take waste material, often loaded from overhead chutes, from inside and drag it out and up to the surface before tipping.

Because of where they have to work, AD55s have a few extra features to make life a bit easier for those who work with them in such a demanding environment. The fully enclosed offset cab is air-conditioned, and fitted with a reversing camera. And because of the enclosed mining environment, the turbocharged Cat 3456E engine is designed to put out fewer emissions and less smoke than an overground counterpart would. The top speed of an AD55 is a heady 34mph (55km/h), although in narrow and inclined passageways, 6mph (10km/h) is a more realistic figure.

RHAM 100HD LOAD HAUL DUMPER

Huge dump trucks are not the only vehicles that work underground. Something has to load the mine's waste material into them, which is where machines like the RHAM 100HD Load Haul Dumper come in.

The best modern mines are colossal feats of engineering, with tunnels of such impressive proportions that size doesn't really matter any more. And this means that machines like the RHAM 100HD Load Haul Dumper—the biggest underground load haul dumper of them all—can cope well far below the surface.

SPECIFICATIONS

Country: South Africa
Year built: 2002
Dimensions: N/A
Weight: N/A
Load capacity:
38.5 tons (35,000kg)
Power: 600hp (447kW)
Cost: N/A

Low to the ground

Powered by a 600hp (447kW) Caterpillar turbocharged 3456E diesel engine—which usually makes part interchangeability between other machines onsite easier, thanks to Caterpillar's dominance in this engineering sector—what distinguishes the RHAM 100D from its siblings working up above is the low-profile bodywork, with the cab roof as near to the ground as possible. So while the loader is a sizeable machine in width and length, it's very squat, and able to get into quite tight spots. The articulated chassis, with a pivot behind where the shovel is mounted, also aids its practicality.

Power to move heavy loads

Capacity of the 100HD's hefty shovel is 38.5 tons (35,000kg), which is not unimpressive for a surface loader. But this is even more impressive when you consider that its nearest rival can manage just half this capacity, according to RHAM. Another feature the 100HD boasts is hydrostatic drive—something of an RHAM trademark—where the maximum torque available can be instantly applied to the wheels, meaning that there's always a large amount of low-down power available, however big the load.

RIGHT AND ABOVE: The capacity of the 100HD's shovel is 38.5 tons (35,000kg) and the two figures amply demonstrate the size of its scoop.

THE LARGEST OFF-HIGHWAY TRACTOR

CATERPILLAR 784C

ABOVE: With its powerful 1290hp (926kW) engine, there's not much the Caterpillar 784C tractor isn't able to tow, under any conditions.

What's the difference between an off-road truck and an off-road tractor?
Well, the tractor is merely a mobile power unit that can hitch up and tow
anything. And in the case of the enormous Caterpillar 784C, there's very
little this machine can't cope with.

Big enough in its own right, it's when Caterpillar's 784C tractor unit couples up to something that its true might becomes apparent. Operating the way an articulated truck does on the road, these tough workhorses have a hitch on their rear that allows a trailer to be attached. However, it's where they can pull this trailer—and how much can be loaded inside it—that would humble an ordinary highway rig.

The size of railroad wagons

Intended for off-road mining work, the 784C's powerful 1290hp (962kW) diesel engine and huge tires allow it to handle rough terrain while pulling coal and ore wagons the size of which wouldn't disgrace a railroad freight train. A typical load for a 784C is 240 tons (218,000kg), but they can go beyond that limit. Once the destination has been reached, the material is deposited from the bottom of the trailer, hence the (usual) triangular shape of the wagon so that the coal or ore naturally flows out.

Although the tractor is ruggedly built, the frame of the 784C, and that of any trailer it is pulling, are still subject to colossal pressure. To counteract this, the yoke-type hitch on the back oscillates four ways to reduce pressure on the frame. Also installed on the tractor are turn stops that prevent the trailer from rotating too much in either direction. As a driver, with hundreds of tons behind, the last thing you want is to be involved in a jackknifing incident.

THE LARGEST BULLDOZER, CURRENT

KOMATSU D575A "SUPER DOZER"

"Super Dozer" is an apt description for the Komatsu D575A bulldozer. Bigger than anything else of its type, and capable of scooping up objects the size of a fairly substantial car with its enormous blade, it is a true king of earth pushing.

Back in 2001, the president of one of the first firms to use a Komatsu D575A in the USA commented: "These things are made for knocking down mountains and could push downtown Dallas into rubble in two weeks."

Dig, carry, or dump

It is a slight overstatement perhaps, but then again, maybe not, because the Japanese-built D575A is not the kind of machine to do things by halves. Its V12 engine is powerful enough to allow its 103 yard^3 (82.3m^3) blade to push up to 240 tons (217,724kg), and when one of the first "super dozers" in America was put to work on a Texas landfill—utilizing its blade to rip the earth because dynamite couldn't be used—crowds turned up simply to watch it in action. And it isn't just a machine for pushing things around either. The blade can be set to three different positions—dig, carry, or dump—meaning it is more versatile than most other bulldozers.

Now used more commonly in strip coalmining operations, where it can even match the massive walking draglines in the amount of material it can move around, the D575A remains the largest and most powerful bulldozer around today. With a top speed of 7.5mph (11.6km/h), however, it probably isn't the fastest. In fact, it is so huge that when it needs to move on to another job, it has to be dismantled and transported in up to eight trucks.

ABOVE, BELOW, AND LEFT: The front blade of the D575A is one of its most impressive features, whether just on display or working hard.

SPECIFICATIONS

Country: Japan	
Year built from: 1996	
Dimensions: 39ft (11.7m) long; 24ft (7.4m) wide	
Weight: 150 tons (136,077kg)	
Power: 1150hp (858kW)	
Blade height: 11ft (3.25m)	
Cost: $380,000	

THE LARGEST WHEELED BULLDOZER, CURRENT

KOMATSU WD600-3

Not every job is suitable for a conventional bulldozer, which is why many heavy engineering companies also offer a "wheeldozer" in their product lineup as well. Wheeldozers sport rubber tires instead of steel tracks. The current production model by which all others are judged is Komatsu's WD600-3.

BELOW: The rubber-wheeled WD600-3 is faster and more versatile than its tracked rivals and does less damage to track surfaces.

Think of a bulldozer, and you probably think of something with caterpillar tracks. But wheeldozers also have their special niche in the world of mega machines. They're popular as clean-up machines for stockpiling coal and other minerals at very large surface mines, where their ability to travel more quickly than conventional bulldozers means that they are more productive. They are even useful for giving loader scrapers a helping push from behind.

Speed machine

Any of these jobs are tasks at which the Komatsu WD600-3 would excel. With 522hp (389kW) of power and a blade with a maximum capacity of 29.5 yards^3 (22.5m^3), its potential for hard and tough jobs is almost as big as the WD600-3 is itself. However, with a top speed of 22.5mph (36.2km/h), it is extremely nippy when compared to its tracked equivalent and, in reverse, it's even faster, capable of reaching 30mph (40km/h).

A big industrial bruiser it may be, but for the operator, the WD600-3 is quite a luxurious machine when contrasted with other "dozers." The rubber tires make it more comfortable and quieter than a tracked vehicle and, inside the cab, there's a five-mode air-conditioner, a radio and cassette player, lunchbox holder, electric windows, and a seat with air suspension. Even the cab itself is mounted on silicone rubber. It's almost a relaxing place to be in, as if getting to play with one of the world's most impressive wheeldozers wasn't enjoyable enough already!

SPECIFICATIONS

Country: Japan

Year built from: 2003

Dimensions:
30ft 6in (9m) long;
9ft (2.5m) wide

Weight: 47 tons
(42,900kg)

Power: 522hp (389kw)

Maximum blade size:
19ft (6m) wide

Cost: N/A

THE LARGEST WHEEL LOADER, OVERALL

LETOURNEAU L-2350

It may sound French, but the LeTourneau L-2350 hails from Texas. And it's rather fitting that such a giant machine should come from such a giant state.

I n the world of wheeled loaders, nothing surpasses Le Tourneau's L-2350—and that's according to *The Guinness Book of Records*. Intended for the tough environments of coal, copper, and hard-rock mining, the bucket of the L-2350 is so large that it often gets used simply to transport material around a site, the same way as a dump truck does.

Loader of choice

Of course, that's not its true purpose. Something has to load the incredibly gigantic dump trunks now used at many mines, and in many cases, the L-2350 is the vehicle of choice. With its standard 63 yard^3 (48.5m^3) bucket installed, one of these can load a truck with a capacity of 319 tons (290,299kg) in just four passes, and the lift height of 24ft (3.5m) and reach of 11ft 6in (7.3m) means it's able to load trucks of up to 400 tons (362,874kg) with ease. Its tires are the largest ever made for a loader, towering 13ft (4m) tall and weighing nearly 8 tons (7,260kg). It takes a four-person crew 17 hours (with an additional 24 hours in cure time) to make each.

Such a monster machine requires a monster power unit, and the 16-cylinder Detroit Diesel engine of the L-2350 weighs in with a capacity of 3967in^3 (65 liters). To put that into perspective, that's around the equivalent of 16 modern Jaguar saloons. No wonder it can pump out a colossal 2300hp (1750kW).

ABOVE AND LEFT: A complex system of rugged hydraulics is necessary to allow the L-2350 to lift and swivel its front bucket.

THE LARGEST WHEEL LOADER (DIESEL-MECHANICAL DRIVE)

CATERPILLAR 994F

One of the few machines comparable to LeTorneau's L-2350 wheel loader is the Caterpillar 994F, which can boast of being the world's largest diesel-mechanical drive wheel loader, even if it isn't (quite) the largest overall.

LEFT AND ABOVE: Big dump trucks need big loaders to serve them, with enough reach to be able to quickly deposit loads for transportation.

According to some sources, Caterpillar's 994D is the largest wheel loader around. What is also certain is that it's one of the biggest machines that the American firm builds (and by far the biggest of its loaders), and is the largest wheel loader to feature mechanical drive. With this system, power from the 1577hp (1176kW) engine is supplied directly to all the wheels, not via an electric motor as with the vehicles like the L-2350. Despite the hefty engine output, the 994F is more about low-down grunt rather than sheer speed, so it is geared to have a top speed of just 15mph (24km/h).

Choice of buckets

So that the 994F proves useful in a number of different environments, it can be fitted with an extensive selection of buckets, the largest of which measures 21ft (6.3m) wide and can scoop up 47 yards³ (35.9m³). Such sizes are primarily intended for shifting coal, however, and the buckets for other mining and quarrying purposes are smaller, but tougher, in order to deal with the harder rocks the 994F is likely to encounter.

Up in the cab, the 994F is quite technologically advanced compared to its rivals. A single joystick is used for direction, gear selection, and steering, rather than the several controls that once did all this. There's even a rearview camera. However, a few basic creature comforts haven't been forgotten—the second (trainer) seat can fold down to be used as a drinks tray, and underneath it, there's space for a lunch cooler.

THE LARGEST TRACKED LOADER

CATERPILLAR 973C TRACKED LOADER

For really tough loading jobs on difficult terrain, only a tracked vehicle can tackle the challenge. This is where machines like the Caterpillar 973C come in, because it is capable of going places that a wheeled loader wouldn't dare to tread.

SPECIFICATIONS

Country: USA
Year built from: 1990s
Power: 242hp (178kW)
Dimensions: 17ft (5.2m) long (without bucket); 9.2ft (3m) wide (without bucket)
Weight: 29 tons (26,373kg)
Bucket capacity: 4.19 yards³ (3.2m³)
Cost: Approximately $350,000

BELOW: Try doing this in a rubber-tired wheel loader! Under difficult steel mill conditions like this, tracked loaders come into their element.

Wheeled loaders do have their limitations. On loose, rough, or very muddy ground, they can get bogged down. In addition, landfill sites, where the piles of garbage can provide a very difficult surface for normal tires to get any adhesion on, can be a challenge.

Better distribution and grip

Under such circumstances, a tracked loader is the obvious option instead. Because the tracks distribute the load and grip of the machine over a greater area, such loaders are more adept at working—even if they're not that maneuverable on "normal" ground.

It is a small wonder that the Caterpillar Company (which is actually named after the tracks it bought the patents for at the turn of the twentieth century) should be at the forefront of tracked vehicles to this day. The 973C is its largest tracked loader. Looking rather like a bulldozer, for all its bulk, the 973C can be quite a dexterous machine, thanks to its hydraulic arms that allow it to raise and lower its front bucket to a variety of different angles and positions. It can act as a grader, flattening soil into roads with some finesse, although it's also capable of churning it up with the assistance of the three big rippers on its rear. Other common usages are demolishing buildings and even shoveling hot materials in steel mills. The 973C is quite a "Jekyll and Hyde" machine, but immensely practical and versatile because of all the different jobs it can carry out.

THE LARGEST STRIPPING SHOVEL (DRAGLINE)

BUCYRUS-ERIE 1150-B DRAGLINE "ODDBALL"

Walking draglines have been around since prior to World War I, but once they've outlived their usefulness, they're usually just scrapped. The Bucyrus-Erie 1150-B, named Oddball, is different though. It has been preserved in the UK so the public can see how epic these machines are.

B uilt in 1948 in the US and shipped over to the UK in 1950 to work at opencast coal and ironstone mines, the Bucyrus-Erie 1150-B Dragline weighed a colossal 1350 tons (1,220,000kg) and was capable of moving 20,000 tons (18,140,000kg) per day over 24 hours. It was known as a "walking" dragline because the propelling of this giant machine was by way of shoes, built so as not to sink into soft ground, moving one after the other. In 1999, after a decade of lying idle, the mains electrically powered "Oddball" was saved as a museum piece. To date, at the size of 60 double-decker buses, it is one of the biggest engineering machines to have been preserved.

Christened Oddball because its electrical equipment was different to the other, similar, draglines that it worked with, the 1150-B was able to travel to its final resting place, some 164ft (50m) from where it had been laid up, under its own power. After a decade

BELOW AND ABOVE: This isn't Oddball itself, but a comparable Bucyrus-Erie 1550-B dragline, showing the complicated arrangement of cables and booms needed to operate the bucket.

SPECIFICATIONS

Country:	USA
Year built:	1948
Dimensions:	N/A
Weight:	1350 tons (1,220,000kg)
Power:	N/A
Bucket capacity:	26 yards³ (20m³)
Cost:	N/A

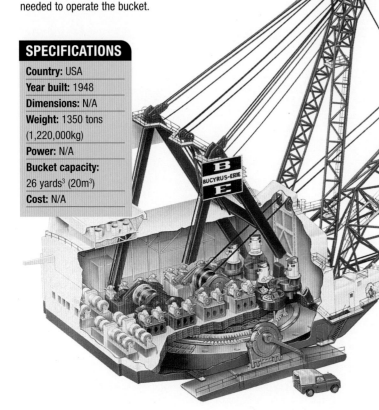

out of use, some of the vital motor equipment needed to be refurbished, and new generators temporarily installed (as well as a trailer-mounted one wired up to follow the dragline), so Oddball could take its last walk. Controlled remotely using a handheld console operated by one person—such have been the huge advances in technology since Oddball was new—the dragline took six hours to make the short journey. Its top speed was a mere 0.025mph (0.04km/h)!

THE LARGEST CRAWLER DRAGLINE

MARION 305-M DRAGLINE

The absolute biggest dragline excavators are mainly fitted with feet so they can "walk" as they work. However, under some circumstances, crawler tracks are preferred as they allow a machine to be more mobile. One such machine is the Marion 305-M.

Until it was taken over by rival Bucyrus-Erie, the Marion Power Shovel Company was known as one of the foremost manufacturers of giant engineering machines, and had been responsible for building Big Muskie—the biggest walking dragline ever. Thus, when an Australian customer required a one-off large electric dragline to be built with caterpillar tracks instead of the more usual "feet," Marion was the obvious company to ask.

The only one

The resultant machine was the 305-M, and was a development of the previous two-crawler draglines that Marion had built in the past. However, it was much larger than any of these, and proved to be the biggest machine of its type anywhere when construction was completed in 1990. To date, only one 305-M has been built, and the electrically powered machine, which drags its supply cables out behind it as it works, is still going hard at it in an Australian mine. It's now unlikely that anything of similar proportions, using tracks to travel, will be manufactured in the near future.

Weighing in at a sizeable 1350 tons (1,225,000kg), the 305-M has a boom of 255ft (77.8m) and can support a bucket capable of scooping up 28.8 yards³ (22m³) of material. However, perhaps its most impressive feature is simply the size of its crawlers: Each one alone is 10ft (3m) wide!

SPECIFICATIONS

Country: Australia
Year built: 1990
Power: N/A
Dimensions: N/A
Weight: 1350 tons (1,225,000kg)
Bucket capacity: 28.8 yards³ (22m³)
Cost: N/A

ABOVE: Crawler draglines are slightly smaller but much rarer than their walking counterparts.

DRAGLINE WITH LARGEST BOOM EVER

MARION 8750 WALKING DRAGLINE

A dragline, with its huge boom, could easily be mistaken for a crane. However, these huge machines—among the biggest land machines in existence—are more involved with destruction than construction.

SPECIFICATIONS

Country: Canada
Year built: N/A
Weight: 7275 tons (6,600,000kg)
Power: 38,000hp (28,337kW)
Bucket payload: 126 yards^3 (97m^3)
Boom length: 4520ft (1378m)
Cost: $50–100 million

Although it may not be the largest walking dragline around in terms of sheer size, the Marion 8750, employed by Fording Coal Ltd. at one of its mines in Alberta, Canada, is worthy of inclusion in a book on mega machines simply because of the length of its boom. At 420ft (128m) in length, it is the longest ever to be installed on a dragline. Coupled with its bucket of 126 yards^3 (97m^3), the 8750 is a pretty impressive piece of kit as it digs coal to supply the nearby city of Edmonton. The length of the boom allows Fording Coal's 8750 to dig further and deeper into the ground than many of its rivals.

Using its feet

Draglines such as these are intriguing to those who appreciate innovative engineering. Instead of running on wheels or crawlers, a walking dragline has two shoes on each side of the machine's frame. A powerful electric drive rotates the shoes in a circular motion, allowing the dragline to perform steps. Invariably, a walking dragline walks away from what it is digging, and it's not unknown for draglines to occasionally cut too close to where they are, causing a landslide that also sends them falling into the trench. Recovering something the size of a dragline is no easy task!

ABOVE: The 8750 hard at work. The Fording machine's oversize boom means that it doesn't need to get too close to the edge of the trench it is cutting, giving it an extra margin of safety.

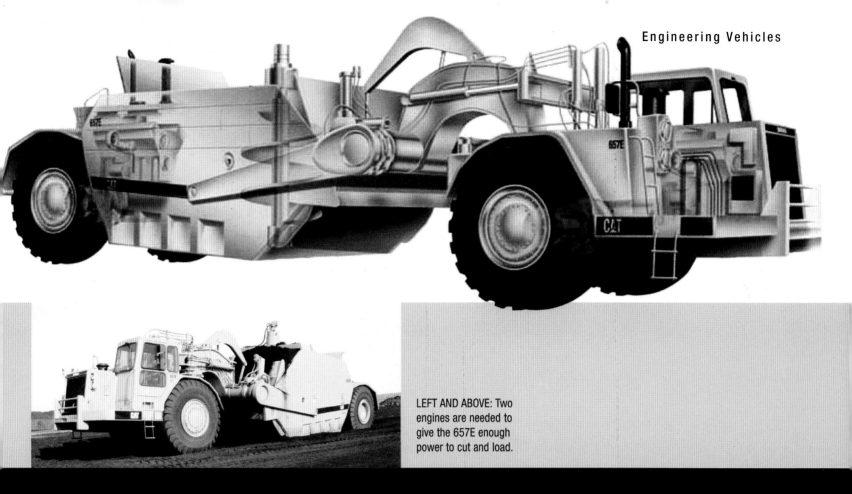

LEFT AND ABOVE: Two engines are needed to give the 657E enough power to cut and load.

CATERPILLAR 657E WHEEL TRACTOR SCRAPER

Invented back in the 1930s, wheel tractor scrapers are high-speed earthmovers that don't just load material, but haul and dump it as well. Versatile indeed—and that's especially true of Caterpillar's huge 675E model.

SPECIFICATIONS

Country: USA
Year built: 2006
Weight: 80 tons (72,224 kg)
Maximum speed: 31mph (50km/h)
Power: 1045hp (779kW) from two engines of 605hp (451kW) and 440hp (328kW)
Bowl capacity: 72 yards³ (55m³)
Cost: Approximately $1,235,000

Machines don't always need a shovel or bucket to dig the earth. Modern wheel tractor scrapers do the job by towing moveable hoppers with a sharp horizontal edge at their front, which can be raised or lowered to cut into the soil. As the scraper travels forward, material is scooped up into the hopper. When it's full, the scraper simply heads off to the dumping zone, gets rid of its load via its back panel, and then starts the whole process again.

Two diesel engines

Usually employed for road construction or bowl mining (where the ground is gradually hollowed out), many scrapers usually require a push from another vehicle to help

them achieve their aim. Not the Caterpillar 675E though. This huge and very long machine is fitted with two powerful diesel engines, one for the main front tractor, and the other for powering the scraper. Working in tandem with each other, one engine drives the front wheels, the other powers the rear set. In addition, the 675E also has an auger mechanism inside the hopper that helps raise the earth into the bowl.

Caterpillar's biggest scraper is no slouch when it's working either. The top speed of the vehicle is 31mph (50km/h), which may not sound like much for an ordinary road vehicle, but it's pretty impressive for something that is taking a large bite out of the surface below it as it goes.

CATERPILLAR 24H MOTOR GRADER

When Caterpillar unveiled its gigantic 24H motor grader in Las Vegas in 1996, it immediately humbled every other grader in production. Caterpillar already had the world's largest grader—the 16H—in its lineup, but the 24H was more than double the weight.

Graders are simply machines for flattening the soil so it can either be built upon or driven over easily by other vehicles. But today's machines have come a long way since the earliest graders, which were little more than a board pulled by a horse.

Grading elite

The Caterpillar 24H is the current elite of graders. It's not the largest grader ever built—there have been some one-off monsters built in the past for special projects that have surpassed it—but it's currently the largest grader that customers can buy "off the shelf."

Intended to maintain large surface-mine haul roads—the type of tracks that the monster dump trucks travel over—the 24H sports a blade that is 24ft (7.3m) wide and can be hydraulically lifted, lowered, and angled to adapt to the surface of whatever it is grading. The blade of a 24H can cut down to a depth of about 26in (657mm). Even more impressive is the 24H's ability to hydraulically move its blade to the left or right, so it reaches out beyond the side of the grader, to a distance of 127in (3229mm). This gives the 24H the ability to grade slopes by the side of the main track or even flatten an adjacent ditch.

BELOW: This is the normal operating position for the 24H's blade. However, it can extend up to 127in (3229mm) either side of the grader to let it flatten slopes and ditches.

SPECIFICATIONS

Country: USA
Year built from: 1996
Dimensions:
52ft (15.8m) long; 136ft 6in (41.65m) wide
Weight: 68 tons (61955kg)
Maximum speed: 23mph (38 km/h)
Power: 500hp (373kW)
Cost: N/A

GOMACO GP-4000 PAVER

With roads and airport runways getting ever bigger, the machines that make them have had to increase in size as well. Meet Gomaco's GP-4000 Slipform paver, capable of paving surfaces up to 50ft (15.24m) wide.

A s strange and complicated-looking as the GP-4000 appears, the job it does is one of the most important when it comes to new roads, highways, or runways. This is the machine that lays and levels the concrete that makes the actual surface on major projects.

How it works

Travelling very slowly—at between 15ft and 30ft 6in (5m and 9m) per minute, the GP-4000 passes over a layer of aggregate (a mixture of sand and gravel) that will form the road bed. Hot asphalt—carried on the paver and constantly vibrating to get rid of air bubbles—is then put over the top of this using a screed, a large flat plate the same width as the pavement. What is left behind is a concrete surface that just needs to be further smoothed before it fully dries—and the job is complete.

That's how all modern pavers work, but what makes the GP-4000 stand out is its width. Because its design is modular,

SPECIFICATIONS	
Country: USA	
Year built from: 1994	
Dimensions: 31ft (9.4m) long; 58ft (17.68m) wide	
Weight: 57 tons (52,164kg)	
Power: 450hp (336kW)	
Cost: Approximately $1 million	

ABOVE AND BELOW: When extended to its maximum breadth, the modular GP-4000 is capable of laying highways and runways in one sweep.

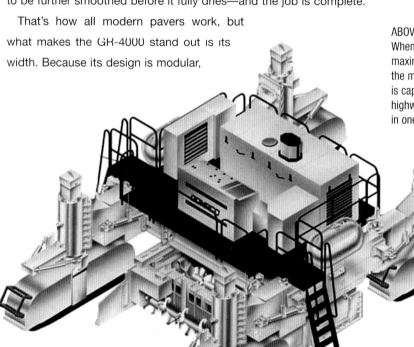

and it has a telescopic framework, it can extend or retract itself to suit the job at hand. At its smallest setting, it paves 12ft (3.66m) across. But it can extend right out to 50ft (15.24m) and down to a depth of 19in (483mm). With the main runways of a major airport like New York's JFK having a width of 150ft (46m), it would only take three of these machines to build something fit for modern passenger jets to land on.

ROADTEC RX-900 COLD PLANER

Once big highways and airport runways have been laid out, they need to be maintained and, every so often, resurfaced. Enter the RX-900 cold planer, a big machine for the biggest of repaving tasks.

SPECIFICATIONS

Country: USA

Year built from: 2004

Dimensions:
55ft (16.8m) long;
9ft (2.7m) wide

Weight: 41 tons
(37,195kg)

Maximum speed:
3.2mph (5.1km/h)

Power: 950hp
(708.5kW)

Cost: Upward of
$550,000

ABOVE: A cold planer like the RX-900 is far quicker and more cost-effective than having men do the same job manually with drills.

However well built a road or runway is, the constant pounding of vehicles eventually takes its toll on its surface. That's when it's time to call in a cold planer. Such equipment is used to remove old concrete or asphalt so it can be repaired.

Cutting through road surfaces

Cold planers can be small (as used for repairing driveways), large or, in the case of RoadTec's RX-900, rather massive. Thanks to its highly powerful engines—the largest unit available is a 950hp (708.5kW) Caterpillar diesel engine—the RX-900 is able to exert enough force to cut down through a solid road surface to a depth of up to 14in (355mm) and to a maximum width of 12ft 6in (3.81m). It's not exactly quick about the task, with a maximum working speed of just 128ft (39m) per minute, but few other cold planers are so versatile. It certainly beats using men with pneumatic drills to do the same thing!

Available with four caterpillar tracks or just three (two at the front and one at the rear, which makes the RX-900 look like an extremely strange back-to-front tricycle), one of the RX-900's more noticeable features is the covered conveyer belt that emerges from the front of the machine. Capable of swinging 60 degrees to either side, the belt is almost 23ft (7m) long and is used to transfer the waste surface material into dump trucks that travel along with the cold planer.

THE LARGEST CABLE EXCAVATOR

P&H 5700 CABLE SHOVEL

Just five of the enormous P&H shovels were built, and not all of them managed to survive their employment intact. One of them ended up being titanic in more than sheer size alone.

S till regarded as the largest two-crawler shovels ever, P&H's 5700 series of excavators was conceived during a time of economic optimism. Unfortunately, by the time these giants were ready for production, economic recession meant that P&H had trouble finding customers. From 1978 to 1991, just five of these white elephants were built.

Electric marvels

Known as cable shovels because their power came from electricity supplied by large cables strung out behind them, the first 5700 weighed in at 1775 tons (1,610,253kg). But the breed grew larger still during its limited lifetime, with the final two machines tipping the scales at 2100 tons (1,905,088kg). Shovel capacity also varied, rising from 29.8 yards^3 (22.8m^3) to 68.8 yards^3 (52.6m^3).

Four of the machines were used for loading oversized dump trucks at mines in Australia and America, but the third one to be built was something of a curiosity. It ended up mounted on a large barge being used for dredging the Great Lakes off Illinois. However, the Chicago, as the 5700 was christened, came to an unfortunate end while being moved across the North Sea to Denmark. It was hit by a high wave, capsized, and sank to the bottom of the ocean. And because a salvage operation to bring it up is regarded as simply too expensive, that's where it remains to this day.

BELOW: This was the fourth 5700 to be built, upgraded to XPA specification and employed at a mine in New South Wales, Australia.

SPECIFICATIONS

Country: USA
Year built: 1978–91
Dimensions: N/A
Weight: 2100 tons (1,905,088kg)
Shovel Capacity: 68.8 yards^3 (52.6m^3)
Boom Length: 90ft (27.4m)
Cost: N/A

THE LARGEST HYDRAULIC EXCAVATOR

O&K RH400 HYDRAULIC EXCAVATOR

Towering above other vehicles of its type, the O&K RH400 has been the world's largest hydraulic shovel since its introduction in 1997. This is a machine that can turn its hand to virtually any earth-moving construction task.

H ydraulic excavators have largely taken over from cable-operated excavators as one of the dominant forces in moving earth. Hundreds of companies all over the planet now make these very practical engineering workhorses, but none of these surpasses O&K's RH400, which was first seen in 1997.

Fluid hydraulics

The German firm originally designed the RH400 for a Canadian company that mined oil sands (oil trapped in a mixture of sand, water, clay, and other natural materials) in order to improve productivity when loading big dump trucks. Thanks to its 80 ton (72,575kg) capacity, it is able to fill a 240 ton (217,724kg) truck in just three passes. However, it's

the speed with which it is able to achieve this feat that makes the RH400 such a useful tool.

Its hydraulics are so efficient that, in the hands of a skilled operator, a pass can take just 29 seconds. All those hefty pistons controlling the lifting boom also allow it to dig up to heights of almost 54ft (16.5m) and extend out to over 57ft (17.3m). Those are long reaches indeed.

The RH400 is a hard worker too. Its 4227 gallon (19,216 liter) fuel tank allows it to run for 28 hours between refills. Its human operators, however, usually work 12-hour shifts. Creature comforts adjacent to the cab include sleeping quarters, a microwave, refrigerator, oven, and a decent stereo system, just to make the job a little more pleasant.

SPECIFICATIONS

Country: Germany
Year built from: 1997
Dimensions:
28ft (8.5m) long;
30ft (9.1m) high
Weight: 787 tons
(713,954kg)
Power: 3400hp
(2535kW)
Bowl capacity:
78.5 yards^3 (60m^3)
Cost: Approximately
$7 million (2000 price)

LEFT: The RH400's side profile shows off the hefty hydraulic pistons.

THE LARGEST DITCHING MACHINE, CURRENT

TRENCOR 1860HD CHAIN DITCHER

There's pretty much a specialist machine for every engineering job these days. Take Trencor's 1860HD, for example. This is a machine designed just to cut ditches through rock and tough soils.

LEFT AND ABOVE:
Digging a ditch made
simple—biting down
deep into the ground
is what the 1860HD
was built to do.

Digging ditches might not seem like a task that could call for a machine the size of Trencor's 1860HD. However, this beast is designed to create cuts that are both wider and deeper than other ditchers are able to achieve. And the 1860HD can even cope with digging through rock at the same time.

Super slicer

Slung out in front of the Trencor, but in between its caterpillar tracks, is a device like a massive chainsaw, equipped with very tough picks tipped with tungsten carbide. Gradually lowered to the required depth, this belt moves at high velocity, tearing into the rock or soil and cutting a passage beneath the machine as it slowly travels along. Waste material from the cutting mechanism is scooped back into the 1860HD and then ejected, through a waste chute with a conveyer belt, from either side.

This is a bulky and powerful machine. An 1200hp (895kW) engine drives the chain, while a second 300hp (224kW) unit powers the track, conveyer, and other auxiliary functions. Digging attachments of different sizes can be fitted to it, letting the Trencor reach down to a maximum of 35ft (10.7m) below itself. The chain can be up to 8ft (2.5m) across.

Another innovative feature is a cab that can be hydraulically raised by up to 39in (1m) for better visibility.

TRENCOR 1260RS ROCK SAW

No, it's not just a trencher. The 1260RS made by Trencor of Texas is intended to be brought in for conditions that would defeat even the biggest and best conventional trenchers, because this machine is the world's largest rock saw.

The literature for Trencor's 1260RS insists "It is NOT a converted chain trencher." As good as modern trench cutters are, sometimes they have to give up. While something like Trencor's 1860HD is designed to cope with a certain amount of rock, if large chunks break off it can jam the mechanism and bring the machine to a halt.

Super saw

However, this amazing machine, which would seem quite at home appearing in a James Bond movie, isn't likely to let a little bit of hard rock put it off its stroke. The lethal and scary-looking blade at the front likes nothing better than to slice through rock at a maximum speed of 21.8 revolutions per minute, either so cables can be laid in the resultant gap, or to soften up the ground for other trenchers to follow along.

Based on Caterpillar technology—both the diesel engine and the crawlers come from the bigger US company—the front blade is lowered into place hydraulically when the 1260RS begins work. Different types of saw wheel can be fitted, ranging from 8in (11.5cm) to 16in (30.5cm) and capable of digging down to a depth of 54in (137cm). The saw wheel can also be reversed, so instead of cutting while the tractor pushes, it does so while being pulled—a process that generally makes less of a mess with waste material.

SPECIFICATIONS	
Country: USA	
Year built: current	
Dimensions:	
33ft (10m) long;	
11ft (3.2m) wide	
Weight: 50 tons	
(45,400kg)	
Power: 525hp (392kW)	
Cost: N/A	

ABOVE: No rock is safe from the mean-looking Trencor 1260RS and its fearsome saw.

THE LARGEST PIPELAYER, PRODUCTION

CAT 589 PIPELAYER

After the ditching machines have done their job, it's time for the pipelayers to come in to lay pipes. Biggest of the current Caterpillar lineup is the 589, able to handle the biggest tubes with its heavy-duty winch and hook system.

BELOW: A Cat 589 makes light work of manhandling large sections of pipework into place.

Pipelayers like the Cat 589 don't usually work on their own. Intended for the bigger construction projects, they normally operate as part of a team, and the sight of several of these monsters lined up in a row, manhandling a continuous length of gas or oil pipe into place, rarely fails to impress.

As much as they look like little more than winches or small cranes, a purpose-built pipelayer is somewhat more complicated than this. The chief difference is the counterweight that is hydraulically extended out of the side when the pipelayer is in action, to improve load balance and clearance, and prevent the machine from toppling forward.

Elevated drive sprockets

However, as the flagship of the Caterpillar pipelaying range, the 589 comes with certain features that you won't find with pipelayers from other manufacturers. The boom is longer than usual, at 24ft (7.3m), and can lift up to 113 tons (103,330kg). Down on the undercarriage, the main drive sprockets are elevated above the crawler wheels, so the tracks take on a triangular appearance. This helps protect them from damage from objects on the ground, as well as contribute further to the 589's balance.

But what the majority of operators will appreciate most of all is the provision of a fully enclosed cab—many pipelayers don't even have this. However, because the 589 often finds itself out in very inhospitable locations, such as Alaska, it has to offer good protection from the weather. There's even a cold-weather package as an optional extra. It also makes the 589 very distinctive in profile, in common with other Caterpillar machines that use this form of drive.

SPECIFICATIONS

Country: USA
Year built from: 1990s
Dimensions:
19ft 6in (5.9m) long;
22ft (6.7) wide
Weight: 72 tons
(65,336kg)
Maximum speed:
6.8mph (10.9km/h)
Power: 420hp (313kW)
Cost: N/A

THE LARGEST TUNNEL-BORING MACHINE

HERRENKNECHT S-300 EPB SHIELD TUNNEL-BORING MACHINE

Among the largest and most visually impressive items of engineering equipment around are the massive tunnel-boring machines, used to cut today's long-distance highway and railroad tunnels. However, few people can appreciate these tunnel-boring machines because they spend most of their lives underground.

Tunnel boring machines (TBMs) are the unsung heroes of civil engineering. They're primarily responsible for some of the world's greatest and most recent civil engineering projects, such as the Channel Tunnel. Yet they work out of the public eye, only seen above ground in their entirety before a project begins, or after it has been successfully completed.

The largest TBM currently around is Herrenknecht's S-300 EPB Shield TBM which, at the time of writing, was being used to bore a motorway tunnel in Madrid, Spain. With a diameter of 50ft (15.2m)—the equivalent of a five-storey building—and a weight of 4810 tons (4,364,000kg), it's quite some drill.

Giant mechanical worm

The German-built machine—which has been christened Dulcinea by the Spanish employees who work with it—has the potential to cut through 98ft 6in (30m) of ground per day. This is accomplished by a huge rotating cutting wheel at the front, typically spinning between 4–10rpm. The rear section of the TBM is braced against the wall by hydraulic jacks, while the head is pushed forward to cut—with the S-300 possessing enough power to lift a fully loaded jumbo jet. Once the TBM meets its maximum telescopic extension, the front is then braced against the walls, the rear dragged forward, and the whole process starts again. Once it has cut its tunnel, it is disassembled onsite, as it is far too large to be removed in one piece.

ABOVE: The 50ft (15.2m) diameter of the S-300 tunnel-boring machine dwarfs the mobile crane by its size, shortly before embarking on its long, hard trip through the ground in Spain.

UDR 5000 DRILL

As the world's resources start to run low, there's an increasing need to explore ever deeper below the Earth's surface in the search for oil, gas, and minerals. For really deep shafts, the tool of choice is the UDR 5000, acknowledged as the biggest and toughest exploration drill on Earth.

When just a piece of drilling equipment has to be flown somewhere by a Russian Antonov cargo plane (the world's largest aircraft) you know it's something rather special. But that was exactly what was required when one of the then-new UDR 5000 drills was flown out to Mongolia a few years ago to search for gold and copper.

Deep below the crust

The UDR 5000 is far from an ordinary drill. It's capable of burrowing down up to 2 miles (3.2km) below the Earth's crust in its search for valuable resources. Powered by a 438hp (326.5kW) diesel engine, its bit can revolve at speeds of up to 2250 revolutions per minute, or even go as low as just 5 revolutions per minute if required.

Because of the depths that the UDR 5000 reaches, and the hardness of the rock it meets en route, its construction has to be extremely robust. The drill bit, therefore, consists of a metal cylinder, onto which industrial diamonds are embedded at the open end of the cylinder. With diamonds being the hardest substance known to man, there isn't much the UDR 5000 can't eat through eventually. This process of drilling is known as diamond coring.

Once the UDR 5000 has attained its required depth, samples of the material it has reached can be analyzed to see if they're of value or not. If they are, that's when the real drilling, by permanent rigs, starts.

The UDR 5000 can be disassembled, packed up and sent off to anywhere that its abilities are required.

BELOW: The UDR 5000 hard at work. The temporary nature of the drill's location is illustrated by the makeshift corrugated iron shack that has sprung up to protect it.

SPECIFICATIONS

Country: Australia
Year built from: 2003
Dimensions: N/A
Power: 438hp (326.5kW)
Maximum force: 100,000lbf (450kN)
Cost: N/A

SPECIFICATIONS

Country: Denmark

Year built from: 1990s

Dimensions: 394ft (120m) high; 480ft (146.3m) total diameter

Weight: 11,023 tons (10,000,000kg)

Lifting weight: 120 tons (108,862kg)

Swing speed: 0.4 revolutions per minute

Cost: N/A

THE LARGEST TOWER CRANE (CONSTRUCTION)

KROLL K-10000 TOWER CRANE

As buildings get ever larger, so do the cranes that build them. The giant of them all, however, is the Kroll K-10000, which is almost as magnificent and towering a creation as the structure it helps to build.

Denmark may not be a country associated with soaring skyscrapers, but without a machine built by a Danish company, some of the world's tallest buildings would have been far more difficult to construct.

Kroll's K-10000 tower crane dwarfs other cranes. At 394ft (120m) tall, it's almost three times the size of the Statue of Liberty, which stands at 151ft (46m) high, and five times that of a conventional tower crane. In fact, it is so lofty that it has a smaller service crane mounted on top of the main frame so essential items can be hoisted up to it. Despite its stature, it can withstand winds of over 174mph (280km/h).

Everything about the Kroll-10000 seems larger than life. It's capable of lifting the objects the equivalent weight of two large military tanks.

When it swings its 300ft (91m) boom, the diameter it covers is the size of six football fields.

Moving the K-10000

There are very few K-10000 cranes around, so when one is needed for a project, it will be shipped anywhere in the world. A recent job in Indiana saw the Kroll arrive on 320 separate truckloads. Because even the base takes up so much space and the crane has to be anchored in concrete, the Kroll is often placed directly in the center of the construction site, and the structure built up around it. And what becomes of the hole that is left once the building is close to completion? That usually ends up as the main lift shaft.

THE LARGEST MOBILE CRANE

MAMMOET PLATFORM TWINRING CONTAINERIZED MOBILE CRANE

Perhaps it's only fitting that the Mammoet Platform Twinring Containerized mobile crane has such a long and convoluted name. It is, after all, the biggest mobile crane in the world, and not exactly used to going unnoticed.

Fortunately, the moniker of Mammoet's gigantic piece of lifting equipment can also be shortened to PTC, although "Momo" is a nickname that is commonly used as well. When installation, repair, or construction jobs are too heavy for a conventional trailer-mounted crane to deal with, the PTC comes into its own.

Although not a "true" mobile crane insomuch as it arrives on site at jobs fully assembled and ready to work, the PTC's modular construction allows it to be easily packed away in standard shipping containers of 20ft x 40ft (6m x 12m) for easy relocation elsewhere. However, it does occupy 88 of those containers, and for one job in the USA in 2001, it turned up in 169 trucks.

Mounted on a huge ring supported by jacks, the latest PTC can lift up to 2204 tons (2,000,000kg). It has a "superlift" mode allowing it to handle ultra-heavy weights whereby a ballast load is suspended from its boom support arm and hangs out over the rear of the crane. Under usual circumstances, this counterweight is normally hung within the circumference of the rotating ring.

ABOVE AND LEFT: The Mammoet needs a complicated system of booms and cables, plus a large counterweight for balance.

SPECIFICATIONS

Country: Netherlands
Year built from: 2000
Weight: 2315 tons (2,100,000kg)
Lifting weight: 2204 tons (2,000,000kg)
Lifting height: 656ft (200m)
Time to rotate through 360 degrees: 8 minutes
Cost: N/A

Arguably, it was agriculture that prompted the first machines. Mankind started cultivating crops around 9500BC, and with that came the development of tools to make the job easier. Ploughs, pulled by oxen or horses, were among the first big machines, albeit very basic. For centuries, they, and other items of farming equipment, stayed simplistic, until the dawn of mechanization changed everything. The Industrial Revolution was just as much an agricultural one as well.

Although in some countries, plowing is still done the traditional way, by horse, other large animals, or even by hand, in countries where the effects of the Industrial Revolution were most far reaching, engineering minds were quick to look at the world of agriculture and apply new technology to it.

Traditionally, plows had been made of wood or iron for thousands of years: That changed to more durable steel from the 1830s onward. And once the structure became tougher, so the equipment got larger and bulkier. One of the largest plows from this era still exists, in a museum in Bakersfield, California. The enormous 1874 wheeled contraption—known as the Souther Ditch Plow—could cut 5ft (1.5m) wide and 3ft (0.9m) deep, and required 40 oxen to pull it. But even so, it wasn't that successful, and was abandoned in 1875.

Needless to say, it wasn't long before steam power was applied to the plow, but it was the advent of the tractor that ushered in the most radical changes in agriculture, allowing jobs to be done at a speed and on a scale previously undreamt of. The first tractors were hardly refined, and were essentially heavy steam engines with huge wheels to stop them sinking into the mud. They were unreliable and

so complicated as to be dangerous to their operators. Typical of the type was the Reeves 40-140 Cross Compound engine from the early part of the twentieth century, examples of which are still around today, still in operational condition as showpieces. Looking at one, the resemblance to a railroad steam locomotive is very noticeable but possibly explains why they really weren't that much good in the fields!

Tractors with gas-powered internal combustion engines started to catch on from 1910 onward, and were widespread by the 1920s. As engines became more powerful and more refined, so tractors grew up. The largest tractor to be built between World Wars I and II was the Minneapolis Twin City 60–90. This was an enormous beast, weighing upwards of 28,000lb (12,700kg) and was fitted with a 2230in^3 (36.5-liter) six-cylinder engine. Even today, they don't come much more monstrous, although the

ABOVE: Even before the era of mechanization, some agricultural machines—like this plow—were built on epic scales.

LEFT: The Minneapolis Twin City 60-90 tractor, weighing an incredible 28,000lb (12,700kg).

ABOVE: Tractors are produced in vast quantities at the Minneapolis factory.

TOP: The "Big Roy" tractor was so large and powerful that there wasn't enough for it to actually do!

Versatile Manufacturing Ltd. did build something to humble even this in the late 1970s. The "Big Roy" 1080 eight-wheel drive tractor was by far the biggest of its type ever and with 600hp (447.5kW) from its 1159.5in³ (19-liter) diesel engine, it was enormously capable. But only one prototype was built, after which it was realized that there wasn't any equipment around that could challenge its abilities, and it was canceled.

According to the USA's National Academy of Engineering, agricultural mechanization is one of the 20 greatest engineering achievements of the twentieth century. At the beginning of the century, one American farmer could produce enough food for 2.5 people. Now, it is 130. In the chapter ahead are some of the mega machines that have helped make this happen.

THE LARGEST TRACTOR EVER

BIG BUD 747

Almost all farms have a tractor or two, because they're among the most vital pieces of agricultural machinery. But only one farm—the Williams Homestead in Montana—has a tractor like the Big Bud 747, the largest in the world.

ABOVE AND BELOW: Four wide tires to each axle make Big Bud quite the agricultural monster and able to tackle any conditions. However, it does make the machine a little less useful when trying to negotiate fields of crops.

Montana is one of the biggest farming states in the USA. It's therefore fitting that this should be the home of the biggest tractor around as well, and that it's still hard at work. The Big Bud 747 has become a legend, and has even had a book devoted to it.

The Big Bud was originally built in Havre, in Montana, in 1977, intended for a cotton-farming operation in California operated by the Rossi Brothers. The huge, V16-engined machine stands over 14ft (4.3m) tall. Out in California, it was used for deep ripping (a function where prongs are dragged through the soil in order to let water drain). The machine stayed employed there for 11 years. It then found itself sold to Florida—for more deep ripping on another farm—before being retired. Or so it seemed. However, the Big Bud was eventually to get another lease of life.

Big Bud goes home

That was until 1997, when the Big Bud went back home to Montana, bought by the Williams Brothers of Big Sandy. They restored the tractor to its original condition and put it back into operation, albeit to pull a cultivator (a device for stirring and loosening soil) on their homestead farm. However, its sheer size ensured it was destined to be more than just a mere working machine, and it wasn't long before the Big Bud had become a local tourist attraction, too. It has been made the subject of a book as well, which isn't an accolade too many single tractors acquire.

The 747's original power output was remarkable enough at 760hp (567kW), but it now pumps out an awe-inspiring 900hp (671kW), which means its mass is also backed up by its abilities. Truly the Big Bud is the king of all tractors.

SPECIFICATIONS

Country: USA
Year built: 1977
Dimensions: 28ft 6in (8.7m) long; 21ft (6.35m) wide
Weight: 55 tons (50,000kg)
Maximum speed: 8mph (13km/h)
Power: 900hp (671kW)
Cost: N/A

THE LARGEST TRACKED AGRICULTURAL TRACTOR

CHALLENGER MT800B

Tracked agricultural tractors used to be rare on farms. As rugged as they were, they simply couldn't provide the speed and comfort of their wheeled rivals. However, in 1986, tracked-technology leader Caterpillar came up with a new system, and the true potential of these tractors was finally realized.

What Caterpillar came up with was a tough rubber track system that offered all the capabilities of a steel track system, but had a smoother, faster ride that didn't try to chew up every road it went along. Caterpillar dubbed the innovation Mobil-trac, and installed it on its new Challenger. It was so successful that a whole series of tracked Challengers followed. Other rival manufacturers, such as John Deere and Case-IH, who had traditionally only built wheeled tractors, introduced variations on the Mobil-trac theme as well.

However, the original still proved to be the best and, in the case of the MT800B, also the biggest. The Challenger line was bought out by AGCO in 2002 and the top tracked machine in the current range is the hefty MT875B, a potent 570hp (425kW) variant of the breed.

SPECIFICATIONS	
Country: USA	
Year built from: 2003	
Dimensions: 22ft 6in (7m) long; 12ft (3.5m) wide	
Weight: 25 tons (22,679kg)	
Maximum speed: 9mph (15km/h)	
Power: 570hp (425kW)	
Cost: N/A	

High-tech wonder

Most people think of tractors as being quite simple machines, but the MT800B series is a high-tech wonder, with a degree of technology that wouldn't disgrace an expensive sportscar. The transmission is electronically controlled, with nine clutches, and it has six onboard computers controlling the mechanics to ensure that everything operates as efficiently and flexibly as possible. However, that's pretty much where the sportscar resemblance ends, because even with all that power, and eight gears, the range-topping MT865B is only capable of 9.3mph (15km/h).

ABOVE: With triangular-shaped tracks, the Challenger MT800B tractor is distinctive. Different widths and types of belt can be fitted for different roles.

ABOVE: The MT900B's size makes articulation practically a necessity—with steering being done by the back wheels rather than the front.

THE LARGEST FOUR-WHEEL DRIVE TRACTOR
CHALLENGER MT900B

The Challenger range also encompasses "conventional" wheeled tractors. "Conventional" is probably not quite the right word to describe something as imposing as this agricultural monster, with four chunky tires to each axle.

SPECIFICATIONS

Country: USA
Year built from: 2006
Dimensions: 25ft (7.6m) long; 17ft (5m) wide
Weight: 30 tons (27,000kg)
Power: 570hp (425kW)
Maximum speed: 25mph (40km/h)
Cost: N/A

Fancy something of the size and power of Challenger's MT800B range of tractors, but would prefer it to have wheels instead of tracks? The MT900B series is practically the equivalent of the big tracked Challengers, except that it is fitted with wheels in each corner instead.

All-wheel drive, rear-wheel steer

There are four MT900B tractors, with the MT975B undoubtedly the flagship of the range, thanks to its Caterpillar turbocharged C18 ACERT diesel engine, which delivers a not-inconsiderable 570hp (425kW). However, despite the resemblance to the tracked '800s, the '900s are more than just the same machines with tires instead of tracks. The chief difference (apart from slightly increased dimensions and the obvious eight stocky tires, with two on each hub) is that the tractors are articulated behind the cab. This makes them more maneuverable than they would be with a rigid frame. Unusually though, it's the back wheels that do the steering—the front ones stay fixed, parallel to the front bodywork. However, with all the wheels powered, having the rear ones doing the turning makes the tractors more versatile because they can achieve a tighter turning circle.

There's one aspect of the M900B that puts one over on its tracked stablemates, and that's speed. The maximum speed that one of these is capable of is 25mph (40km/h). Maybe that's not much by usual vehicle standards, but over a muddy plowed field while towing a scraper or a harrow, that's a pretty outstanding pace.

THE LARGEST ROW-CROP TRACTOR

JOHN DEERE 8530 ROW-CROP TRACTOR

A row-crop tractor is a machine that typically has an adjustable tread width and a higher ground clearance than other tractors. This enables it to work in fields planted with tall crops planted in rows. Typical of the biggest of this type is John Deere's 8530 model.

The original John Deere was born in 1804 in Vermont. He was a blacksmith by trade but moved in to making agricultural machinery. The company he founded remains one of the oldest in America, and is much respected in the agricultural world. Vehicles like the 8530 are only likely to further enhance that reputation.

It isn't just the size of the John Deere 8530 that makes it so notable. It's the power as well. By their nature, row-crop tractors have to be more delicate than other agricultural machines because they need to be able to make their way accurately and carefully down lines of crops, doing as little damage as possible. However, the 8530 still manages to be muscular and mighty, without compromising those needs. At 275hp (205kW), it is the most powerful row-crop tractor ever built.

Narrow and tall

The chief features of the 8530 are its narrow bodywork, needed to negotiate crop passageways (although the double rows of tires do increase the total width significantly), as well as the tall cab, dubbed the Command View by John Deere. The cab comes complete with a computer display allowing the operator to monitor all aspects of what the tractor is doing, and how well it's doing it. What isn't obvious from looking is the innovative gearbox, known as Infinitely Variable Transmission (IVT), which allows smooth gear changes without the need for a clutch.

SPECIFICATIONS

Country:	USA
Year built from:	2005
Dimensions:	N/A
Weight:	12.5 tons (11,400kg)
Power:	275hp (205kW)
Maximum speed:	26mph (42km/h)
Cost:	$216,265

BELOW AND RIGHT: The John Deere 8530 can be fitted with two tires to each wheel for when those farming jobs get tough. Narrow body and high ground clearance allow the 8530 to pass over crops without damaging them.

THE LARGEST COTTON PICKER

JOHN DEERE 9996 COTTON PICKER

Once upon a time, laborers used to harvest a crop of cotton by hand. That changed from the 1950s onward, with the gradual introduction of the cotton picker, a machine that can work more than one row at a time. In fact, one machine can accomplish the equivalent of what once took up to 240 people to achieve.

Looking almost like a mutated vacuum cleaner, the John Deere 9996 is a common sight around the cotton states of the USA. This substantially built and complicated-looking machine travels down a row of plants removing cotton lint and seed, and is able to do up to six rows simultaneously. It achieves this using barbed spindles that rotate at high speed and separate the seed-cotton. The seed-cotton is then passed through to a basket, where eventually a "brick" of cotton is created, which can be easily stored back at the main farm.

Four-wheel drive to eight tires

The 9996 is among the elite of cotton pickers. The ability to pick six rows at once makes it stand out as a highly productive tool, and with its six-cylinder turbocharged diesel engine rated at 350hp (261kW), there's little to compare with it in terms of sheer power. Four-wheel drive (and two tires on every axle hub as standard) gives it the ability to tackle rough ground, and its large-capacity basket of 15,069ft³ (427m³) allows the machine to keep harvesting after many other rival machines have to stop and be emptied.

The console allows smooth fingertip control, and easy speed control. The basket is monitored electronically, so when it is full, a light comes on the cab and a horn sounds for three seconds. Unmistakable signals, no matter how wrapped up the driver is in his work.

ABOVE AND RIGHT: The forward-mounted, high-positioned cab gives the 9996 operator excellent visibility while working. Picked seed is stored in the cage at the back.

SPECIFICATIONS

Country: USA
Year built: Current
Dimensions: 28ft (8.5m) long; 17ft 6in (5m) tall
Weight: 22.5 tons (20,400kg)
Maximum speed: 12mph (19km/h)
Power: 350hp (261kW)
Cost: $430,000

SPECIFICATIONS

Country: USA
Year built from: 2004
Weight: 22 tons (19,850kg)
Maximum speed: 21mph (30km/h)
Power: 516hp (385kW)
Grain tank capacity: 360 bushels (12,500 liters)
Cost: $308,000

THE LARGEST COMBINE HARVESTER

CLAAS LEXION 590-R COMBINE HARVESTER

ABOVE: The wide cutting blade makes harvesting a snip—the 590-R can gather 26ft (8m).

The largest machines found on most farms are combine harvesters. So a combine harvester that's bigger than any of the others has to be something pretty amazing—an appropriate description indeed for the mega machine that is the Lexion 590-R.

The Lexion 590-R, and its sister machine, the 595-R, are two of the biggest machines in agriculture. Not only are the two machines the largest combine harvesters ever built, but they're also the most powerful. The difference between the two is that the 590-R has wheels, while the 595-R has tracks at the front and wheels at the rear.

Installed in front of the Lexions are headers, a set of removable cutters that are interchangeable depending on the crop. The combine harvester travels through the field, threshing the crop and passing it through the throat of the machine where the seed is separated. The seed passes through a chute on to a truck running by the side of the harvester, leaving the hay as a separate by-product.

Power, size, and technology

A few features make the 590/595-Rs stand out from the others. The 516hp (385kW) of power it wields is not an inconsiderable amount for any vehicle. Its size is substantial too, with the largest header measuring a full 26ft (8m) across. The technology inside is almost like something from a computer-game console. Driving speed and direction are controlled by a joystick, which is also used to adjust the cutter height, start and stop the loading process, and even activate the autopilot. Yes, there really is an autopilot—these machines are that advanced. They are definitely masters in their field.

THE LARGEST LOG HARVESTER

KOMATSU VALMET 941

Once upon a time, humans with saws used to fell trees. These days, where speed and scale are essential, a log harvester is used instead. These machines are capable of bringing down forests with almost brutal precision and speed.

ABOVE AND BELOW: Fitting the front wheels with a track gives the 941 more ability to cope with difficult forest conditions such as those shown here. The cab tilts with the crane/cutting arm so the operator gets the best view of operations.

SPECIFICATIONS

Country: Finland/Japan
Year built: Current
Dimensions: 10ft (3m) wide; 13ft (4m) high
Weight: 26 tons (23,500kg)
Power: 277hp (204kW)
Cutting diameter: 28in (700mm)
Cost: N/A

Trees are generally quite substantial items, one of Mother Nature's more robust creations, and quite a challenge when it comes to shifting them. But they are no match whatsoever for something like Komatsu's Valmet 941 log harvester. Looking a little like a hydraulic digger, this mega machine's specialty is more destruction than construction.

The design of the Valmet 941 is such that everybody involved in the process of logging is safe inside the machine. Inside, they are in no danger of being crushed by falling trees or being injured by a chainsaw, as they would be if they worked on the forest floor. In order to obtain the best visibility possible during felling and lifting jobs, the cab of the 941 also revolves and tilts.

Well armed

The crane arm of the 941 is designed to allow it to handle the largest and heaviest timber, and has a reach of 32ft 6in (10m). It's a versatile tool in the 941's armory, equipped with delimbing knives to remove branches, strong rollers to both hold the tree and allow the arm to move up and down the trunk, and, of course, a powerful chainsaw. After the tree has been stripped, the arm grasps the bottom, and the chainsaw bursts into life. In just seconds, the tree has been felled.

Fitted with six wheels, one novel feature of the 941 is that the twin axles at the front can be fitted with tracks. This gives the 941 more opportunity to get into difficult or muddy terrain where just having wheels might leave it stranded.

THE LARGEST MOWER

SPEARHEAD MACHINERY 820 ROTARY MOWER

So, you've got a lot of grass to cut, but can't afford, or don't have room for, something like a Claas Cougar self-propelled mower. Then simply opt instead for something like a Spearhead Machinery 820. Towed behind a tractor, it's capable of clearing a lot of ground.

BELOW AND RIGHT: The 820 demonstrates its on- and off-road practicality. Wide when working, it folds up for road transport so that it's about the same width and height as the tractor pulling it.

Y ou won't find a wider towed mower on the market than Spearhead's 820. At 27ft (8.2m) wide, its fanlike structure—hence the name—and 15 cutting blades underneath allow it to cut up to 220 acres (89 hectares) in a typical 10-hour day.

Auto technology in the field

It can be powered from whatever it is attached to, as long as it's got more than the minimum 150hp (112kW) required to pull and drive the 820's blades. The 250hp (186kW) gearbox on the mower sends drive to five rotors, which revolve at high speed. Each rotor has three blades mounted on it. Capable of cutting at heights between 1in (25mm) and 16in (400mm), the suspension of the 820 borrows from car technology, employing a Hydra-Gas system, where fluid and gas are mixed to soften shocks and stress. This method of springing was used on a number of popular British cars from the 1970s onward.

After use, the whole mower can be folded up, so it can be transported using just the inner four wheels instead of the full eight. Despite this, the

continuously welded frame is still very strong. Spearhead's brochures show the mower withstanding having a tractor driven over it.

SPECIFICATIONS

Country: UK
Year built: Current
Dimensions:
20ft (6.15m) long;
27ft 6in (8.4m) wide
Weight: 4.5 tons
(4100kg)
Power: Up to 250hp
(186kW)
Blade speed: 292ft/sec
(89m/sec)
Cost: N/A

RIGHT AND BELOW:
Hydraulic jacks at the front steady the TH580B as it extends its retractable arm upwards.

TH580B TELEHANDLER

It's a close-fought thing between Caterpillar's TH580B and JLG's G12-55A machines in the battle for telehandler supremacy. The JLG may have more power and be able to carry more, but the Caterpillar is bigger and can reach just that little bit higher.

Telehander is actually a contraction of "telescopic handler" and is one of the more widely used machines in large-scale agriculture. Essentially, it's a more versatile forklift truck, with a telescopic boom instead of a sliding lift mechanism, which means it can stretch forward as well as upward. Different attachments can be fitted to the end of the arm, and the handler has the ability to traverse tougher terrain than a forklift would be able to manage, thanks to its chunky tires.

Long and far

One of the undisputed kings of the type is Caterpillar's TH580B, which has a quite astonishing height and reach. It can lift objects up to 56ft (17m) above the ground, and its boom can stretch out up to 42ft (13m) away from the vehicle. However, this practicality comes at a cost. The more the TH580B extends its arm, the less it can carry, as the boom acts as a giant lever and makes it unstable—even with hydraulic jacks extended. Maximum capacity is a not-inconsiderable 11,000lb (5000kg), but at maximum lift height, it can only manage around 5500lb (2500kg). It's even more "puny" at full reach, when just 2500lb (1333kg) is the max—and that's with stabilizers. Nevertheless, these kind of weights are still well beyond the vast majority of other telehandlers. Most of the lifting operations are done through just one very versatile joystick, down by the righthand side of the driver. There are also three different steering modes: Two wheel, crab, and circle steer. All it takes to toggle between them is just a single, three-position switch.

SPECIFICATIONS

Country: USA
Year built from: 2003
Dimensions:
21.73ft (6.6m) long; 8ft 3in (2.54m) wide
Maximum speed:
25mph (40km/h)
Maximum reach:
56ft (17m)
Maximum weight:
11,000lb (5000kg)
Cost: $125,000

THE LARGEST PLANTER

JOHN DEERE DB90 PLANTER

BELOW: The yellow box in the center of the DB90 is the "Central Commodity System"— the hopper that holds the seeds for distribution to the 36 trailing arms.

The most important agricultural job is to grow things, and that process starts with the planting. As with almost everything else in the world of farming, the job isn't just fully mechanized now, but has its own mega machines.

SPECIFICATIONS

Country: USA

Year built: Current

Dimensions:
55ft (17m) long;
90ft (27.5m) wide

Weight: 17 tons
(15,400kg)

Maximum speed: N/A

Recommended tractor power: 280hp (209kW)

Cost: $214,769

Once upon a time, planting was simply done by hand, by scattering the seeds on plowed land. Not any more though. To get the highest crop yields, and to plant the fields in neat little rows that other machines can negotiate when the plants are growing, is now a highly precise job.

Extra wide for extra productivity

These days, the job calls for something like the John Deere DB90 planter, one of the latest generations of extra-wide planters capable of seeding an area 90ft (27.5m) wide in one go as it is towed behind a tractor. When being transported between jobs, however, the planter can be folded up into five sections, reducing its size to a mere 17ft 6in (5.36m).

Spread out over its breadth, the DB90 has 36 rows, each one finishing in a seed dispenser. Fed by a main central hopper, and with electrical power provided via the tractor, these dispensers distribute seeds in a flow regulated by the operator. Naturally, of course, it's all high-tech, with electronic systems monitoring every aspect of the seeding process. Powerful springs keep each row as close to the soil as possible so as not to waste any seed, and the flexible frame means the whole apparatus bends with the lie of the land. So, if a field isn't flat, then it is no problem, because as wide as it is, the DB90 can still cope.

KALMAR LMV 88 FORKLIFT TRUCKS

Forklift trucks are small and agile, and primarily intended to carry only small loads so they don't fall over. That's usually the case—except for the three trucks built by Kalmar back in 1991, which were anything but diminutive.

Today, the largest forklift truck made by Swedish firm Kalmar can lift 50 tons (45,360kg), while another has a tall enough lifting arm to allow it to stack a modern shipping container on top of four others. Either of these machines are worthy enough to earn Kalmar a place in this book.

Record still unsurpassed

However, these achievements pale into insignificance compared to the three trucks that Kalmar built back in 1991. The company was specially commissioned to build machines that were capable of lifting a staggering 195 tons (176,000kg), which is still something unsurpassed by any other maker. It was also enough to earn Kalmar a place in *The Guinness Book of Records*.

Built for an industrial concern, these diesel-engined, rubber-tired heavy lifters were able to achieve this feat by being very long and counterbalanced with ballast at their rear. This meant that the weight of what they were carrying was balanced by the vehicle's own rear mass. However, despite this design, the loading height was somewhat limited, with the forks only able to raise objects up to 7ft 6in (2.5m). Anything beyond this, and the trucks would have been in serious danger of becoming unstable and pitching forward.

Since these incredible Kalmar vehicles were made, nobody else has come close to constructing a forklift that has the same or even close to their impressive level of lifting ability.

ABOVE: Industrial forklift trucks can cope with different shapes—the tilting arm and prongs allow this Kalmar to carry pipework without it rolling off.

TRANS-GESCO TG88D LOG SKIDDER

Log skidder? Sounds complicated. What modern log skidders do is exactly the same thing that teams of horses and mules used to do in centuries gone past—they literally drag felled trees through a forest using sheer brute force, so they can be loaded on to trucks or trains.

TOP AND ABOVE:
Crawler tracks and a hefty engine allow the TG88D to successfully manhandle and drag logs.

SPECIFICATIONS

Country: Canada	
Year built: Current	
Dimensions: N/A	
Capacity: 35 tons (31,750kg)	
Power: 400hp (298kW)	
Price: N/A	

Suffice to say, such a job requires a lot of grip and power, something a machine like Trans-Gesco's imposing TG88D log skidder is able to offer by the pail. This tracked 400hp (298kW) turbocharged diesel-powered beast is the planet's largest skidder and forwarder. It is fitted with a 45ft² (4.2m²) grapple that is able to cope with the larger and longer trees that typically grow in North America. The boom that the grapple is mounted on can reach out as far as 26ft (8m).

When the going gets rough

The TG88D has three variants: The grapple skidder (fitted with, as its name suggests, a big grapple); a clambunk skidder (which has a different attachment where timber can be gradually loaded instead of grasped all at once as a grapple does); and a forwarder (which carries the logs clear of the ground on a trailer, in order to avoid damage to trees and soil, although this does limit the size of the timber that can be moved). The forwarder can cope with a payload of 25 tons (22,700kg), while the others can manage 35 tons (31,750kg), but the grapple skidder offers the further benefit of being able to use its hydraulic boom (normally folded out of the way when traveling, to aid the TG88D's balance) to push itself along if the ground gets too rough.

THE LARGEST TRACKED LOG LOADER

JOHN DEERE JD 800C

Time is money in today's mechanized logging industry. Fast loading—and unloading—of timber is essential to maximize profits. Enter the John Deere JD 800C, the world's biggest and fastest loader.

ABOVE AND BELOW: The JD 800C's excavator origins are noticeable but it has proved itself highly adept as a log loader.

SPECIFICATIONS

Country: USA
Year built from: 2003
Weight: 235 tons (213,115kg)
Power: 454hp (338kW)
Track length: 21ft (6.5m)
Cost: Approximately $1.5 million

John Deere's JD 800C didn't start life as a logging machine. In 2002, the type was introduced as one of the company's top-of-the-line excavators. Most hydraulic excavators can be fitted with arm attachments to allow them to perform different functions, and the potential of the 800C was soon realized.

From excavator to grapple

Because the 800C was a big excavator to start with, its transformation into a forestry machine automatically awarded it the status of the largest log loader in the world. Modifications were carried out to the cab, the tracked undercarriage, the boom, and, naturally, the end of the arm,

which can stretch to 51ft 6in (16m), and was fitted with a grapple capable of grasping logs. The revamped vehicle tipped the scales at 235 tons (213,155kg), and was powered by a 957in³ (15.7 liter) diesel engine, giving 454hp (338kW) in total.

But how well does the 800C do its job in comparison with the competition? One of the first companies to start using it for unloading logging trucks reported it was doing the job 50 percent faster than before—managing to unload an entire large trailer packed with timber in just five minutes. When it came to sending the logs on elsewhere, the 800C managed to fill a trailer in six minutes where 12 to 15 minutes had been the norm, and that had been with two smaller log loaders as well.

THE LARGEST WHEELED LOG LOADER

LIEBHERR A974 B

Liebherr's gigantic A974 B log loader is a truly unusual machine. For starters, it has eight wheels instead of the more usual tracks, and is the largest forestry loader to have this arrangement. It also has a cab that can be raised or lowered (even down to ground level if necessary) on an arm.

The enormous Liebherr A974 B is the world's largest wheeled material handler. It is essentially a versatile jack-of-all-trades, able to cope with most handling tasks. However, one field where the A974 B excels is as a forestry machine for loading and unloading timber.

Sprouting from the center of this eight-wheeled monster is a massive boom, capable of reaching over 69ft (21m) away from the vehicle, and swinging wood through a 160-degree radius, with a full 360 degrees of rotation. Even more novel, though, is the smaller arm beside it that supports the cab and allows this to also move up to 26ft (8m) away, giving the driver an unparalleled high-level view of operations.

Because of its size and wheel configuration (its turning circle is 69ft [21m]), the A974 B is generally confined to flatter, easier terrain than its tracked counterparts. It is often used as a static machine, prevented from toppling over by the four jacks that emerge from each corner and lift the whole vehicle, including the wheels, off the ground. The A974 B weighs around 140 tons (127,000kg), even before it has started throwing bits of tree around, so that's a lot of bulk to support.

Typical grapple capacity on the A974 B is 106ft³ (3m³) and the boom can support 8 tons (7257kg), so a lot of logs can be grabbed in one go.

ABOVE AND BELOW: With its cab mounted on a hydraulic arm, the Liebherr A974 B takes on an almost science-fiction appearance. During grappling, all the wheels are jacked up to prevent toppling.

SPECIFICATIONS

Country: Switzerland
Year built from: 1998
Dimensions: 57ft 6in (17.5m) long; 20ft (6m) wide
Weight: 140 tons (127,000kg)
Maximum speed: 6.2mph (10km/h)
Power: 431hp (317kW)
Cost: N/A

THE LARGEST LAWNMOWER

CLAAS COUGAR

Lawnmowers are traditionally quite compact—even the ones you sit on. Not so the Claas Cougar. This is a machine so large that its main problem is finding somewhere with enough grass for it to cut.

ABOVE: Retractable arms spread out from the Claas Cougar to allow it to cut areas much wider than the vehicle's breadth.

You won't find too many of these in the average suburban garden, trimming the lawn on a Sunday. The Claas Cougar mower is the big boy of the mowing world, a 480hp (350kW) monster that can clear up to 50 acres (20 hectares) an hour under ideal conditions.

From wide to narrow

The Cougar bristles with five limbs, to which grass-cutting attachments can be fixed. Full control from the cab allows these to be manipulated into any position to maneuver them around obstacles, or fold them out of the way completely. This is just as well because, with the Cougar being able to cut at widths of 46ft (14m), it needs a big area to play with. However, with the arms folded up, the whole machine shrinks to just 11ft (3.5m) wide.

Its top speed is 15mph (24km/h) while cutting, or 25mph (40km/h) when just traveling between jobs. One of the Cougar's more novel features is that its cab can be rotated through 180 degrees. When the machine is working, it faces the blades. When just driving normally, it points the other way, so the lethal cutting edges are safely tucked away at the rear. For this reason, the four-wheel drive machine also has all-wheel steering as well, so that it handles (more or less) in the same way, whichever direction it is being driven in. When you're in something with this many sharp edges, accidents really aren't advisable!

SPECIFICATIONS	
Country: Germany	
Year built from: 2004	
Dimensions: 38ft (11.5m) long; 44ft (14m) wide	
Weight: N/A	
Maximum speed: 25mph (40km/h)	
Power: 480hp (350kW)	
Cost: N/A	

THE LARGEST COMPACTOR (ROLLER)

AL JON INC VANTAGE 600 COMPACTOR

Today's landfill sites need specialist machines to squash all the waste of modern life, and not much surpasses Al Jon's Vantage 600 when it comes to rolling rubbish. The Al Jon Vantage is simply the biggest compactor money can buy.

Why compact trash? Well, law regulates most landfills, so they are only allowed to reach a certain height. And, if nothing else, a huge pile of rubbish is hardly the most attractive of sights.

Traditionally, bulldozers have been the usual machines to work on landfill sites, but because their load is spread out, they don't do a great job of actually compressing what's below them. Compactors, though, are specialized machines intended specifically to pile down waste.

Weight, size, and power

Weight is the key to success, which puts the Vantage 600 right at the top of its league. At 63 tons (57,000kg), it is heavier than any of its rivals, as well as being larger and more powerful. Trundling along on menacing-looking spikes, a hydrostatic transmission applies constant torque to the wheels, meaning it has superb adhesion and the ability to change direction without losing power. A blade of more than 17ft (5m) wide at the front allows the 600 to push heaped rubbish over so it can drive on top of it, and the operator hasn't been forgotten either. In order to combat, let us say, the fragrance of a landfill site, the cab is fitted with a system that filters fresh air from outside to make the job a little less smelly. There's also a rearview camera with a monitor, just in case the driver wants to check if a bit has been missed.

SPECIFICATIONS	
Country:	USA
Year built:	Current
Dimensions:	31ft 6in (9.6m) long; 15ft 6in (4.7m) wide
Weight:	63 tons (57,000 kg)
Maximum speed:	5mph (8kph)
Power:	600hp (447.5 kW)
Cost:	Approx $500,000

TOP RIGHT AND BELOW: It may not be pretty, but with that blade and those heavy spiked wheels, the Vantage 600 gets the job done.

3 LAND VEHICLES

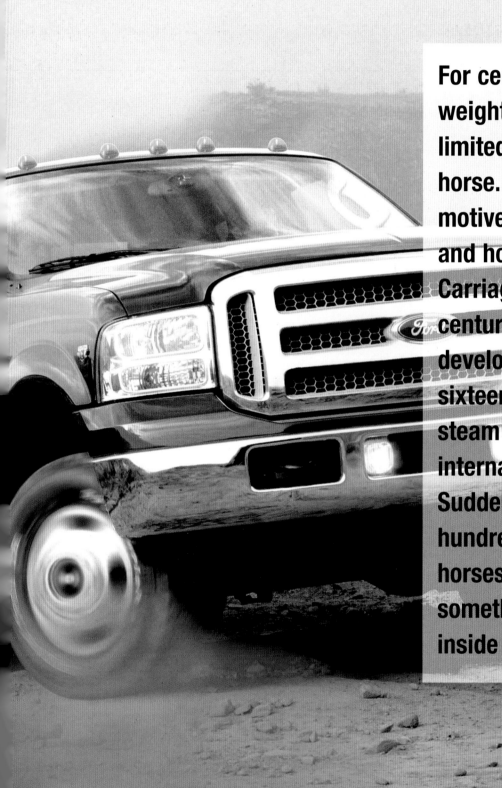

For centuries, the size and weight of land vehicles was limited by one simple factor: the horse. As the principal form of motive power, this dictated what and how much could be pulled. Carriages of the eighteenth century showed only marginal development from those of the sixteenth. And then came the steam engine and, later, the internal combustion engine. Suddenly, the work of tens, hundreds, even thousands of horses could be carried out by something that could be fitted inside a vehicle.

Suffice to say, land vehicles started to put on weight with the arrival of mechanization. Although there had been, and throughout the nineteenth century continued to be, experiments with steam-powered road vehicles, it was railroads that saw the first great mobile land machines of the Industrial Revolution.

The first practical steam locomotive to run on rails, invented by engineer Richard Trevethick in 1804, has every right to be called a mega machine because there was simply nothing else like it around at the time. But, as one of the chief tools of the Victorian era, and the only form of high-speed, long-distance travel, the development of railroads was rapid. In larger countries, such as Australia, India, and especially America, the train opened up the nation. This resulted in some impressive nineteenth-century machines—one of the more notable of which was El Gobernador (The Governor), a 4-10-0 steam built by the USA's Central Pacific Railroad in 1883. It had five driving wheels in a row, in addition to its other wheels, and, as the biggest steam locomotive in the world at the time, had to be transported in five pieces to the location where it was to do most of its work because it was thought too heavy for the bridges en route.

Steam power on the rails eventually gave way to diesel and electric power, and although less romantic than the atmospheric and visibly potent steam engines they replaced, extra efficiency and reliability allowed trains to grow larger and stronger still. Some magnificent machines were produced, one of the more famous types being the Deltic diesel-electrics, which took over the top link express duties from steam on Britain's premier London to Scotland trains. At their advent in the 1950s, they were the most powerful single-unit diesel locomotives in the world, with 3300hp (2461kW) from their two engines.

However, railroads had also given birth to some more threatening machinery, such as the "Paris" big gun. Mounted on a rail wagon, this

TOP: Ford's F-150 pickup has been the world's favorite light truck for decades.

ABOVE: Although the style of the F-150 may have changed, its impressive load-lugging abilities remain constant.

LEFT: More than 21,000 DUKWs were built during World War II—proving their worth in situations like this where river crossings were destroyed.

ABOVE: El Gobernador, of the Central Pacific Railroad, was a massive machine for its era.

ABOVE: The "Paris" big gun was the largest artillery weapon ever seen, when it was built during World War.

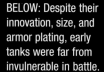

BELOW: Despite their innovation, size, and armor plating, early tanks were far from invulnerable in battle.

enormous canon was used by Germany to bombard Paris in 1918. Its 92ft (28m) long barrel could hurl shells at the city from 80 miles (130km) away. World War I was also responsible for the emergence of the first true massive non-rail mobile land machines, in the form of tanks. The invention of the successful, small gasoline engine had seen the birth of the automobile by the end of the nineteenth century, but these pioneering vehicles were small and lacking in strength. World War I monsters like the French Char 2C Heavy Tank of 1918, the biggest of its era, broke new limits with what could be achieved with vehicles using the internal combustion engine. By World War II, there were ingenious machines such as the USA's DUKW amphibious vehicle, effectively a boat as well as a transport truck.

The bestselling vehicle in the world today—indeed, the bestselling for over the last two decades—is the Ford F-150 pickup truck. It's not exactly diminutive, and its continuing success suggests that, despite environmental concerns about big land vehicles, they aren't likely to be disappearing anywhere soon.

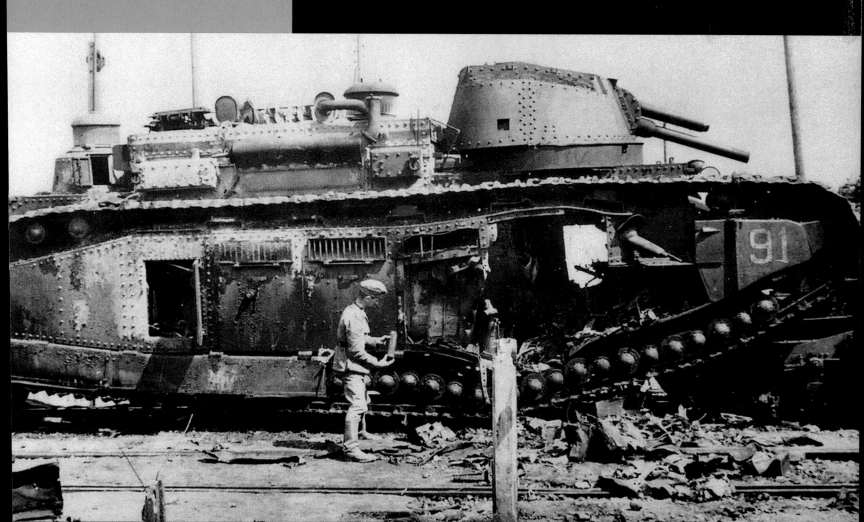

THE LARGEST JET-PROPELLED CAR

THRUSTSSC

The world's largest jet-powered car isn't the obvious record that comes to mind with ThrustSSC. This was, after all, the car that broke the land speed record and also became the first vehicle to travel faster than the speed of sound on the ground.

BELOW: The two enormous General Electric J79-GE-17A jet engines dwarf the rest of the bodywork. With two wheels at the back and one at the front, ThrustSSC can also lay claim to being the world's fastest three-wheeler.

When a car's specification features two afterburning engines from an F-4 Phantom II jet fighter, it's a fair bet it isn't being constructed to amble around town on the daily commute. ThrustSSC (SuperSonicCar) was built with just two purposes in mind: To be the fastest car of all time, and to reach Mach 1.

Up against America

The brainchild of Richard Noble—who had taken the land speed record in 1983 with Thrust2—ThrustSCC was put together between 1994 and 1996, and taken to the Black Rock Desert in Nevada for the speed attempt in 1997. It had competition from a US rival, Spirit of America, but

repeated engine problems for the US car meant that it was ThrustSSC, driven by RAF pilot Andy Green, that was able to achieve Mach 1.016, or 1227.99km/h (763.035mph), just one day after the fiftieth anniversary of Chuck Yeager achieving the same thing in the air. An extraordinary photo taken of the run showed the sonic shockwave spreading out from ThrustSSC as it achieved Mach speed—something that had never been photographed before.

ThrustSSC now resides in a museum in Coventry, in the UK, where its 54ft (16.5m) length and 12ft (3.7m) width, along with its 15ft 6in (4.73m) long engines, can be appreciated up close—even if the Thrust's ability to reach 600mph (1000km/h) in just 16 seconds can't.

SPECIFICATIONS

Country: UK

Year built: 1994–96

Dimensions:
54ft (16.5m) long;
12ft (3.7m) wide

Weight: 11.5 tons
(10,500kg)

Maximum speed:
Mach 1.016/
763.035mph
(1227.99km/h)

Thrust: 50,000lb
(223kN) from two
engines

Fuel consumption:
0.04 mpg (5500 liters
per 100km)

Cost: N/A

THE LARGEST ENGINE CAPACITY, CURRENT

BUGATTI VEYRON

When Volkswagen revitalized the famous Bugatti racing marque in 1999, it was the Veyron sportscar that made all the headlines. It's the most powerful, most expensive, and fastest car currently available, which would make it enough of a true mega machine even if it didn't also have the world's largest capacity engine too.

TOP AND ABOVE: Whether at rest or in motion, the Veyron looks spectacular.

It's taken a long time for the Bugatti Veyron to reach production, although with a mere 70 or so cars built during 2006, production isn't quite the word. The world's most exclusive sportscar was seen at various car shows and events across the world for seven years before building models for customers started properly in 2006.

Speedy but thirsty

Still, there's little about this car that is like anything else on the roads. Top speed of the Veyron is an almost unbelievable 253mph (407km/h), although it could go faster if only current tire technology would allow it.

At those kind of speeds though, it manages a fuel consumption of 2.1 miles per gallon (125 liters per 100km), which is enough to empty the gas tank in a mere 12.5 minutes.

At the heart of this road-going rocket is a W16 engine of 488in³ (7993cc), the biggest engine by capacity of any car built today. The design is essentially two V8 engines mated together, with a total power output of a rather impressive 1040hp (775.5kW).

The current price for the Bugatti is around $1,440,880. Still, it's even more expensive for Volkswagen, as it has been estimated that each car costs the German car firm over $9,250,000 to make.

SPECIFICATIONS

Country: USA
Year built: 1913–18
Dimensions: 12ft (3.7m) wheelbase
Weight: Varied depending on model type
Power: 66hp (49kW)
Engine displacement: 825in³ (13.5 liters)
Cost: $7200 (Landau model)

LEFT: Despite the enormous engine, the Pierce-Arrow 66 was far from powerful by modern standards. It had an imposing road presence though.

THE LARGEST ENGINE CAPACITY EVER ON A CAR

PIERCE-ARROW 66

During the early days of the automobile, engines were generally very inefficient, with large-capacity motors often turning out the sort of power figures that even the smallest-engined car could easily exceed today. The years 1912 to 1918 saw three cars that shared an engine capacity of 824in³ (13.5 liters), the greatest there has ever been.

Those three cars were the Pierce-Arrow 66 from 1913 to 1918, the Peerless 6-60 of 1912 to 1919, and the more obscure Fageol of 1916 to 1917, all of which were built in America and had six-cylinder engines of equal (and enormous) size. The Pierce-Arrow was the most notable of this trio, with the company being preferred by American presidents of the era. Its 66 model, rated at 66hp (49kW), was available in several guises, from stately limousine down to the basic open-top Raceabout model. Its power and performance made it popular among Prohibition-era alcohol smugglers, who eventually ended up racing their cars and went on to found NASCAR.

Powerful and pricey

Almost as prestigious, the Peerless 6-60 was somewhat less powerful at 60hp (45kW), but it was the Faegol that almost surpassed both these put together in output. Its immense six-cylinder Hall & Scott engine gave it 124hp (92.5kW), but at prices ranging from $9500 (for just the chassis!) to $17,000, it was far too expensive to succeed.

All three companies had disappeared from car-making before the beginning of World War II, with Fageol vanishing in 1917, Pierce-Arrow surviving until 1938 after being bought by Studebaker, and Peerless moving into brewing in 1931. It still exists today as the maker of Carling beer.

THE LARGEST CAR OF ALL TIME

BUGATTI ROYALE

ABOVE AND BELOW:
Nothing discreet about a
Bugatti Royale—a car
designed to impress! At
the top is a Napoleon
Coupe de Ville version,
while the bottom car has
coachwork by Binder.
Note the elephant
mascot that adorns
all Royales.

There has never been a more extravagant car than a Bugatti Royale—or a bigger one. These huge French cars were the last words in elegance and power, intended to surpass Rolls-Royces and Cadillacs as the ultimate luxury road machine. Although the intention was only ever to make 25, a mere six were built.

The radiator mascot of the Bugatti Royale was an elephant, somewhat fitting for a car that was larger than anything else and, ultimately, one of motoring's biggest white elephants. After an Englishman told Ettore Bugatti that "If one desired to be fastest, one must choose a Bugatti, but it was evident that if one wanted the best, one must choose a Rolls-Royce," Bugatti vowed to come up with something that would change this.

Grand scale

And the massive Type 41 Royale was just such a car. First seen as a prototype at the German Grand Prix in 1928, everything about it was to a grand scale. An extensive hood housed a 779in³ (12,763cc) engine of around 300hp (224kW), and the rest of the bodywork was built to the same epic scale, with overall length stretching to over 20ft (6m). Every one of the further six built had a different body, ranging from low, sleek roadster, to very stately limousine, the latter intended for European royalty.

Competition

But, there was a competitor from America in the shape of the almost as grand, but cheaper, Duesenberg, and many of the customers intended for the Bugatti bought one of these instead. It was a blow to Ettore Bugatti's pride, and production was halted, although the powerful engine design later went on to be used in French railcars.

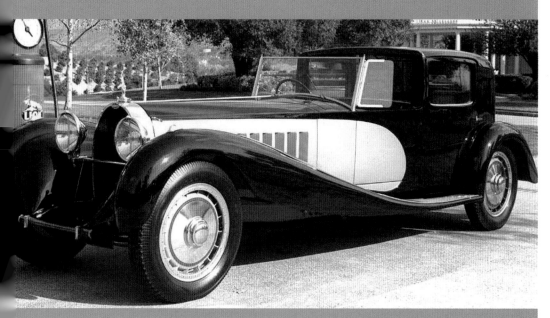

THE WIDEST CAR OF ALL TIME

KOENIG COMPETITION

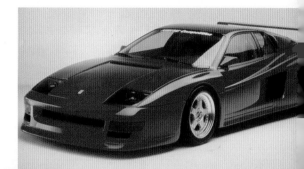

BELOW: The Koenig Competition was based on the Ferrari Testarossa, but tuned to perfection and sporting a body kit to make it even more visually exciting. Coupe and convertible versions are illustrated.

Koenig is a German tuning firm that started tuning Ferraris in 1974. Its most successful model was the Koenig Competition, based on the 1980s Ferrari Testarossa. Among the changes carried out were broader body kits and bigger wheels, thus creating the widest car in the world.

When Ferrari unleashed its Testarossa in 1984, it was a stunner. With a 301.5in³ (4942cc) 12-cylinder engine and a top speed of 181mph (291km/h), there was little else around at the time to compare for performance and handling. Its distinctive side cooling slats also made it into the widest production car around, at 6ft 6in (1.97m).

Powering up

For those who just wanted a bit more than Ferrari could offer, Koenig had its extreme Competition tuning package. Among the options, wealthy customers could select were a 1000hp (745kW) twin turbo engine—enough to send the car rocketing up to 230mph (370km/h)—plus brake and suspension modifications so the driver could keep control at that kind of speed.

To make the Koenig-modified Testarossa even more special, these mechanical changes could be accompanied by new body kits, and a convertible version. It was the front and rear wing extensions, made of carbon-kevlar or glass fiber, that bulked the Koenig Competition out to almost 7.2ft (2.2m), an increase of 8.7in (22cm) over the standard Ferrari, and by far the broadest car in the world. Of course, all this did mean that you also needed a very wide road to enjoy a Koenig Competition.

SPECIFICATIONS

Country: Italy (built), Germany (modified)

Year built: 1984–92

Dimensions: 14ft 6in (4.5m) long; 7ft (2.2m) wide

Weight: 3500lb (1589kg)

Maximum speed: 230mph (370km/h)

Power: 1000hp (745.5kW)

Engine displacement: 301.5in³ (4942cc)

Cost: $94,000 for standard Testarossa (1985 price)

DUESENBERG SJ

Duesenberg was one of the most glamorous of all American car marques, rivaling European firms like Rolls-Royce and Bugatti for exclusivity and luxury. Its greatest model was the SJ, a supercharged version of the already very special (and expensive) Model J. These cars became the longest cars—bar limousines—ever built.

BELOW: Finished to the highest standards, the SJ was sheer opulence on wheels and built on a giant scale, with the length of some versions stretching 20ft 6in (6.25m).

Introduced in 1928, the Duesenberg Model J was a no-expense-spared attempt to build the best car in the world. And, with customized bodywork coming from the best coachbuilders in Europe and America, several of the cars undoubtedly were the greatest of their kind. But such luxury came at considerable cost. At launch, the top model cost $25,000, the equivalent of almost $360,000, or over eight times the annual salary of a doctor of the era.

Supercharging arrives

But there was more to come. In 1932 came a supercharged version of the J, dubbed the SJ. Sheer power, 320hp (235.5kW), and speed, 135–140mph (217-225km/h),

were just two of the features that made this type particularly stand out, but some of the body styles customers could choose were the longest ever on a nonstretched production model. For example, the SJ Town Car stretched a vast 20ft 6in (6.25m).

Unfortunately for Duesenberg, the price and opulence of its cars made it very vulnerable to economic conditions, and the financial depression throughout the 1930s meant that it was rarely that far away from going out of business. In 1937, the inevitable happened, and Duesenberg, along with sister car firms Cord and Auburn, collapsed. Some of the most fantastic American cars ever were suddenly no more.

SPECIFICATIONS

for SJ Town Car

Country: USA

Year built: 1932–37

Dimensions:
20ft 6in (6.25m) long;
6ft (1.88m) wide

Weight: 6400lb
(2905kg)

Maximum speed:
106mph (170km/h)

Engine displacement:
420in³ (6884cc)
supercharged

Power: 320hp (238kW)

Cost: $9500 for basic
chassis

THE HEAVIEST PRODUCTION CAR, CURRENT

ZIL 41047 LIMOUSINE

The heaviest passenger car currently in production is the ZIL 41047 limousine, Russia's answer to Rolls-Royce, Mercedes-Benz, and Cadillac. Intended for government officials, including presidents, only very few of these cars are built every year. They are rarely seen outside Russia and the Commonwealth of Independent States (CIS), and are way beyond the pocket of ordinary citizens.

SPECIFICATIONS

Country: Russia
Year built from: 1985
Dimensions:
21ft (6.33m);
7ft (2m) wide
Weight: to 4.5 tons
(4110kg)
Maximum speed:
118mph (190km/h)
Power: 315hp (232kW)
Engine displacement:
470in³ (7700cc)
Cost: N/A

TOP AND ABOVE:
ZIL limousines are
now only built in
tiny numbers, and
despite their outdated
1980s design, are
still very expensive.

Introduced in 1985, the ZIL 41047 limousine has remained largely unchanged and is regarded as something of an anachronism, a motoring relic from USSR days that has, somehow, managed to survive into the twenty-first century free-market days of the former Soviet Union.

Seven-seater

There's little about the ZIL that reflects modern design. With its looks based on contemporary American designs of the late 1970s and early 1980s, much of the mechanical underpinnings of the ZIL date back even further—one of the main reasons the car is the heaviest of all models built today. A hefty V8 of 470in³ (7.7 liters)—still using old-fashioned carburetor technology—lurks within substantial, robustly constructed bodywork. The car is capable of seating seven occupants, including the driver. This amount of space inside extends the length of the ZIL to 21ft (6.33m), helping total weight to mount up to 4.5 tons (4110kg).

However, quite what is in store for the 41047 is uncertain. The opening up of Russia to the West has seen luxury marques from other European companies being chosen as government transport. And while ZIL's future as a truck and bus manufacturer looks secure, the outlook for the old-fashioned cars it builds is less optimistic.

THE LARGEST STRETCHED LIMO

JAY OHRBERG STRETCHED LIMO

For some people, an "ordinary" stretched limo simply isn't enough. They have to go a little bit further, or, in the case of customizer Jay Ohrberg of California, about 22 wheels further. He's the man behind the world's longest car, which has 26 wheels and stretches for 100ft (30.5m).

W hat wouldn't you expect to find on a limousine? A satellite dish maybe? Well, they're pretty common these days. How about a king-sized waterbed? Not that difficult to put in, especially if the limousine is long enough. A swimming pool, complete with diving board? Okay, well that's a little less likely. What about, as the *pièce de résistance*, a functioning helicopter pad? That must be impossible.

Limo like a truck

Actually, all these are features of Jay Ohrberg's longest limo on Earth, which is more akin to a mansion house on wheels. And of course, it has more of those than any other car as well. Thanks to its size, it's not a particularly practical vehicle, as sharp turns present a major problem, even though it can bend in the middle, like an articulated truck. The swivel point is situated after the seventh axle. However, even with this little touch of practicality built in, the limo had spent much of its life being exhibited at shows, or appearing in movies or on TV.

Based on a Cadillac Fleetwood, the rear of the car is open like a pickup truck. But instead of a loading bay, this is where the swimming pool is situated. Ideal for those hot Californian summer days and nights.

Jay Ohrberg has been behind many other weird and wacky automobile creations, including another Cadillac transformed into a giant pink guitar. Which would probably be worthy of its own entry in this book as the world's biggest mobile guitar.

ABOVE: Imagine replacing all those tires! At 100ft (30.5m), this is a stretched limo with a lot of luxury.

SPECIFICATIONS

Country: USA
Year built: 1970s
Dimensions:
100ft (30.5m) long;
7ft (2m) wide
Speed: N/A
Engine: 500in³
(8194cc) V8
Cost: N/A

ABOVE AND LEFT: The sleek shape of the Eliica aids its speed and range. Each wheel has an electric motor on it, with the front two responsible for the steering.

SPECIFICATIONS

Country: Japan
Year built: 2005
Dimensions: 17ft (5.1m) long; 6ft (2m) wide
Weight: 5291lb (2400kg)
Power: 60hp (480kW) from eight engines
Maximum speed: 230mph (370km/h)
Cost: $320,000 development costs

THE LARGEST ELECTRIC CAR, CURRENT

ELIICA ELECTRIC CAR

Although electric cars have been around almost since the early days of the automobile, they've always been handicapped by their range and power. It takes a lot of batteries, and therefore a lot of space, for an electric car to achieve the potential of a conventional car. However, the futuristic Eliica may just be able to prove that electricity can beat gas.

First shown at the 2005 Japanese Motor Show, the Eliica electric car—currently the largest and most successful of its kind—looks like something from another planet. And it might well be, because the technology it uses is very advanced. The aerodynamic body sits on top of a hollow chassis containing the bank of 80 batteries, supplying current to a 80.5hp (60kW) motor on each wheel (of which there are eight), with the front four responsible for the steering. When the car brakes, the motors turn into generators instead, gaining power from the disc brakes. Such attributes give the Eliica the ability to go for 200 miles (320km) between charges, although it does take 10 hours to recharge. However, this can be done using a domestic electricity supply.

Electric supercar

Unlike most long-distance electric cars, the Eliica doesn't sacrifice performance. Top speed of one of the two prototypes built so far, on a high-speed test track, was 230mph (370km/h), and it can accelerate to 60mph (96.5km/h) from rest in under four seconds. Such characteristics rank it alongside the ultimate petrol supercars available today.

Although only two test versions have been built so far, the results have been so promising that there is a plan to build 200, to be sold commercially. Could this be the future of personal road transport?

THE LARGEST PRODUCTION SUV, STREET LEGAL

HUMMER H1

Originally built for military purposes, the civilian version of the Hummer went on sale in 1991. The original H1 version is the biggest production sports utility vehicle ever to be sold to the public, unless you count the even more outrageous stretched limousine H2 model.

A ccording to popular legend, it was Arnold Schwarzenegger, the action-movie actor now turned Governor of California, who convinced the AM General company to start selling the High Mobility Multipurpose Wheeled Vehicle (HMMWV or Hum-Vee) outside the closed military market. Hummer was the more user-friendly name chosen, and "Big Arnie" was, naturally, the first to own one.

Fighting machine for the street

Although the Hummer range has expanded under General Motors (who took over in 1999), it's the first H1 version, discontinued in June 2006, that is still regarded as the definitive model. It's definitely the largest interior, being based on the standard military version, with only a few extra creature comforts such as more comfortable seats, a stereo system, and air-conditioning. But the big V8 diesel engines, body, and suspension are the same as those serving with US forces around the world, although, obviously, the street models don't get the protective plating. Or the weaponry.

Although the H2 version of the Hummer is smaller overall, it has become a popular basis for "stretching" into a limousine, thus making it one of the few road vehicles able to make an H1 Hummer look humble!

As popular as they are with those who've bought them—no other personal form of transport is more imposing on the roads— Hummers are disliked by many others because of their size, how much fuel they consume, and their potentially damaging effects on the environment.

SPECIFICATIONS	
Country:	USA
Year built:	1991–2006
Dimensions:	15ft (5m) long; by 7ft (2m) wide
Weight:	4 tons (3680kg)
Maximum speed:	83mph (133km/h)
Power:	300hp (224kW)
Cost:	$140,796

TOP RIGHT AND ABOVE: Just the sort of terrain the Hummer loves—although many seem to spend all their time on road instead of off it!

THE LARGEST TOUR COACH

DESERT STORM TOUR BUS

Based on a standard American school bus, the coach known as Desert Storm, used on tours around the sand dunes north of Perth in Western Australia, now has little in common with its educational-use sisters. Converted to four-wheel drive and running on huge tires to allow it to negotiate the dunes, it's claimed by its owners to be the largest 4x4 tour bus in the world.

ABOVE: It may be a bus used to school runs, but military-style suspension and heavy-duty off-road tires mean Desert Storm is now happy to tackle loose sand dunes.

The idea to run adventure trips so that tourists could explore the 1.5 mile (4km) square area of desert and dunes around Lancelin in Western Australia was envisaged in 1997, but an immediate barrier was the lack of a suitable vehicle. There was nothing capable of taking passengers over loose sand hills sometimes up to 164ft (50m) in length.

Monster-truck tour bus

So, the tour company decided to have its own made. A standard 32-seat school bus was shipped over from America, but a few changes were carried out. Heavy-duty military-specification suspension and four-wheel-drive mechanics were fitted, with the whole ensemble topped off by four "Monster Truck" type tires to give Desert Storm a height of 13ft (4m)—the usual height for this kind of vehicle is about 10ft 6in (3m). The lower bodywork was extended downward to cover up the running gear, but Desert Storm still has superb ground clearance. And to emphasize the contrast between it and a standard school bus, the traditional yellow livery was retained. Desert Storm has Terra 5ft 6in (1.7m) tall tires, four-wheel steering, and a 1000-watt sound system!

THE LARGEST BUS

FOREMOST TERRA BUS

Take a normal bus off-road and it's likely to only be a matter of seconds before it becomes totally stuck. Not the Foremost Terra Bus, though. It's the toughest, most rugged bus around, with all its six wheels driven, a 250hp (187kW) engine, and impressive off-road capabilities, but a top speed of just 25mph (40km/h).

That 25mph (40km/h) speed limit speaks volume about the Terra Bus. It's really at its happiest off the road rather than on it—especially when you take into account its turning circle of 72ft (22m), far wider than most streets will allow.

Off-road passenger carrier

Built by Canadian heavy-load specialist Foremost, the diesel-powered Terra Bus can carry up to 56 passengers, practically anywhere they want to go, thanks to the six-wheel-drive, which can cope with almost any terrain. The 5ft 6in (2m) tall Terra tires are designed to run on low pressures, so there's less chance of a blowout in the snow, mud, and desert environments the Terrabus is most at home in. The tires are also high floatation, should the Terra Bus find itself having to cross any less-solid areas of ice.

Primarily intended as a transporter for getting personnel out to difficult locations, the 13ft (4m) Terra Bus has also been finding popularity as a tourist vehicle, especially in areas where snow conditions prohibit less competent passenger-carrying vehicles. With windows all around, including on the roof, the Terra Bus can provide views few other busses would be able to. And that's before it has gone to places that no other bus would be able to reach, either.

BELOW: The Foremost Terra Bus is able to take its passengers to environments where other busses fear to tread.

SPECIFICATIONS

Country: Canada
Year built: Current
Dimensions:
48ft (15m) long;
11ft (4m) wide
Weight: 33 tons
(29,940kg)
Maximum speed:
25mph (40km/h)
Power: 250hp (187kW)
Cost: N/A

VOLVO B12M BI-ARTICULATED BUS

An articulated bus is a common enough sight these days, but what about a bi-articulated bus? Volvo's current B12M high-capacity passenger model is more akin to a truck or even a train, with two passenger compartments linked to the main body of the bus by two large swivel joints. All together, they make the vehicle the world's longest commercially available bus.

SPECIFICATIONS

Country: Sweden/Brazil

Year built from: 2004

Dimensions:
88ft (27m) long;
8ft (2.5m) wide

Passenger capacity:
270

Weight: 44 tons
(40,500kg)

Power: 340hp (250kW)

Cost: N/A

ABOVE: Why use one bus, when you have three all in one go?

They don't come any longer than this. Designed for heavily populated cities where single, or even articulated, busses are unable to cope with passenger numbers, the three-section B12M is the very inventive solution to shifting lots of people in one go. In total length, it measures 88ft (27m) and can hold 270 passengers. To put that into perspective, a standard single B12M bus, which is regarded as large in its own right, is 33ft (10m) long, and can hold about 50 people.

Bendy bus

A vehicle of this size and capacity—often referred to as a "bendy bus"—needs a lot of engine to move it, and doing the service in the B12M is a 732in^3 (12 liter) six-cylinder diesel unit of 340hp (250kW). Computer controls monitor all the vital functions of the Volvo, including giving the driver a warning if turntable angles are excessive. Air suspension is used throughout.

Built on a specially strengthened chassis, the eight-wheeled Volvo is so large that most cities operating it have dedicated bus lanes and specially sited stops. Routes have to be planned out carefully. Too sharp a corner, or too narrow a street, and the B12M could find itself stuck. Backing up a vehicle of this size isn't exactly easy.

ABOVE AND TOP: So long is the B12M that special routes have to be built for it, employing gradual bends (as bottom).

THE LARGEST BICYCLE EVER

DIDI SENFT BICYCLE

Didi Senft is one of life's eccentrics—a passionate German cycling enthusiast who turns up at every Tour de France event dressed as a devil, just for the fun of it. However, he's also an inventor, who has created over 100 cycles, one of which is listed by *The Guinness Book of Records* as the biggest on the planet.

LEFT AND BELOW: Didi Senft's bike is so tall, it has trouble fitting through bridges and tunnels.

SPECIFICATIONS

Country: Germany
Year built: N/A
Dimensions: 25ft 6in (8m) long; 12ft (4m) high
Weight: N/A
Power: One person power
Cost: N/A

If you're ever watching the Tour de France and a very cheerful Satan with a German accent pops up beside you brandishing a pitchfork, don't be too concerned. It's likely to be Didi Senft, and somewhere nearby will probably be one of the largest bicycles in the world. For most events that Didi attends, he tows a huge bike behind his van.

Beyond an ordinary bike

However, this cycle isn't the largest in the world. That one stays behind when Didi is on the road, because it's so tall that, he says, he has trouble transporting it under bridges and through mountain tunnels. Which isn't really much of a surprise as it is 25ft 6in (8m) long and 12ft (4m) tall. The wheels alone measure over 10ft (3m) tall. Despite being twice the size of an average person though, the bike can be ridden, although it does require a few helpful people around to hold it up while the rider gets on. Braking and getting off again can also be a little tricky too.

Bicycle chain

The mechanism of the aluminum-framed bike is conventional (and the same size as you'd find on an ordinary-sized version), but the chain has to go through some complicated linkages to make it able to reach the back wheels and still be linked to pedals that can be used by the rider.

THE LARGEST MOTORCYCLE EVER

GREG DUNHAM MOTORCYCLE

RIGHT AND BELOW: You can see just how large Greg Dunham's motorcycle is when it is compared with a car and a truck.

When friends of California man, Gregory Dunham, bet him he wouldn't be able to build the world's largest rideable motorcycle, he told them he could. Of course, it did take three years of work and cost him about $300,000 to do so. But at least he made it into *The Guinness Book of Records*.

M ost people probably wouldn't take a bet to build the biggest operational motorcycle on the planet that seriously. After all, when Greg Dunham's friends made the wager, there was a massive motorbike already in existence. Called Big Toe and powered by a 326in³ (5343cc) Jaguar V12 engine, it had been finished in Sweden in 1998 and measured 8 ft (2m) high by 15ft (5m) long. If Dunham really wanted to beat that record, he'd have to build something pretty incredible.

Stepping on the Big Toe

However, he managed it. Despite the three-year timescale and the substantial amount of money, by 2005, Dunham

had constructed something that eclipsed even Big Toe—in most dimensions. His motorbike was over 3ft (1m) taller and nearly 5ft (1.5m) longer. Its tires alone—at 6ft (2m)—were almost as big as Big Toe was high in its entirety, and at 502in³ (8.2 liters), the engines were more substantial.

Safety features

Because the "proper" handlebars are in scale with the rest of the bike, the actual steering (plus the other controls) is from a small cage mounted below this part of the bike. And, although ostensibly a two-wheeled machine, this most grownup of bikes does need small stabilizers on the rear wheels, to stop it falling over.

SPECIFICATIONS

Country: USA
Year built: 2003–05
Dimensions: 25ft (6m) long; 11ft (3m) high
Weight: 3 tons (2950kg)
Engine size: 502in³ (8.2 liter)
Maximum speed: N/A
Cost: $300,000

THE LARGEST MOTORIZED TRICYCLE

HARLEY-DAVIDSON ANACONDA

It may look like a motorbike but this much-expanded Harley-Davidson is the world's biggest tricycle. Behind the idea was Steve "Smokey" McGill of Kansas City, who simply wondered why nobody had created a limo motorcycle. And when he couldn't come up with a decent reason, he decided to build it himself.

ABOVE: The Anaconda can accommodate one driver plus 10 passengers. That front engine is the nonfunctional one, just there for display.

SPECIFICATIONS

Country: USA
Year built: 2003–04
Dimensions:
19ft 6in (6m) long
Weight: 1420lb (644kg)
Maximum speed:
Approximately 90mph
(145 km/h)
Power: Upwards of
60hp (43.8kW)
Cost: N/A

It was in 2004 that Steve "Smokey" McGill's Anaconda—fittingly named after the longest snake in the world—made its public debut, after being inspired by a customized Harley-Davidson trike he'd seen in a shop. That machine had impressed him but he felt it could be longer. He xeroxed some pictures of it, stuck them together until he'd created a 10-seater machine, and then started to think about to make it a reality.

Three-wheeled limousine

The Anaconda took almost 650 hours to build, over a six-month period, using a 1998 Harley-Davidson Electra-Glide motorcycle and a trike kit. Of course, in between, there was a rather long, heavy-duty steel frame to fabricate as well, that would be capable of taking the weight of 10 passengers. Now primarily used for advertising and promotional purposes, as well as shows, the Anaconda is not used as a limo on the road because the insurance would be too high. However, it does occasionally haul passengers on private land where there is no traffic. The trike is completely street-legal when just being ridden normally. But tight corners can be rather a challenge.

Although it looks like the Anaconda is twin-engined, only the one at the rear, which is the Harley's stock Evo motor, actually works. The one at the front is simply a dummy one, made out of glassfiber, and there to add visual balance.

THE LARGEST EVER THREE-WHEELER VEHICLE

DAVIS DIVAN SEDAN

The Davis Motor Company story is one of ingenuity but, ultimately, failure. Set up in 1946 by Gary Davis, its main creation was a futuristic-looking and extremely big three-wheeled car, capable of accommodating seven people. But by 1949, the company had been wound up amid allegations of fraud, after just 18 cars had been built. Behind it was left the legacy of the world's largest three-wheeler.

You have to admire Gary Davis's dream. At the end of World War II, he purchased a one-off racing car that had been converted into a three-wheeler. He was so impressed by it that he decided it would make a great basis for a production economy vehicle, and founded his own motor company to build the cars. Having managed to raise $1,2000,000, the first two prototypes were built in 1947. Dealers were intrigued, and over 300 took franchises, lured by the promise of eventual production reaching 1000 cars a day. But it never happened.

Three wheels, but seven inside

The Davis Divan sedan was certainly quite something for a three-wheeler. Four people could be seated abreast in a very sleek, aluminum-crafted body, featuring hidden headlamps. At a push, seven people could squeeze inside. In length, the Divan measured more than 14ft (4m), but it was underneath the hood where the three-wheeler was really packing a punch. Most three-wheelers have tiny engines, but Davis's car had a 2600cc Continental engine. One model even wound up with a Ford V8.

Size and power couldn't save the Davis Divan though. Amid fraud claims and court cases, the company was closed down, with all its assets being sold in May 1950. It was a sad, but perhaps inevitable, end to a brave vision.

SPECIFICATIONS	
Country: USA	
Year built: 1947–49	
Dimensions: 14ft (4.3m) long	
Weight: N/A	
Maximum speed: Approximately 65mph (105 km/h)	
Power: Upwards of 34kW (47bhp)	
Cost: N/A	

ABOVE AND TOP: Four people abreast was the normal capacity of the Davis Divan, but with the roof off, it could manage seven.

SPECIFICATIONS

for Van Hool T915
Acron Jumbulance

Country: UK

Year built: 1998/1999

Dimensions: 39ft (12m) long; 8ft (3m) wide

Weight: N/A

Power: 410hp (301kW)

Cost: N/A

THE LARGEST AMBULANCE

JUMBULANCE

Operated by a British charity, a Jumbulance is a custom-made ambulance based on a coach body. Part bus, part medical transport, and (almost) part aircraft, the vehicles are used to take extremely sick and severely handicapped people on holidays abroad, in as much comfort as possible.

The Across Charity of the UK was set up to provide a means of taking ill—often terminally ill—and handicapped patients to the Christian shrine of Lourdes in France. Because travel in an ordinary coach or via aircraft might have been too stressful and difficult for many, the concept of the Jumbulance was invented. Essentially, a Jumbulance is a commercial coach converted into a more "medical-friendly" vehicle, with the longest Jumbulances articulated in the middle to provide more capacity and comfort for occupants.

A hospital on wheels

They are classed as ambulances, and, as such, are by far the largest of this type of medical vehicle to ever have been constructed. Some can be as long as 60ft (18m), and as high as 13ft (4m). Jumbulances have appeared in several different guises since they made their debut in the 1970s, with most based on Van Hool bodies, with articulated TG821 variants being the largest of all.

At present, the charity operates two Jumbulances, which are fitted with amenities such as eight aluminum trolley beds, 16 recliner sleeper-chairs, a fully equipped kitchen, a disabled toilet, hydraulic lift, PA system, oxygen supply and medical equipment, a large storage capactiy to accomodate wheelchairs, and air-conditioning. There is a cabin that allows the drivers to stay in the busses whilst on the route to France.

ABOVE: All Jumbulances are big, but this 1980s Van Hool T821 was the largest type of all. Fitted with beds and medical equipment, it was more like a traveling hospital than ambulance!

SPECIFICATIONS

Country: USA
Year built: 1963–65
Dimensions: N/A
Weight: N/A
SP Truck power:
255hp (190kW)
Pump power: 2400hp
(1789.5kW)
Total hosing length:
2438ft (8000m)
Cost: $875,000

THE LARGEST PUMPER FIRE TRUCK

MACK SUPER PUMPER FIRE ENGINES

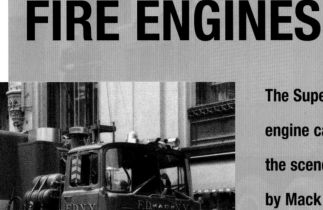

The Super Pumper was, as its name suggests, a fire engine capable of pumping a large amount of water at the scene of significant incidents. Only one was built, by Mack Trucks, and it went into service in the American city where everything is on a bigger scale than anywhere else—New York.

ABOVE AND BELOW: This is the Super Pumper itself—the tractor-trailer fitted with the powerful Deltic-engined pump. Other trucks carried hoses that attached to its outlets.

Actually, the Super Pumper was more of a system than just a fire engine—there was one massive truck, bigger than any other pumper in operation, along with four hose units that worked with it at major fires. The idea was the brainchild of marine engineer and architect, William Francis Gibbs who, in 1938, had designed a fireboat for the Fire Department of New York (FDNY). Named the *Fire Fighter*, it is still the most powerful of its type in existence. Back in the 1960s, Gibbs wanted to come up with the land equivalent, capable of replacing 10 conventional fire units.

As powerful as a train

Gibbs worked alongside Mack Trucks to turn his concept into reality. The main pump and machinery were mounted on a tractor-trailer unit, with power coming from a Napier Deltic 18-cylinder diesel unit. Its engine was so strong that, in the UK, the same engines were used to power express railroad locomotives. This then supplied another tractor-trailer carrying 2000ft (610m) of hose and able to blast out 10,000 gallons (37,854 liters) of water per minute, plus three other smaller rigs, which could deliver 4000 gallons (15,142 liters) per minute through their monitors.

In service from 1965 to 1982, one of the Super Pumper's more notable achievements was pumping nonstop at one fire for a remarkable 12 hours and 35 minutes.

THE LARGEST AERIAL FIRE TRUCK, CURRENT

BRONTO SKYLIFT F101 HLA

Buildings have never been taller than they are today and so fire trucks have had to grow to keep up. The Bronto Company of Finland builds the world's highest truck-mounted fire and rescue platform. It's called the F101 HLA, and it can extend a staggering 331ft (101m) upward.

LEFT AND ABOVE: The reach of the F101 HLA is truly staggering—yet it all folds neatly away into the size of a large truck.

The first of Bronto's High-Level Articulated (HLA) range of aerial rescue platforms was built more than 20 years ago, and the family—and the heights that can be reached—have been growing ever since. Up until 2006, the maximum reach was 295ft (90m), but then came the Skylift F101 HLA, with a 331ft (101m) reach. That's one-third the height of the Eiffel Tower, or slightly taller than the Statue of Liberty. The platform can also extend 92ft (28m) sideways when in the air, allowing it even greater flexibility during emergencies. The control system, which can be operated from the ground or the top cage, allows an exact outreach to be set, regardless of weather conditions or other external forces. When folded away, the total height is a mere 13ft (4m).

High fire fighting

The F101 consists of hydraulic articulated arms, mounted on a conventional six-axle truck chassis of the customer's choice. An integrated waterway runs up the arms, so fires can be extinguished from the platform at the top, as well as the platform being used to rescue stranded people. To keep the whole contraption from toppling, jacks extend 26ft (8m) out of each side to lift the wheels off the ground and keep the lifting section steady.

SPECIFICATIONS

Country: USA
Year built: Late 1960s
Length: N/A
Liquid capacity:
13,000gallons
(49,210 liters)
Weight: N/A
Power: Approximately
500hp (373kW)
Cost: N/A

THE LARGEST ARTICULATED FIRE ENGINE

CATERPILLAR/ KLEIN C-5A FIRE ENGINE

The biggest articulated airport fire engine—or crash-rescue vehicle, to give it its proper title —was built as part of the US Air Force's C-5A Galaxy program during the 1960s. With two extinguishers, it was able to carry 13,000 gallons (49,210 liters) of foam in case of incident.

ABOVE: Built for the C-5A Galaxy program, the Caterpillar/Klein fire engine was a forerunner to today's enormous airport rescue vehicles.

The apparatus used for dealing with aircraft emergencies is extremely specialized. It has to be, to be able to cope with potentially highly dangerous situations that are created by most incidents because of large quantities of flammable fuel and large numbers of people involved in airplane cargo.

Large breeds large

As planes grew increasingly larger, so did the equipment that had to deal with any accidents, and, during the development of the US Air Force's enormous C-5A Galaxy transport plane in the 1960s, a request went out for a design of fire tender that was capable of responding to the devastation that a C-5A crash would cause. This was, after all, an aircraft weighing 848 tons (769,000lb) fully loaded, and capable of carrying 51,149 gallons (193,620 liters) of fuel.

The result was an enormous articulated crash unit, the largest one of its type in the world. The vehicle was a collaboration between the US Government, Caterpillar (who were responsible for the two-wheeled tractor unit as well as the main body of the machine, similar in layout to the company's scraper machines) and Klein Products of California. The latter designed the tank and nozzle equipment.

Storage capacity was 13,000 gallons (49,210 liters), dispensed via two directional monitors mounted on top of the tank. Two personnel standing exposed on top of the flat-topped container operated these, although, for the purposes of protection, fire-resistant suits were provided.

THE LARGEST PRODUCTION TRUCK, CURRENT

INTERNATIONAL CXT PICKUP TRUCK

The letters stand for Commercial Extreme Truck. International's CXT is the largest pickup truck in the world, making even a Hummer look like a compact car by comparison. However, it's far from being a working pickup, for this flashy flatbed is aimed firmly at the wealthy and well-known.

This definitely isn't the sort of pickup truck you'll find down at your local building site—certainly not at $115,000 a go! If anything, the four-wheel-drive CXT has invented a new niche for itself, that of the celebrity luxury load-lugger, just the kind of thing for bringing multiple Oscars or gold records back from awards ceremonies.

Big on luxury

Based on International's rugged dump trucks and snow plows, twice the weight of a Hummer H2 and standing 9ft (2.7m) tall, little here is subtle. The stated gross vehicle weight of 11.7 tons (11,792.9kg) is carefully calculated—for anything over 13 tons (11,793.4 kg) means it could only be bought with a commercial trucker's licence. Goodies inside include a DVD player, satellite navigation, rear camera, tinted windows, lots of leather, and a very loud sound system. Outside, there's an excess of chrome for extra effect. Production is limited to between 500 and 1000 a year.

Naturally, the engine is big too, a diesel V8 putting out up to 300hp (224kW) from its "MaxxForce" diesel engine—enough to allow the CXT to tow 20 tons (18,144kg) and carry 5.5 tons (4989kg) in its load bay. However, the penalty for all this size and power is that fuel consumption can drop as low as 7–10 miles per gallon (4.3–6.2 km per 3.79 liters).

SPECIFICATIONS

Country: USA

Year built from: 2004

Dimensions: 21ft (6.4m) long; 9ft (3m) wide

Weight (loaded): 13 tons (11,792kg)

Maximum speed: Approximately 80mph (129km/h)

Power: 300hp (224kW)

Cost: $115,000

FAR LEFT, LEFT, AND ABOVE: The CXT looks more big rig than normal road pickup—in fact, it's based on a dump truck!

THE LARGEST MONSTER TRUCK

BIGFOOT 5

The Bigfoot family of monster trucks was born in 1975, when Missouri man, Bob Chandler, modified the family Ford pickup. A few years later he decided to start crushing cars at shows with it. There have been 21 official Bigfoot trucks, but No. 5 was the tallest, widest, and heaviest.

In fact, Bigfoot 5, built in the middle of 1986, isn't just the largest of the Bigfoots. It's the tallest, widest, and heaviest of all pickup trucks anywhere. Although based on a standard Ford F-250—albeit with the body made of glassfiber—what gives No. 5 its extreme dimensions are its tires, which are much bigger and thicker than usual Bigfoot tires. It was especially built to run on special Firestone Tundra tires, which tower 10ft (3m) high and weigh 2400lb (1089kg). Although these wheels had been used on previous Bigfoots, No. 5 was to be their permanent home. And, when the monster truck appeared at its first show, it sported dual tires on each axle. It was this arrangement that clinched its entry into *The Guinness Book of Records*.

From land train to Bigfoot

The original use of the Firestone Tundra tires was on the US Army's unsuccessful Alaskan land train of the 1950s, used at that time to transport troops and machinery across the frozen wastes of Alaska. Bigfoot 5 uses the wheels left over after it was taken out of service.

Bigfoot 5 is mainly retired now, on display at the Bigfoot 4x4 Incorporated headquarters in St. Louis, Missouri. After all, if it punctures too many tires driving over cars at shows, just how do you go about finding replacements?

SPECIFICATIONS

Country: USA
Year built: 1986
Length: 15ft 6in (5m) high; 13ft (4m) wide
Weight: 38,000lb (17,236kg)
Power: N/A
Engine size: 460in³ (7538cc) Ford V8
Cost: N/A

BELOW: The wheels on Bigfoot 5 are so large, they make a handy place to stand when watching the other Bigfoots performing shows! The truck was especially designed to fit these tires.

THE LONGEST PRODUCTION TRUCK, CURRENT

FORD F-350

Actually, it's not just the Ford F-350 that deserves a mention in this book. It's the Ford F-350 Super Duty Crew Cab Long Bed, which, as well as having an inordinately long name, also has a lot of body length. It's currently the longest production pickup truck being built.

ABOVE AND BELOW: The Ford F-350 is practically a monster truck for the street, and in Crew Cab specification (as here), little else of its type can match it for length.

SPECIFICATIONS

Country: USA
Year built: 2007
Length: 22ft (7m) long; by 8ft (2m) wide
Weight: (loaded) 13,000lb (5,897kg)
Maximum speed: Approximately 100mph (161km/h)
Power: 362hp (270kW)
Cost: Starts at $24,075

The F-series of trucks have been, and remain, an incredibly popular series of trucks for Ford. In recent years, they have made up around half of the company's profits, and for 23 years, one variant—the F-150—has been the bestselling vehicle in the world.

So long

The F-150 may be the vehicle that everybody buys, but, no doubt, the F-350 would be the truck that they would choose if money—and room —were no object. The Super Duty Crew Cab Long Bed variant stretches for 22ft (7m), with a typical large car measuring around 18ft (5.5m). Even

the wheelbase of the F-350 is almost 15ft (4.5m); many compact cars don't reach that in total length. That's a lot of road space the F-350 is taking up. Maximum load capacity of the flatbed is 5800lb (2631kg).

Ruggedly built, with a separate box-section chassis and, on the 4x4 models, twin traction beams to cope with any rough stuff, the F-350 features Ford's own 415in³ (6.8 liter) V10 engine, introduced as a response to Dodge's legendary 10-cylinder unit. It offers a massive amount of low-down torque as well as top-end power.

F-350s have become popular as personal "lifestyle" vehicles and they're also popular among modifiers, who give their cars a little "bling."

THE LARGEST FREIGHT TRUCKS

THE "ROAD TRAINS" OF AUSTRALIA

If you want to see the road equivalent of a railroad freight train, then Australia is the place to head for, where the long, flat, and usually deserted Outback highways are the preserve of the road trains—huge "prime movers." It's no surprise that the record for the world's longest truck load was broken down under.

Australia doesn't make it easy for transport. Its vast, mostly uninhabited, and usually hostile environment makes any travel challenging, but particularly the carriage of heavy freight. In places without the benefit of good railroad links, road trains are the answer.

Tricky overtaking

Consisting of a powerful truck towing (usually) four or five trailers, road trains are a common sight in the Outback regions of Western Australia, Queensland, and the Northern Territory—and a bane to any car driver that gets stuck behind them. On the dusty roads of the Outback, getting past is practically impossible, unless it's a helpful truck driver in front.

Breaking the record

Over the last decade, there have been several attempts to claim the record for the longest road train. The current record was set by 70-year-old John Atkinson in early 2006, when a new Mack Titan tri-drive truck moved its load a mere 32ft (100m) near Clifton in Southern Queensland. That doesn't sound like much until you consider that the Titan was attached to 113 loaded trailers, the equivalent of 100 times its own weight. The total length was 4,837ft (1,474.3m). That would have been a difficult one to overtake.

BELOW: The world's longest road train gets underway, behind a single Mack Titan truck. Its load stretched back 4,873ft (1,474.3m).

BOTTOM: A three-trailer road train, a specialist long-haul truck, parked.

SPECIFICATIONS

for record attempt

Country: Australia

Year built: 2006

Dimenions: 0.91 miles (1.47km) long

Weight: 6433 tons (5,835,910kg)

Power: 620hp (463kW)

Engine capacity: 915in³ (15000cc)

Number of gears: 18

Cost: N/A

"BIG BOY" STEAM LOCOMOTIVE

Some steam locomotives have been heavier. Some steam locomotives have been more powerful. But no mainstream steam locomotive has ever been larger than the "Big Boy" engines built by the USA's Union Pacific Railroad in the 1940s to pull its heaviest freight trains over mountain passes.

Only 25 "Big Boys" (as the UP's 4000 class 4-8-8-4 locos have been so aptly nicknamed) were built between 1941 and 1944. Yet they have become one of the best-known railroad engines of all time, thanks to their sheer size and the awe-inspiring sight they made when working hard. Although austere in appearance, there was also a strange grace and beauty to their tremendous strength.

Mountain beaters

They were constructed to be able to pull long, high-speed goods trains, weighing up to 3640 tons (3,300,000kg) over the Wasatch Mountains in the Midwest where, previously, helper locomotives had been needed because the gradients were so steep. The delays had been slowing down service times as well as causing extra expense, but the "Big Boys" soon eradicated these. Massively powerful, but also very fast for an articulated freight loco (speeds of 80mph [130km/h] were possible) the Big Boys soon earned a fine reputation, not just for their load-lugging abilities but also for being easy to drive, despite their mass.

The rapid dieselization and electrification of the US railway system meant that all the "Big Boys" were withdrawn from service by 1959, years before the end of their useful life. However, they were still among the last steamers to continue running in regular service in America. Eight have been preserved, although none is operational. One problem with restoring one to working order is that there would simply be nowhere to run it.

SPECIFICATIONS

Country: USA
Year built: 1941–44
Dimensions: 133ft (40.5m) long
Weight: 604 tons (548,279kg)
Maximum speed: 80mph (130km/h)
Power: 6300hp (4698kW)
Tractive effort: 135,375lbf (602.18kN)
Cost: N/A

TOP AND ABOVE: The main driving wheels of a "Big Boy" were on bogies, to allow the enormous locomotives to negotiate corners. Even with these, though, they were still too large for most UP routes.

THE LARGEST OPERATIONAL STEAM LOCOMOTIVE

UNION PACIFIC CHALLENGER NO. 3985

SPECIFICATIONS

Country: USA

Year built: 1936–43

Dimensions: 122ft (37m) long

Weight: 850 tons (771,924kg)

Maximum speed: 70mph (113km/h)

Power: Approximately 4500hp (3355.5kW)

Tractive effort: 97,350lbf (433kN)

Cost: N/A

Slightly smaller in size to their "Big Boy" close relations, the Union Pacific's Challenger class steam locomotives were more widespread, with 105 built between 1936 and 1943. However, only two managed to escape scrapping when withdrawn. One of those—No. 3985 —is in working order as the world's largest and most powerful operational steam locomotive.

ABOVE AND LEFT: The Challengers were more versatile than the closely related "Big Boys"—which is one of the reasons why a No. 3985, was preserved in working order—there were more places to run it.

Because their dimensions weren't quite as extreme as the similar-looking "Big Boys," the UP's Challenger locomotives, with a wheel arrangement of 4-6-6-4 (in other words, two fewer main driving wheels than the 4-8-8-4 Big Boys) were able to operate all over the company's system, their articulation allowing them to tackle tight curves despite their overall length of 122ft (37m). Primarily used for freight, they found some use on passenger trains as well, especially in mountainous areas where their huge reserves of power came in handy for severe gradients. They got their name because they were able to tackle routes that would be a challenge to anything else, and the design was so successful that other railroad companies had their own versions built. In total, 252 examples were spread between nine systems.

The end, except for 3985

Withdrawals started in the 1950s, with practically all of the class eventually retired to the scrap heap. One loco that escaped was No. 3985. It remained in use until 1957, but retired in 1962 after which it was stored in Wyoming. In 1975 it was displyed near the depot at Cheyenne. However, in 1981, a group of enthusiastic UP employees got together to restore 3985 and get it hauling trains again. It was a big undertaking, but they succeeded, and 3985 is now back to doing what it does best—hauling excursion trains around, the Union Pacific Challenger delights the crowds that always turn up to watch this magnificent locomotive in operation. It used to burn coal, but was converted to oil in 1990.

THE LARGEST DIESEL LOCOMOTIVE, EVER

UNION PACIFIC CENTENNIAL DDA40X DIESEL LOCO

The Union Pacific's reputation for using massive locomotives continued beyond the Big Boy and Challenger steam era (see pages 93 and 94), and into the diesel epoch. Its DDA40X class of freight locomotives, purchased to do exactly the same sort of duties carried out decades earlier by the Big Boys and Challengers, were the largest and most powerful diesel-electric types ever built.

It was on May 10, 1869, that a golden spike was driven to mark the completion of the USA's first transcontinental railroad. One hundred years later, one of the companies involved, Union Pacific, celebrated the anniversary by taking delivery of the first of its colossal Centennial class of diesel locomotives, also known—rather less memorably—as the DDA40X series (with the "X" standing for "experimental," as EMD intended studying them as working testbeds for new technology). The first locomotive was numbered 6900 to commemorate the events of '69.

Twin diesel power

The Electro-Motive division of General Motors built 47 of these distinctive yellow machines between 1969 and 1971, and nothing else around was bigger or more powerful. Weighing almost 275 tons (250,000kg) and measuring 98ft 6in (30m) in length, total power output was 6600hp (4900kW), albeit generated by two V16 engines. Paralleling the careers of Big Boy and Challenger, they were withdrawn well before their time, in 1980, as a result of an economic downturn. In 1984, 25 were returned to service, but by 1986 they were all gone for good from regular service. Thirteen have been preserved, one (No. 6936) by Union Pacific itself, which uses it for special excursions.

SPECIFICATIONS

Country: USA
Year built: 1969–71
Dimensions:
98ft 6in (30m) long;
10ft 6in (3m) wide
Weight: 273 tons
(247,400kg)
Maximum speed:
90mph (145km/h)
Power: 6600hp
(4900kW)
Tractive effort:
136,000lbf (605kN)
Cost: N/A

BELOW: The side view illustrates the vast size of the Centennial diesel loco.

THE LARGEST FREIGHT TRAIN EVER

BHP IRON ORE TRAINS, AUSTRALIA

Thanks to its wide-open, unpopulated landscape and vast area, Australia is able to operate enormously lengthy freight trains. The longest and heaviest trains on the planet currently travel on the iron ore line from Port Hedland to Newman, and can run up to 336 cars long.

SPECIFICATIONS

Country: Australia
Year built: 2001
Length: 4.5 miles (7.5km)
Wagons: 682
Weight: 109,940 tons (99,734,000kg)
Maximum speed: N/A
Total power: 48,000hp (64,369kW) from eight locomotives
Cost: N/A

The state of Western Australia is one of the most isolated places on Earth, separated from the more populated areas of the country by deserts and the Outback. With sometimes huge distances between towns, railroads are still the dominant force in moving freight, particularly heavy mineral cargos from far-flung mining locations. On the 265 mile (426km) line between Port Hedland and Newman in Western Australia, operated by BHP Billiton Iron Ore, trains stretching more than 2.2 miles (3.5km) are normal rather than exceptional. Providing power for these epic movements are some of the most powerful diesel-electric locomotives in the world, General Motors' AC6000CW type, generating 6000hp (447kW).

The longest ever

However, even for an area used to massive railroad operations, the events of June 2001 were unprecedented. To demonstrate the capabilities of its system, BHP Iron Ore decided to assemble the longest train ever recorded —by quite a considerable margin. The formation consisted of 682 wagons, loaded with 90,680 tons (82,262,000kg) of ore, and hauled by eight AC6000CW locos, all of which were controlled by a single driver. The total weight came to practically 110,231 tons (100,000,000kg) and the train stretched to 4.5 miles (7.5km) in length. Neither was this just a static display. The train actually traversed, complete and fully laden, the 171 miles (275km) from Yandi to Port Hedland.

LEFT AND TOP: The orange and black BHP diesel locomotives are a familiar sight hauling the longest trains in the world.

THE LARGEST PASSENGER TRAIN, REGULAR SERVICE

AMTRAK AUTO TRAIN

ABOVE AND BELOW: Double-decker Superliner passenger coaches and car carriers give the Auto Train a lot of capacity, yet a typical train is still about 40 cars long.

The question of the longest passenger train in regular service in the world is a contentious one. Many cite the Eurostar sets between London, Paris, and Brussels as the holders of the record, with their 18 carriages and two power cars stretching 1293ft (394m). However, Amtrak's Auto Train in the USA also has a good claim to the title.

SPECIFICATIONS

Country: USA
Year built from: 1971
Length: Approximately 0.5 miles (0.8km)
Wagons: Approximately 40
Weight: N/A
Maximum speed: 110mph (177km/h) P42DC Genesis locomotive
Average speed: 52mph (83.6km/h)
Total power: 8000hp (6000kW) from two locomotives
Cost: N/A

Unlike Eurostar, the Auto Train, which runs the 855 miles (1376km) between Lorton (near Washington, D.C.) and Sanford, Florida, isn't a pure passenger train. It also has vehicle-carrying wagons, known as autoracks, allowing passengers to bring their cars and vans with them. The passenger coaches and autoracks combined add up to the longest train of its type currently in operation.

Long train coming

Operating nonstop (except for one fueling and crew change) between its terminals, the first Auto Train ran in 1971, with a typical setup comprising between 30 and 64 coaches and wagons, pulled by up to three locomotives. Amtrak took over in 1983 after the original company went bankrupt. A typical train is now formed of two General Electric P42 Genesis diesel-electric locomotives and around 40 railcars, depending on demand, with the usual length of a train about 0.5 miles (0.8km). Because the service operates overnight, sleeping cars are also included in the formation—something else that contributes to making an Auto Train so long.

Operating every day, with trains at both ends leaving at 4 p.m. and arriving the following morning at 8 a.m., it has been estimated that 200,000 passengers opt to let the Auto Train take the strain rather than drive on the congested highways between the northeastern seaboard of the USA and the popular holiday destination of Florida.

SPECIFICATIONS

Country: USA
Year built: 2002
Dimensions: Power car 69ft 6in (21m) long; 10ft 6in (3m) wide
Weight: N/A
Maximum speed: 150mph (240km/h)
Power: 5000hp (3750kW)
Cost: Approximately $41 million on development

THE LARGEST JET RAILWAY LOCOMOTIVE

JETTRAIN

Yes, the name really is accurate. Based on the successful Acela Expresses, which operate on the electrified east-coast tracks of the United States, the experimental JetTrain uses a gas turbine engine, more usually found in aircraft, instead of electricity for propulsion.

Electrifying long-distance, high-speed routes is a costly undertaking. This is one of the reasons the JetTrain was developed by Bombardier Transportation—to show that rapid railroad transport wasn't just the preserve of wires and gantries. Jet trains aren't anything new—there have been experimental ones running since the 1950s, but many of these have been on a small scale, used for military testing of missiles on purpose-built tracks. The lightweight JetTrain is a serious attempt at a practical, full-scale passenger-carrying type for the twenty-first century, to compete with both diesels and electrics. It is the largest of its type operating today.

ABOVE: Although only a prototype at the moment, the maker of the JetTrain hopes railroad companies will consider the aircraft-engine powered train as an alternative to electrification.

Aircraft power in a train

At the heart of the JetTrain locomotive is an aviation Pratt & Whitney Canada PW150 gas turbine, capable of an output of 5000hp (3750kW). Speeds of 150mph (240km/h) are the usual top speed, but in testing, a JetTrain managed to achieve 205mph (330km/h), setting a new world record in the process.

In normal service, the JetTrain runs with tilting coaches (again, similar to those used on the Acela Expresses), but actually finding anywhere to use it has proved problematical. Proposals to introduce it in regular service in the USA have all fallen through, usually because of budgetary constraints. There are some tentative future plans to use them in the United Kingdom on long-distance diesel routes, however.

THE LARGEST MAGLEV TRAIN, REGULAR USE

SHANGHAI MAGLEV TRAIN

Maglevs are being touted as the future of rail transport, a high-speed, mass-transit system where the "trains" are suspended above the "track" by electromagnetic forces. The biggest and most successful of the current maglev systems is that which operates between Shanghai and Pudong International Airport.

Most maglevs are simply experimental at the moment, technology testbeds for some of the many systems that are proposed for the future. However, the line that runs from Shanghai city to its international airport has been operating commercially since the beginning of 2003.

Flying on the ground

For passengers getting off aircraft, the maglev must seem almost like a continuation of their flight—as indeed, it almost is, since there is no actual contact between the train and the track when in motion. The Shanghai Maglev Train (SMT) is capable of reaching 267mph (430km/h) during its journey, and can accelerate up to 220mph (350km/h) in just two minutes. No other land-based transport system is capable of such feats, and during a test run in 2003, one train even hit 311mph (501km/h), a new record for its type. Although the track is 19 miles (30.5km) long, journey time is a mere seven minutes and 20 seconds. The three trains, built by the German Transrapid company, operate at 15-minute intervals during the day.

The success of the Shanghai maglev has prompted the Japanese government to extend the line, and other systems are now being proposed throughout the world, with speeds of up to 404mph (650km/h), the sort of performance that will put them into direct competition with short-haul aircraft, assuming the lines can be made long enough.

SPECIFICATIONS

Country: Japan
Year built: 2001–03
Dimensions: 19 miles (30.5km) long
Weight: N/A
Maximum speed: 267mph (430kpm/h)
Power: N/A
Cost: Approximately $1.2 billion

BELOW: The Shanghai Airport Maglev is the world's first commercial magnetic levitation transit system, and has managed speeds of 311mph (501km/h) in tests.

THE LARGEST TRACKED RECOVERY VEHICLE

M88A2 HERCULES ARMORED RECOVERY VEHICLE

ABOVE AND BELOW: When the heaviest US tanks get into trouble, they need recovery by the best: The M88A2.

What do you do when the biggest and heaviest tanks around break down or get damaged, and need rescuing? You call in an M88A2 Hercules—the largest armored recovery vehicle (ARV) around, and one of the few tracked battlefield units that can make an M1 Abrams Main Battle Tank look puny by comparison.

As tanks have got bigger, so have the machines that support them. The M88 was first seen in 1961, with an upgrade in 1977 to the M88A1. The current variant is the M88A2, which appeared in 1997, and is the largest by far of all the types—able to deal with the US Army's mainstay M1 Abrams.

Foldaway crane

Essentially, the M88A2 is a turretless tank fitted instead with a foldaway A-frame type crane on top for towing, winching, and hoisting. Fitted with 280ft (85m) of strong cable, the ARV has the ability to lift the equivalent of its own weight (77 tons/70,000kg), meaning that the average Abrams is no trouble. Other abilities include the facility to start stranded tanks that have run out of electrical power, using the M88A2's two online generators, plus the means to fuel or defuel vehicles. There's also a large blade at the front that can be used for pushing and clearing obstacles, although it is more commonly deployed to keep the ARV stable during winching operations.

Because the M88A2 is intended to operate while under fire, it is equipped with armor that is resistant to nuclear, biological, and chemical attacks, and also has a smokescreen generator as well as a heavy machine gun.

SPECIFICATIONS

Country: USA
Year built from: 1997
Dimensions:
28ft (8.6m) long;
12ft (4m) wide
Weight: 77 tons
(70,000kg)
Maximum speed:
26mph (42km/h)
Power: 1050hp
(783kW)
Cost: $2,050,000

THE LARGEST TANK, CURRENT (BY WEIGHT)

CHALLENGER II MAIN BATTLE TANK

Typical of the modern breed of enormous main battle tanks, the Challenger II is very large, very heavy, and very deadly. Mainstay of the British Army, it is also used by the Royal Army of Oman, and has seen action in the major conflicts of recent years, including the last Gulf War.

ABOVE AND BELOW: The Challenger II is designed to fight around the world, in any conditions, under any circumstances.

Although it uses the same hull and much of the same mechanical equipment as the earlier Challenger I tank (introduced in 1982), the Challenger II of 1994 is resolutely a tank for the twenty-first century. Equipped with the latest in weaponry and target-finding equipment, it is one of the most advanced—and potent—armored fighting machines around today, as well as being the heaviest.

Heavy weapon, heavy armor

Its main armament is a 4.7in (120mm) rifled gun, designed to take out other tanks, vehicles, and buildings. Also fitted are a chain machine gun and an antiaircraft gun. Computer and digital systems are included to make the weapons more effective, as are a laser rangefinder and night vision.

Very tough Chobham armor is intended to provide protection against all kinds of attack, including chemical, nuclear, and biological.

Time for tea

The Challenger II is crewed by four personnel, with power coming from a 12-cylinder Rolls-Royce Perkins diesel engine. Combined with the novel Hydragas suspension (a system using fluid and air, in somewhat smaller form, on several popular British cars such as the Austin Allegro, Princess, and Metro from the 1970s onward), this allows the Challenger II a comparatively high top speed of 37mph (60km/h). Being a British vehicle, one of its most essential pieces of equipment is the water boiler, used to make tea.

SPECIFICATIONS

Country: UK
Year built from: 1994
Dimensions: 27ft (8m) long; 11ft 6in (3.5m) wide
Weight: 69 tons (62,500kg)
Maximum speed: 37mph (60km/h)
Power: 1200hp (894.8kw)
Cost: Approximately $1.2 billion

THE LARGEST BRIDGE LAYER, CURRENT

M104 WOLVERINE

Tanks may have a reputation of being able to go anywhere, but pit them against a major river or fissure, and they're likely to be defeated. The solution is a specialist armored combat engineering vehicle such as the immense M104 Wolverine Heavy Assault Bridge, capable of spanning gaps of 79ft (24m).

ABOVE AND BELOW:
The M104 Wolverine demonstrates how it works: The bridge unfolds above, and is then maneuvered into position. The front blade is used as a jack to stop the vehicle tipping forward.

For much of the last quarter of a century, the US Army had a problem. Its main armored bridgelaying vehicles were based on tank designs that had first appeared in the 1950s, and were increasingly unable to keep up with modern tanks like the M1 Abrams. In addition, its bridging equipment was having trouble coping with the weight of the army's latest vehicles.

The tank that builds bridges

The solution needed was a high-performance bridgelayer, and as it had to be capable of running alongside the Abrams Main Battle Tank in action, it was logical to use that vehicle as a basis. The resultant vehicle was the M104 Wolverine, the first of which entered service in 2003.

It's quite a machine. The bridge, in two sections, is carried above the hull. The Wolverine anchors itself in place opposite whatever needs to be crossed, joins the two parts of the bridge together, extends it out across the gap, and then drops it in place. Amazingly, all this takes a mere five minutes, to "build" a 12 ton (10,886kg) bridge capable of supporting a 70 ton (63,503kg) weight moving across it at up to 10mph (16km/h). After use, it takes a mere eight minutes to retrieve the equipment again and all without the two-man crew having to leave the safety of the Wolverine.

SPECIFICATIONS

Country: USA
Year built: 1999–2006
Dimensions:
43ft (13m) long;
32ft (4m) wide
Weight: 69 tons
(62,313kg)
Maximum speed:
45mph (72km/h)
Power: 1500hp
(1119kW)
Cost: Approximately
$4 million

PANZERKAMPF WAGEN (PZKPFW) MAUS SUPER-HEAVY TANK

The ironically named Maus (mouse) wasn't just the largest and heaviest tank to be built during World War II, it remains the biggest tank ever constructed. However, by the time it was ready to go into production, Germany was on the verge of defeat, and only two prototypes were completed.

ABOVE: The first Maus undergoing tests, with a dummy turret fitted. Ultimately, just two prototypes were built, both proving to be quite useless.

Described as "this gigantic offspring of the fantasy of Hitler and his advisers," the Maus was more a propaganda weapon than a useful fighting machine. It would have done the Nazi war effort no harm at all if it were to be made known that the country possessed the largest and most powerful tank in the world. But in reality, the Maus was too expensive, too heavy, too slow, and too complicated.

Mammoth to mouse

Originally known as the Mammut (Mammoth), the inappropriately titled Maus was designed by Ferdinand Porsche, also responsible for the Volkswagen Beetle and whose son would go on to build Porsche sportscars. The first prototype was completed by the end of 1943—albeit with a mocked-up, nonfunctional turret—and a second followed in 1944, this time fully operational.

Too heavy

Fitted with a huge 5in (128mm) gun, parts of the Maus' armor were 9in (240mm) thick in places. This pushed the weight up to a staggering 210 tons (191,000kg)—too heavy for the V12 gasoline-engined tank to maneuver effectively or have any useful speed. It was too heavy for most bridges too, so a snorkel device was incorporated to allow it to go under water to a depth of 45ft (13m).

Both versions of this behemoth of a tank were damage in combat and captured by the Russians, who made them into one complete vehicle, which is still on display at the Russian Tank Museum.

SPECIFICATIONS

Country: Germany
Year built: 1943–44
Dimensions: 33ft (11m) long; 12ft (4m) wide
Weight: 210 tons (191,000kg)
Maximum speed: 12mph (20km/h)
Power: 1080hp (783kw)
Cost: N/A

THE LARGEST STEAM TANK

US ENGINEER CORP STEAM TANK

The first tanks went into action in 1916, during the Battle of the Somme in World War I. This radical new military technology—the stealth fighter of its day—was still under development at the time, with various countries experimenting with different forms of propulsion. One fascinating offshoot was the US Engineer Corp steam tank.

That steam should have been thought a potential form of motive power for newfangled tanks wasn't as strange then as it seems now. After all, tanks were then about the size of a small railroad locomotive, about as heavy, and the gasoline engines of the era had their jobs cut out moving such weights under difficult battle conditions and staying reliable.

Boston-built

Based on the design of the British Mk IV tank, the single machine had two railcar kerosene-fired steam boilers and engines, giving around 500hp (373kW), far more than the 150hp (112kW) of the same type with a gasoline engine.

Built in Boston, Massachusetts, the tank had a crew of eight and, instead of a conventional gun, was fitted with a flame thrower driven by steam. It also had four machine guns.

Great things were expected of the tank, and after much razzmatazz over it in public parades around Boston (during which it broke down just the once), it was shipped to France in June 1918. Once there, it was named "America" to boost moral. But it proved pretty inept in service, with the conditions for the crew almost unbearable due to the heat. Reliability was also an issue, as was the amount of fuel that needed to be carried. And then there was its vulnerability—even a small hit on the boilers or kerosene tanks could destroy it. Unsurprisingly, no more were built.

SPECIFICATIONS

Country: USA
Year built: 1918
Dimensions:
35ft (10.5m) long;
12ft 6in (4m) wide
Weight: 56 tons
(50,800kg)
Maximum speed:
3.7mph (6km/h)
Power: 500hp (373kW)
Cost: N/A

ABOVE: The steam tank tried to offer the solution of more power for early tanks, but proved unreliable and too hot inside for its crew.

THE LARGEST GUN EVER

SCHWERER GUSTAV BIG GUN

Epic and deadly in equal measure, the German Schwerer Gustav 31.5in (80cm) railroad gun of World War II was the biggest artillery weapon to have been both built and fired in anger. However, during its four-year life, it fired just 78 shots under battle conditions, before being deliberately sabotaged to stop it falling into Allied hands.

BELOW: So big was the Schwerer Gustav that it had to run on two parallel railroad lines, specially built at its firing position. Range was 23.5 miles (38km).

The original reasoning behind the Schwerer Gustav big gun, conceived in 1934, was that it was to be used by the Germans to destroy concrete fortresses on the French Maginot defensive line, in the event of any future German invasion. It was a massive undertaking—the calculation calling for an artillery piece that could fire a 8 ton (7000kg) shell from long range beyond the reach of enemy weapons, with the barrel over 98ft (30m) long and weighing well over 1102 tons (1,000,000kg). The final gun would be so large that it would need to be transported by rail.

Mobile WMD

But, by the time this mobile weapon of mass destruction was finally complete, in 1942, France had already fallen. So the Schwerer Gustav went to Russia instead. The train that carried all its equipment was 25 wagons long, stretching 1 mile (1.6km). Deployed against the besieged city of Sevastopol, it took 200 men three days to assemble the gun, with new railroad track having to be laid by 2500 men to get it into suitable firing positions. The 48 rounds fired, from June 5–17, did considerable damage, and Sevastopol fell on July 4.

A proposed attack against Leningrad was canceled, and, as the war turned and the Germans started to retreat in 1944, the gun came with them, firing 30 rounds into the Warsaw Ghetto during the 1944 uprising. It was destroyed in early 1945 to prevent its capture.

SPECIFICATIONS

Country: Germany
Year built: 1941–42
Dimensions:
155ft (47m) long;
23ft (7m) wide;
38ft (12m) high
Weight: 1490 tons
(1,350,000kg)
Total power: 1853hp
(1382kW) from two
diesel locomotives
Barrel length: 107ft
(32.5m)
Cost: N/A

THE LARGEST HALF-TRACK VEHICLE

SDKFZ9 18-TON HALF TRACK

Half-track vehicles were extensively used by most armies during World War II, but became unpopular soon afterward. So it's very unlikely the SdKfz9 18-ton half-track built by the Germans during World War II will ever be surpassed as the largest hybrid wheeled/tracked vehicle ever built.

As tanks grew ever larger in the lead-up to World War II, there was a requirement for ever-bigger vehicles to recover them if they became stuck or were disabled. Thus, in 1936, plans were laid down by the German military for what would be by far the largest half-track vehicle anywhere.

The vehicle that became the SdKfz9 was envisaged as a V12-engined support vehicle to back up the ever-expanding tanks that made up Germany's elite Panzer divisions. Few other machines were capable of towing the fighting leviathans in service at the time, although when it came to the enormous Tiger tanks, it still took two of these half-tracks, working together, to pull one.

Lifting and pulling

Two types were built, one with a 7 ton (6000kg) capacity crane, the other with a 11 ton (10,000kg) ability. This second version required a counterweight jib and outrigger legs to allow it to (or at least try to) recover the biggest tanks. An offshoot without a lifting ability, used for towing the German Army's largest mobile artillery pieces, eventually joined these models.

Third Reich tanks grew so massive and heavy—as typified by the King Tiger type—that it was beyond even the capabilities of the SdKfz9 to help them when in trouble, and production of the half-track ended in 1944.

SPECIFICATIONS

Country: Germany
Year built: 1936–44
Dimensions: 27ft (9m) long; 8ft 6in (3m) wide
Weight: 19 tons (18,000kg)
Maximum speed: 31mph (50km/h)
Power: 250hp (186kW)
Cost: N/A

ABOVE AND BELOW: This is the transport version of the SDKFZ9, for towing artillery and carrying troops.

2S7 203MM "PION" SELF-PROPELLED GUN

SPECIFICATIONS

Country: Russia (USSR)
Year built from: 1975
Dimensions:
43ft (13m) long;
11ft (3.4m) wide
Weight: 51 tons
(46,000kg)
Maximum speed:
32mph (51km/h)
Power: 750hp (559kW)
Cost: N/A

ABOVE AND BELOW:
The long barrel on the
2S7 gives it a range of
29.5mph (47.5km), if
rocket assistance is used
to assist the projectiles.
Chillingly, it is capable
of firing tactical
nuclear warheads.

Counterpoint to the US Army's Howitzer is the former Soviet 2S7M 8in (203mm) self-propelled gun. This is the largest armored vehicle currently employed by the Russian Army, and one of the candidates for the title of largest mobile artillery piece currently in operation in the world today.

The Cold War game of "What you've got, we'll have too" between the Eastern Bloc and NATO made it inevitable that the Soviet Union would build its own 8in (203mm) self-propelled gun to match—and ideally surpass—the US Army's Howitzer of that size. What resulted was the 2S7 "Pion," and when it appeared in the mid-1970s, it was the largest of its type anywhere on the planet.

Nuclear capability

With a muzzle capable of lifting to a 60 degree angle and moving 30 degrees to either side, the usual range of the 2S7 is 23.3 miles (37.5km). However, with rocket assistance, the gun can throw a shell as far as 29.5 miles (47.5km), a record for modern field artillery. In addition to normal high explosive shells, the 2S7 can also fire concrete-piercing, chemical, and even tactical nuclear projectiles. Rate of fire on the improved 2S7M version of 1983 is 2.5 shells rounds per minute, although this pace is exceptional, and a more likely figure is approximately 40 to 50 rounds each hour. Theoretically, the 2S7M is able to fire a couple of shells, and then move to a safer position before the enemy has had a chance to react to it. The latest 2S7M has better communication systems and can carry a total of eight projectiles and charges.

Like the American Howitzer, the 2S7 also usually has a support vehicle following it for storing ammunition and helping transport its crew of 14.

M110 203MM HOWITZER

There has never been a larger US self-propelled gun than the M110 type of Howitzer. Able to trace its origins back to guns of a similar caliber deployed during World War I, it is only in recent years that modern technology has rendered this type of huge canon obsolete.

SPECIFICATIONS

Country: USA	
Year built from: 1963	
Dimensions: 35ft (11m) long; 10ft (3m) wide	
Weight: 31 tons (28,300kg)	
Maximum speed: 45mph (72km/h)	
Power: 1500hp (119kW)	
Cost: N/A	

Although the M110 Howitzer is no longer in service with the country that made it—the US Army started phasing out the 1023 examples it operated during the 1990s—this type of heavy artillery weapon is still used by other Western forces such as Spain and Greece. Whatever the argument that current hi-tech weaponry has rendered "old school" pieces like this ineffective, the M110 is still a pretty powerful item of battlefield kit.

Pinpoint accuracy over long range

With a crew of 13—which includes personnel in the support vehicle that carries the ammunition—the more recent M110A2 versions of the Howitzer are capable of lobbing a 200lb (91kg), 8in (20cm) diameter shell a distance of just over 18 miles (29km) with deadly precision. Up to two a minute can be fired. During operations with the US Army, it was found to be the most accurate of its field artillery items. The first examples came into service in 1963, and have been deployed in Vietnam as well as more recent Middle East conflicts.

A distinctive feature of the M110A2 is the large spade it carries at the rear, which can be hydraulically lowered and raised. This isn't for clearing obstacles, but is instead used to anchor the vehicle when it is firing—to counteract the huge recoil caused by launching shells.

ABOVE AND BELOW: A blade at the back of the M110 is lowered into the ground during firing, to eliminate the effects of the recoil, which would otherwise cause the Howitzer to spring backward, despite its weight.

ABOVE AND LEFT: The Rhino Runner is heavily armor-plated all over, hence its angular shape.

Welcome to the toughest bus on the planet—the Rhino Runner. Even the name makes it sound rugged and strong, but that's only the beginning of the story. This is a transport vehicle capable of facing heavy combat conditions, and surviving.

Used for any circumstances where its occupants could face attack en route, the Rhino Runner has seen extensive recent use in Iraq for carrying civilian contractors, military personnel, and VIPs. It has proved its worth most on the dangerous route between Baghdad International Airport and the "safe" Green Zone.

One-way bulletproof glass

Completely custom-built, out of composite armor and special bulletproof glass by Labock Technologies in the USA, the Rhino Runner is intended to be resistant to both armor-piercing bullets and bomb blasts. However, despite the inherent strength of the plating, it's actually so light that sections of it can float on water. Even more innovative are the windows. Although they're bulletproof from the outside, those inside can shoot through out if necessary. Even the usual weak points of a wheeled vehicle—the tires—are able to run while flat, for those moments when getting out to change a wheel really isn't a wise idea.

Because the Rhino Runner is an armored vehicle, most of its specifications are still kept secret, but two things are for certain: It's very big and very tough!

THE LARGEST MILITARY BUS

RHINO RUNNER

The Rhino Runner is a bus only in the loosest possible sense of the word. It's more an armored personnel carrier on tires instead of tracks. It may bear a superficial resemblance to a road vehicle, but is much, much more resilient than your average public transportation vehicle.

4 MARITIME

Nowhere are mobile mega machines larger than on the oceans. From the earliest times, boats have always been a prime way to move people and cargo, and many of the world's greatest-ever machines have been built to sail the seas. Recent centuries have seen ships reach epic proportions, their development accelerated by metal instead of wood construction, and the use of engines instead of sail. And still, the trend is toward ever-larger vessels.

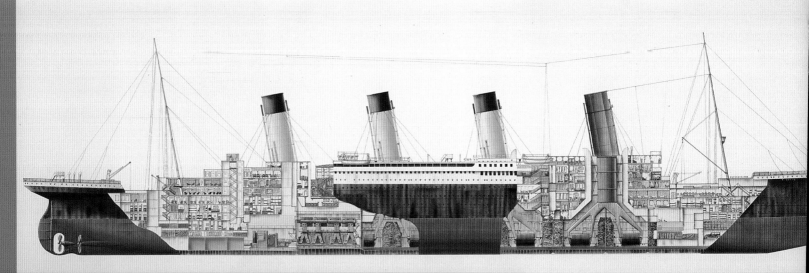

Boats were the first great machines of the world—early civilizations came to depend on them for exploration, conquest, transport, and often mere survival. By 2000BC, man had developed craft for practically all the purposes we use them today, and vessels continued to grow as tools and techniques became better. The societies that prospered were those that understood the importance of the sea, and learned to exploit it with vessels of increasing mass and complexity. The Egyptians pioneered the use of sail, and one of the major reasons the Roman Empire came to dominate much of the known world was through its superior navy. Roman galleys—a formidable naval weapon—were built with multiple decks, could hold hundreds of men, and were comparable in size with some boats of today.

ABOVE: As if the ability to attack unseen wasn't enough, Japanese Sen Toku submarines also carried aircraft.

Sail-powered warships were the giants of the sea for many centuries, their ultimate development being typified by vessels like the USS *Constitution* of 1797 which, despite being made of wood, was nicknamed "Old Ironsides" due to her strength. She still remains in service today, albeit ceremonial. However, the Industrial Revolution of the nineteenth century saw great advances at sea, as it did everywhere else. By the 1850s, sail and wood were rapidly being superseded by metal and steam power, probably the most significant maritime

ABOVE: Britain ruled the waves of the world during the early twentieth century with its fleet of deadly Dreadnoughts.

RIGHT: The *Freedom Ship* is less a conventional boat and more a floating metropolis …albeit one capable of moving anywhere on sea.

ABOVE: She may have been humble in size, but the SS *Meredith Victory* deserves recognition for the scale of her humanitarian achievement.

tried to constantly outdo one another with ever-greater passenger and cargo vessels.

By the turn of the twentieth century, battleships had grown to epic proportions, with the advent of the Dreadnoughts. Fast, thanks to steam turbines, immensely strong due to steel construction, and utterly deadly because of their huge long-distance guns, the ultimate British Dreadnoughts were the Queen Elizabeth class, completed just before World War I. Many regard them as the most impressive battleships of all time. However, by this time, passenger ships were a match in size and speed for military ships. The *Titanic* of 1912 needs no introduction: It was the biggest ship of the age, but its tragic maiden voyage made it even more famous.

Developments above the sea were accompanied by those below it. Submarines had been around since the seventeenth century, but

twentieth-century conflicts saw a marked increase in their use, dimensions, and impact. During World War II, there were even submersible aircraft carriers. The Japanese I-400 Sen Toku class, which could carry three planes, wouldn't be beaten in size until the ballistic missile submarines of the 1960s.

But sheer size isn't always the major attribute for epic maritime achievement. In 1950, during the Korean War, an otherwise humble freighter, the SS *Meredith Victory*, evacuated 14,000 civilian refugees to safety. It remains the biggest rescue operation by a single ship ever.

And what of the future? A proposal has recently surfaced for what is effectively a traveling city. The *Freedom Ship* would be four times the size of the *Queen Mary*, hold 100,000 passengers, tower 25 storeys (350ft [107m]) high, and have its own airport on top. If it happens, no other machine anywhere else on the planet will be able to compare

VALMY, 1847

In the nineteenth century, gaining supremacy of the seas was one of the main concerns of the major European nations. An advantage in the oceans meant profitable colonies, profitable trade routes, and international standing. And although it was the British Royal Navy that ultimately "ruled the waves," it was the French who built the largest sailed warship ever.

SPECIFICATIONS

Country: France
Year built: 1836–47
Dimensions:
210ft (64m) long;
59ft (18m) wide
Weight: 6422 tons
(5,826,000kg)
Speed: N/A
Number of guns: 120
Cost: N/A

ABOVE: This painting depicts the *Valmy* in 1867, by which time she had been renamed the *Borda*.

Size was everything in the 1800s, and in 1847 when the French Navy launched the *Valmy,* named after a battle fought during the French Revolution, she seemed to prove this point. She was the largest warship in the world, and would remain so until the British matched her with the HMS *Duke of Wellington* six years later. However, that ship, although starting as a sailing ship, was converted to steam power while being constructed. That meant that the *Valmy* remained the largest warship powered by the wind, and still does to this day. In fact, it was actually thought impossible at the time that a sail warship could be built bigger, because the extensive rigging required on anything larger would be too complex to be operated just by manpower alone.

Steam supersedes sail

But it also meant she was obsolete very quickly, lacking the new technology of the era, namely, steam engines. Her size—three decks, each loaded with guns—didn't make her that easy to maneuver either. The only time she went into battle, during the bombardment of Sevastapol in the Crimean War, she actually had to be towed by a newer steam warship.

Despite being less than 10 years old, she was deemed past her usefulness by 1855, and became a training ship and renamed. She was scrapped in 1891, at the age of 44. But for only eight of those years had she actually served as a warship, the purpose for which she was built. Perhaps, in the case of the *Valmy,* size wasn't everything.

THE LARGEST PADDLE STEAM SHIP, EVER

SS *GREAT WESTERN*

In an era that produced more engineering geniuses than any previous century, Isambard Kingdom Brunel stood out as a towering example of Victorian ingenuity and enterprise. He was a man who seemed able to turn his hand to anything, but among his greatest achievements were his massive ships.

The SS *Great Western* was more or less a railroad line from London to New York. It was an extension of the London to Bristol Great Western Railway, and could take passengers on to America. Brunel had engineered the railroad line, and so was also put in charge of the design of the ship.

Sail and side paddles

When she was completed in 1837, the *Great Western* was the largest steamship ever built and the first to be intended simply to cross the Atlantic. Her hull was made out of wood, with iron bracing to give her extra strength, and side paddles providing the propulsion. She was also fitted with masts in case of engine failure, since the technology was still quite new, and far from reliable.

Despite her size, the *Great Western* could only carry 148 passengers, because her boilers took up half her hull space. On her first run to America, she raced another rival ship, the SS *Sirius*, and although the *Sirius* beat her to New York by a day, she had started four days previously. The SS *Great Western* was consequently awarded the Blue Riband for the fastest transatlantic crossing, and this was despite an onboard fire en route.

The SS *Great Western* stayed in service between America and Britain until 1846, making 64 trips in total. She then became a troop ship before being broken up in 1856. She is still the largest paddle steamer ever built.

BELOW: Two side paddle wheels provided the main propulsion, with four masts and sails as backup. For the *Great Western*'s first transatlantic trip, she had just seven passengers aboard.

SPECIFICATIONS

Country: UK
Year built: 1833–37
Dimensions:
236ft (72m) long;
58ft (18m) wide
Weight: 1478 tons
(1,341,000kg)
Speed: 9 knots/10mph
(17km/h)
Number of passengers: 148
Cost: N/A

AMERICAN QUEEN

Although steam power has now been largely superseded as a means of motive power for the world's largest ships, there are still many steam-driven ships operating all over the world, and giving faithful service. The largest of these is the *American Queen*, a modern recreation of the classic Mississippi riverboat.

SPECIFICATIONS

Country: USA
Year built: 1995
Dimensions:
418ft (127m) long;
89ft (27m) wide
Weight: 3707 tons
(3,362,935kg)
Speed: 9.5 knots/
11mph (18km/h)
**Number of
passengers:** 436, plus
160 crew
Cost: $60 million

The *American Queen,* operated by the Delta Queen Steamboat Company around the wide rivers of America's Deep South, is not all that she seems. Although she looks decades old, she was actually launched in 1995, as a faithful replica of an historic Victorian riverboat. And although the enormous 28ft (8.5m) paddle at the stern is operated by steam power, it receives a little bit of a helping hand from two propellers mounted on either side of the wheel. These are powered by diesel, and actually provide most of the propulsion when she's underway.

Modern technology, Victorian style

In order to improve the *American Queen*'s handling, the propellers are mounted in pods on the hull, and can be turned to change direction, using a system known as Z-drive. They can even face forward, to cancel out forward motion if the *American Queen* has to be stopped in a hurry.

There are several other concessions that have been made to the modern world onboard the six-deck steamer, which towers 97ft 6in (30m) above the river (although the smokestacks can be lowered for obstructions). Decorated outside with lacy filigree and inside with authentic Victorian opulence, her cabins still contain plenty of wood and antiques, but retain all the mod cons that discerning customers would expect to find on most ships of today, including two lifts that are made necessary by her height. She can carry 436 passengers, along with a crew of 160.

ABOVE AND BELOW: Because the USA's inland rivers are so calm, riverboat decks can extend almost down to the waterline.

THE LARGEST CABLE LAYER

SS *GREAT EASTERN*

Every time Isambard Kingdom Brunel achieved anything truly monumental, he tried to better it. The SS *Great Eastern* was the third and final of his great Atlantic steamships, and was five times bigger than anything else afloat when launched in 1858. But she proved to be a failure, although her later career did see her become the world's largest cable layer.

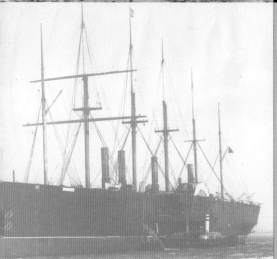

TOP AND ABOVE: The *Great Eastern*'s side paddle wheels were 56ft (17m) in diameter.

SPECIFICATIONS

Country: UK
Year built: 1854–58
Dimensions: 692ft (211m) long; 83ft (25m) wide
Weight: 21,200 tons (19,217,000kg)
Speed: 13 knots/ 15mph (24km/h)
Power: 8000hp (6mW) from five engines
Number of passengers: 4000, plus 418 crew
Cost: £500,000

The SS *Great Eastern* was Brunel's last project. The final photograph of him was taken on her deck in 1859, just before he died. But it was perhaps kinder that he didn't see the ship he loved (referring to her as "Great Babe") become such a floating disaster.

Thousands of passengers

Construction took four years, with the iron-hulled leviathan being incredibly advanced for her era. She even had a double-skinned hull for safety, something that wouldn't become common in ships for over 100 years after her. She could accommodate 4000 passengers, and was powered by five steam engines, four for her side paddles, and one for her propeller. Her sails proved useless because they caught fire from the hot exhaust from the funnels.

Always regarded as an unlucky ship—there were several deaths associated with her—her passenger career flopped. She was too big and unwieldy, and on her first voyage to America in 1860, there were only 35 passengers and 418 members of crew. Her subsequent role as a cable layer was much more fruitful, because of how much she could carry, and she was responsible for laying the first transatlantic cable in 1865. When she was scrapped in 1890, it took 18 months to dismantle her.

THE LARGEST SAIL-POWERED CLIPPER
CUTTY SARK

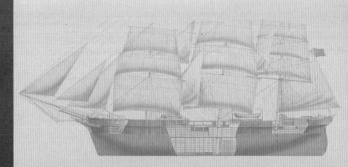

RIGHT AND BELOW: The central mast of the *Cutty Sark*—65ft (19.8m) tall—gave her a graceful appearance. Here, the ship is being presented to the Thames Nautical Training College in 1938.

Today, the *Cutty Sark* is one of London's most famous landmarks, and is permanently preserved in dry dock at Greenwich. But in her heyday she was one of the ultimate expressions of the very fast sailed clippers that plied their trade between China and London.

The *Cutty Sark* was what was known as a clipper, which was a highly maneuverable, very quick cargo ship distinguished by many masts and large sail areas for extra speed. One of the last to be built, she was born into a world where the steamship was becoming increasingly dominant. She would spend just eight years performing her intended role as a tea carrier, during which time she did only eight trips. She found fame in 1872 when racing another clipper back to London with the first tea of the season. Although she didn't win, thanks to losing her rudder en route, it was her captain's decision to press on using improvised steering that made her a maritime star.

Steam supplants sail

When steamships ousted the *Cutty Sark* from the tea routes in 1878, she went in to general service between Britain and Australia. On one journey, she managed to complete the trip in 67 days, which was extremely fast for the time, even by steamship standards. Her long-distance ocean travels came to an end in 1922, when she was restored and used as a training ship. She went into dry dock in Greenwich in 1954, as part of the National Maritime Museum's collection. Thousands of visitors visit the *Cutty Sark* every year, and a major regeneration program has just begun to ensure that the vessel continues to survive.

SPECIFICATIONS

Country: UK
Year built: 1869
Dimensions:
212ft 6in (65m) long;
36ft (11m) wide
Weight: 1080 tons
(978,000kg)
Speed: N/A
Crew: 70
Cost: £16,150

THOMAS W. LAWSON

SPECIFICATIONS

Country: USA
Year built: 1902
Dimensions:
385ft (117m) long;
50ft (11m) wide
Weight: 5850 tons
(5,302,000kg)
Speed: N/A
Crew: 16
Cost: £258,000

Schooners (ships with at least two fore- and aft-rigged masts) were some of the few cargo sailing ships able to compete with steamboats in the later years of the nineteenth and the first years of the twentieth centuries. The culmination of their 300 years of development resulted in the enormous but beautiful *Thomas W. Lawson*, the only seven-masted sailing ship ever constructed.

Built in 1902 for a Boston, Massachusetts, shipping company, the steel-hulled *Thomas W. Lawson* was one of the last-gasp efforts to build a freight craft that could compare in both size and speed to the latest steam-powered vessels. Her seven masts towered to a height of 190ft (58m) and she must have made a stirring sight with all her sails hoisted. Two steam winches performed this operation, meaning that she could operate with a crew of just 16. Her total sail area was 43,000ft² (4000m²), and, because of their number, the crew christened her masts after the days of the week.

Lost at sea

Ironically, her original purpose was to transport coal, the very fuel that made her rivals go. However, her 12,320 ton (11,177,000kg) capacity and her sheer size proved too big for many loading ports, and she was converted into an oil tanker in 1906. However, she didn't last long at this job either, for tragic reasons. In December 1907, on her first transatlantic trip, she sank off the Scilly Isles with the loss of all her crew, except the captain and one other. Nothing like her was ever built again.

RIGHT AND ABOVE: The seven masts were named after days of the week. The graceful appearance quite belied the ship's role as a coal and oil carrier.

THE LARGEST SAILING SHIP, EVER

PREUSSEN

A mammoth even by modern standards, the *Preussen* was the biggest sailing ship ever constructed, a record she still holds today. Built to transport nitrate to Europe, she was such a visually imposing craft that her name (meaning "Prussian" in German) was suggested by Emperor Wilhelm II as a way of spreading the glory and achievements of the Prussian empire.

ABOVE: The *Preussen* had so many sails, it was beyond mere manpower to raise them. Mechanical winches were used.

B y the end of the nineteenth century, the rivalry between French and German companies to transport nitrate from Chile to Europe had gone beyond just commercial competition. It had practically become a matter of national pride. However, with nitrate—an essential ingredient in explosives—it was hardly surprising that such cargos should be hotly fought over by the nations of a politically unstable Europe.

Extreme sail power

In 1902, the main German firm involved in this trade launched the *Preussen*, a ship that wasn't just to surpass anything the French had, but was also the largest sailing ship in the world. Made entirely out of steel, her five tall masts carried 48 sails with a surface area of 17,983m² (59,000ft²), with the largest of them measuring 223ft (68m). She is the only entirely square-rigged sailing ship ever built. Mechanized winches worked all these sails, and she was also one of the first vessels of her type to boast the newfangled wireless telegraphy.

With her hold able to squeeze in 8000 tons (7,257,000kg) of nitrate, 62,000 sacks, she was a very profitable vessel for her owners, up until November 6, 1910, when a cross-channel ferry ran into her in the English Channel. She was towed to Dover, but drifted ashore and was lost.

SPECIFICATIONS

Country: Germany
Year built: 1902
Dimensions:
408ft (124m) long;
53ft 6in (16m) wide
Weight: 5600 tons
(5,081,000kg)
Best speed: 18
knots/21mph (33km/h)
Crew: 46
Cost: N/A

THE LARGEST LINER OF THE PRE-JET AGE ERA

NORMANDIE

So huge was the *Normandie*—the greatest of the pre-World War II liners—that a new dry dock and other facilities had to be built at her home port of St-Nazaire in France. When she went into service in 1935, she offered the grandest, most luxurious way of crossing from Europe to America.

ABOVE AND BELOW: Top view shows the *Normandie* after launch and below is a cutaway showing the inside of the vast ship.

SPECIFICATIONS

Country: France
Year built: 1931–35
Dimensions:
1,029ft (314m) long;
119ft (36m) wide
Weight: 88,800 tons
(80,552,000kg)
Best speed: 37mph
(60km/h)
Power: 200,000hp
(149,140kW) from four
engines
Passengers: 1972 plus
1345 crew
Cost: N/A

When American immigration restrictions forced shipping companies to move upmarket and concentrate on affluent tourists and businesspeople, a series of mighty, very lavish liners appeared in quick succession. The culmination of this building rush saw the appearance of the *Normandie*, a veritable floating palace finished in Art Deco style.

New ship, new technology

Launched in October 1932 in front of a crowd of 200,000, the largest ship ever built created such a big wave at the bottom of the slipway that several hundred people were soaked. She went into service in 1935, and her capabilities were impressive. Her steam turbo-electric engines were the most powerful ever to be put into a ship, and she could reach 32.2 knots/37mph (59.6km/h). Other innovations were an early form of radar and a gyroscopic compass. She easily managed to win the Blue Riband for the fastest transatlantic crossing at her first attempt.

When it was announced that the forthcoming RMS *Queen Mary* would be larger than the *Normandie*, her French owners promptly added a new lounge to her superstructure just so that she could retain the title of the biggest liner in the world. She sank in 1943 in New York. Work to convert her into a troopship started a fire, and the weight of the water used to put it out caused her to capsize.

IMPERIAL JAPANESE NAVY, *SATSUMA*

The *Satsuma* was the first battleship to be built in Japan and, as if foreshadowing that country's later excellence in engineering and technology, she became the largest warship afloat. Soon after she was completed though, her conventional steam engines were almost obsolete compared to newer, steam-turbine designs.

For a country that had never built a dreadnought before, the *Satsuma* was quite something. Although many of the parts for her construction came from the UK, for a small, previously isolated nation to come up with the world's greatest warship was little short of a miracle.

Big-gun battleship

She was designed as an all "big-gun" ship, intended to carry 12in (305mm) armaments to make her capable of hitting targets from a long distance. However, there weren't enough of these monster barrels available, and in the end, only 37 of her 41 guns were of the size originally envisaged.

Launched in 1906, something else the *Satsuma* was missing was steam-turbine engines, the latest advance in marine power introduced soon afterward in the British HMS *Dreadnought*. These were both more efficient and more powerful, and gave battleships equipped in this way the edge in speed. They soon became the standard for new ships. The *Satsuma* was left behind as the largest conventionally engined steam battleship in the world, but not the most cutting edge.

Satsuma was used during World War I, with Japan on the Allied side during this conflict, but was scrapped in 1922. The fate that befell her was to be used as target practice. And, with her size, she wasn't that difficult to miss.

BELOW: The name may seem less than impressive to English ears, but the *Satsuma* was far from small fruit.

SPECIFICATIONS

Country: Japan
Year built: 1905–06
Dimensions:
482ft (147m) long;
80ft (25m) wide
Weight: 21,355 tons
(19,372,000kg)
Best speed:
18.25 knots/21mph
(338km/h)
Power: 17,300hp
(12,901kW) from
20 boilers
Crew: 887
Cost: N/A

THE LARGEST WORLD WAR II BATTLESHIP

JAPANESE BATTLESHIP *YAMATO*

With her sister ship, the *Musashi*, the *Yamato* was the largest battleship ever built, and one of the best equipped. She carried the greatest weaponry, including nine 18in (460mm) guns. Nothing of that size had been mounted on a warship before: Just the turrets themselves weighed around 2500 tons (2,260,888kg), the equivalent of a whole destroyer.

SPECIFICATIONS

Country: Japan
Year built: 1937–41
Dimensions:
862ft 6in (263m) long;
121ft (37m) wide
Weight: 80,250 tons
(72,800,000kg)
Best speed: 27
knots/31mph (50km/h)
Power: 150,000hp
(110mW) from 12
boilers and four engines
Crew: 2750
Cost: N/A

The London Naval Treaty of 1930 prohibited the construction of battleships, which is why, when design work started on the *Yamato* in 1934, it was carried out in total secrecy. Even when she was being built, a special dock was constructed to help mask what was going on. One of the briefs given was that she had to be bigger than anything that America would be likely to build. Because US Navy vessels had to use the Panama Canal, there were limitations on their size. This meant the *Yamato* could be fitted with the type of enormous guns it would have been impossible to fit on an American battleship.

Delayed fighting

She was commissioned in December 1941, just over a week after the Japanese attack on Pearl Harbor. However, despite being on the fringes of several battles and being attacked by a submarine, it wasn't until June 1944 that she actually fired her guns as part of a naval action. In the middle of 1945, when Japan was on the verge of losing the war, she was sent out on a suicide mission against US forces landing on Pacific islands. But an attack by 386 aircraft prevented her reaching her destination. When she sank, only 269 of her crew of 2750 survived.

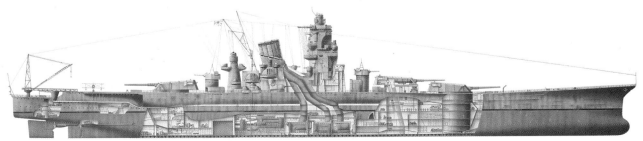

LEFT AND ABOVE:
Despite the *Yamato*'s huge size, and the amount of manpower and materials needed to build her, she was constructed in total secrecy.

SPECIFICATIONS

Country: USA

Year built: 1943–44

Dimensions:
888ft (270m) long;
93ft (28m) wide

Weight: 27,000 tons
(24,584,706kg)

Maximum speed: 33
knots/40 mph (60km/h)

Power: 150,00hp
(11.2mW) from eight
boilers and four
turbines

Crew: 3448

Cost: N/A

THE LARGEST WORLD WAR II AIRCRAFT CARRIER

TICONDEROGA CLASS AIRCRAFT CARRIER

The *Ticonderoga* class of aircraft carriers were the largest to see battle during World War II, and the biggest naval ships on the seas during the era. Capable of carrying 80 to 100 aircraft, it was only after the end of the war that anything would be built to better them.

The first *Ticonderoga* aircraft carrier, christened HMS *Ticonderoga,* was commissioned in June 1944. She was an outsized development of the already huge Essex-class of carrier with the bow reshaped to provide extra room for antiaircraft guns. The modification added an extra 88ft (27m) onto the length of the 820ft (250m) Essex vessels, and sent the *Ticonderoga* into the record books.

World War II and beyond

A total of 13 were built, with four in operation by 1944 and the rest following in 1945. The four of 1944 vintage were able to take part in the Pacific operations that ultimately led to the capitulation of Japan: None was lost in engagements. After the war ended, the gigantic maritime machines were no longer needed, and eight were mothballed. However, the Korean War and the escalation of the Cold War soon saw these pressed back into service. During the 1950s, several were completely rebuilt.

Decommissioning started in the late 1950s, with the final example, USS *Hancock*, which was one of the original craft built in 1944, passing out of the US Navy in 1976.

ABOVE: Conceived early on during World War II, the *Ticonderoga* class took US aircraft carriers to an unprecedented size, but most were completed too late to take an active role in the conflict.

TYPHOON NUCLEAR SUBMARINE

Weighing in at 53,000 tons (48,000,000kg), the Soviet Union's class of Typhoon ballistic missile submarine is the largest type of submersible ever built. And although soon to be retired from service, even its forthcoming successors will be unable to surpass its dimensions.

SPECIFICATIONS

Country: USSR/Russia	
Year built: 1977–88	
Dimensions: 574ft (175m) long; 75ft (23m) wide	
Weight: 53,000 tons (48,000,000kg)	
Maximum speed: 27 knots/31mph (50km/h)	
Maximum depth: 1312ft (400m)	
Crew: 163	
Cost: N/A	

So huge are the Typhoons of the Russian Navy that the facilities onboard them sound more like something you'd find on a civilian passenger ship. There's a smoking room, sports facilities, a sauna, and even a swimming pool, although the idea of going swimming in a huge metal tube hundreds of feet below the surface of the sea is a little ironic.

Six months underwater

But good crew conditions had to be an essential feature of the Typhoon design, as these craft can spend months away from ports. They can stay submerged for up to 180 days if necessary, or even longer in the event of war.

The main reason for the overall bulkiness of the Typhoon series is that they feature multiple pressure hulls, although their ability to carry up to 20 intercontinental ballistic missiles, as well as other weaponry, also increases their mass. There are three hulls to protect the sub overall, meaning a high chance of the vessel surviving if attacked.

Although their size might be considered a handicap to their ability to operate covertly, it actually aids their ability to avoid detection. Because they are so large, noise is minimized by the hull, so they are much quieter than many other military submarines. And they're very maneuverable as well, something else unexpected of vessels of this size.

However, despite the Typhoon's abilities, the era of the class is coming to an end. With even the newest of the six-strong class now nearing its twentieth birthday, they are being phased out to be replaced by the cutting-edge—but slightly smaller—Borei-type submarines.

ABOVE AND LEFT: Nuclear submarines such as the Typhoon class are capable of traveling under the polar ice caps, making them almost undetectable to opponents.

THE LARGEST SUBMARINE, EVER
OSCAR II CLASS SUBMARINE SERIES

Although the largest attack submarines ever built, Russia's secretive Oscar II vessels might have gone unnoticed by the world in general had it not been for a tragic accident. In 2000, one of their members, the *Kursk*, was lost with all hands, despite an international rescue attempt.

The first Oscar submarines were constructed in the early 1980s, but it was their ultimate development into the Oscar II class later on in that decade that took them into the record books, surpassing the American Ohio-class subs. Regarded as unsinkable, thanks to their double hulls, they were also longer, heavier, and able to dive deeper—down to 1968ft (600m)—than their predecessors. But a lot of information on these nuclear-powered and missile-equipped machines remains sketchy. The West learnt more about their construction, though, in the catastrophe that claimed the sixth out of the 10 Oscars IIs to be launched.

Tragedy at sea

In August 2000, during a training exercise, two huge explosions, the second so large it measured 4.4 on the Richter scale, sank the *Kursk*. The accident made the headlines around the world, as did the Russian, British, and Norwegian attempts to rescue the 116 members of the crew, 354ft (108m) down. The efforts were in vain and unfortunately there were no survivors. The cause of the incident was later on blamed on a faulty torpedo.

Kursk's nine sisters remain in service to this day.

SPECIFICATIONS

Country: Russia
Year built: 1986–91
Dimensions:
508ft (155m) long;
60ft (18m) wide
Weight: 18,077 tons
(16,400,000kg)
Speed: 32 knots/
37mph (59 km/h)
Power: 98,000hp
(73,078.5kW) from two
nuclear reactors
Crew: 48 officers, 68
personnel
Cost: N/A

TOP AND ABOVE: The size of the Oscar II series is partly down to the double hulls, one inside the other, to give better survivability in an attack.

SS-N-20 (R39) SUBMARINE-LAUNCHED BALLISTIC MISSILE

Few weapons of mass destruction are as terrifying as a submarine-launched nuclear missile. There's no warning and little chance of destroying the launcher before it fires, as there might be with a landbased site. One of the most frightening of all—because of its size—was the SS N-20 intercontinental ballistic missile (ICBM).

LEFT: An R39 out of its natural Typhoon submarine environment. The tip could carry 10 nuclear warheads.

SPECIFICATIONS

Country: USSR/Russia
Year built: 1979–89
Dimensions:
52ft 6in (16m) long; 8ft (2.4m) diameter
Payload: 5622lb (2550kg)
Weight: 99 tons (90,000kg)
Speed: "Hypersonic"
Range: 13,277 miles (8250km)
Cost: N/A

You can breathe a small sigh of relief. This deadly looking missile—known in Russia as the R39 and in the West as the SS-N-20 Sturgeon—is no longer in use. Introduced in 1983 aboard the USSR's Typhoon Class of submarines, which were then the largest submarines in operation, the last of these weapons was taken out of service in 2004 after the submarines they were used on were scrapped as well.

Five times the speed of sound

Firing differed from a ground-based missile, with the SS-N-20 ejected from the submarine using a gas generator so as not to damage the vessel. Once it broke the surface of the water, the conventional rockets came into play, and the weapon operated like a conventional three-stage booster. Traveling at hypersonic speeds (five times the speed of sound), and with each one having a yield of 200 kilotons, the potential if used against an enemy was deadly, especially as there would be absolutely no defence against them.

Capacity for destruction

Each SS-N-20 could carry 10 nuclear warheads, and each Typhoon could carry 20 of these in total. During the peak usage of these missiles, 120 were deployed on Russian vessels, which meant a total of 1200 warheads. From 1996, the missiles started to be taken out of service as a result of the terms of arms treaties. There were plans to create an even more potent successor, but so many prototypes failed during testing (submarine-launched ICBMs are more complicated than their traditional land counterparts) that the project was dropped.

THE LARGEST AIRCRAFT CARRIER, CURRENT

USS *ENTERPRISE*

BELOW: Seen at the bottom with a deck of F-14 Tomcats, this is, allegedly, the vessel that inspired Gene Roddenberry to name his fictional starship from *Star Trek* the *Enterprise*. The huge size of the ship is seen below, USS *Enterprise* (right) next to USS *Taylor* and USNS *Supply* (T-AOE 6).

Although the Nimitz-class of US Navy aircraft carriers are the heaviest of their type in the US fleet, the USS *Enterprise*, the first nuclear-powered carrier in the world, surpasses them in length. Commissioned in 1961, she is still in service and likely to remain so until superseded by a new generation of larger supercarriers.

Amazingly advanced

Still, when this USS *Enterprise* appeared in the early 1960s, she might well have been from outer space: There was nothing else like her. Longer than any other naval vessel around—an honor she still holds today—she was fitted with eight nuclear reactors, something else that hasn't been surpassed since. For example, America's latest carrier, the USS *Ronald Reagan*, only has two. She even played a role in the USA's initial exploration of space, serving as a tracking station for the country's first orbital space flight in 1962. She was also a major participant in the Cuban Missile Crisis and the 1975 evacuation of South Vietnam.

She was intended as the first of a series of six carriers. However, the huge costs in building what was at the time the most technically advanced machine in the world meant that her sisters were canceled, leaving the *Enterprise* as a unique ship in the US Naval fleet.

Everybody knows the *Enterprise* name of course. It has become famous as the spacecraft of the *Star Trek* television and film series. In fact, one of the kinder nicknames of the current bearer of the name is "the starship" in reference to her fictional successor. She is more commonly referred to as the "Big E," however.

SPECIFICATIONS

Country: USA

Year built: 1958–61

Dimensions: 1123ft (342m) long; 133ft (40.5m) wide

Weight: 93,500 tons (85,000,000kg)

Maximum speed: 33 knots/38mph (61km/h)

Power: 280,000hp (210mW) from eight reactors and four turbines

Crew: 3500 plus 1500 aircrew

Cost: $465 million

THE LARGEST CAR FERRY, CURRENT

ULYSSES

The world's largest car ferry, by capacity, is the MF *Ulysses*, which plies its trade between Dublin in Ireland and Holyhead in Wales. It can hold up to 1342 cars or 260 lorries and coaches, enough to stretch 3 miles (5km) if laid end to end.

SPECIFICATIONS

Country: Finland
Year built: 1999–2001
Dimensions:
686ft (209m) long;
102ft (31m) wide
Weight: 56,150 tons
(50,938,000kg)
Maximum speed: 22
knots/25mph (40km/h)
Power: N/A
Passengers: 2000
Cost: £100 million

Competition on the passenger routes between England and Ireland has always been fierce, but when Irish Ferries launched the towering MF *Ulysses* in 2001, it intensified even more. At a stroke, the *Ulysses* humbled all its rivals. The publicity surrounding the introduction of what was, and still is, the world's largest and most advanced roll-on, roll-off ferry undoubtedly attracted extra customers.

Twelve decks up

Built in Finland, the ship, which is named after James Joyce's novel about Dublin, makes the journey between its two ports in three hours and 15 minutes. In addition to the vehicles, it can also accommodate up to 2000 passengers, although if they all fancy a sleep en route, it could be a problem as there are only 228 beds.

Glass elevator

The *Ulysses'* 12 decks rise to a height of 167ft (51m) from keel to mast, and include shopping arcades, restaurants, bars, a video-gaming area, mini casino, and even two cinemas, in addition to the usual ferry amenities. For passengers who want to get a closeup view of how tall the ship is, there's even a glass-fronted elevator on the outside of the hull—however, it only operates when the *Ulysses* is safely docked in port.

ABOVE: One of the enormous *Ulysses's* more unusual features—its glass-mounted exterior lift—can be seen about halfway along the superstructure in this view.

KNOCK NEVIS

She's been known as the *Seawise Giant*, the *Happy Giant*, *Jahre Viking*, and is currently the *Knock Nevis*. However, whatever the title, there's one thing that has remained constant about this gigantic supertanker: She is the largest ship, of any type, ever built.

SPECIFICATIONS

Country: Japan (built), Norway (owned)

Year built: 1979–81

Dimensions: 1,504ft (458m) long; 226ft (69m) wide

Weight: 622,544 tons (564,763,000kg)

Speed: 15 knots/ 17mph (28km/h)

Power: 50,000hp (37,285kW) from one engine

Capacity: 4.1 million barrels of crude oil

Cost: N/A but last sold for $39 million

When the *Seawise Giant* supertanker was being built at the end of the 1970s, she wasn't quite the biggest in the world. However, after the company that had ordered her went out of business, she was sold instead to a Hong Kong concern, who bought her under the condition that she be lengthened. She was already enormous, at 529,110 tons (480,000,000kg), but the extra metal topped her off at 622,545 tons (564,763,000kg). Officially, this made her the largest vessel in the world.

Sinking and salvage

Too big to navigate the Suez and Panama Canals, or even the English Channel, her early career was spent around the USA and the Middle East, up until the point in 1986 when she was sunk off Iran by Iraqi jets. Had she not gone down in shallow water, her story might have ended there. However, in an epic salvage operation, she was refloated and repaired in Singapore, during which time she became the *Happy Giant* and then the *Jahre Viking* in quick succession.

Operating with a crew of just 40—a very small complement given her bulk—her subsequent oceangoing career was without incident, up until 2004 when she was re-equipped as a floating storage and offloading (FSO) unit. Renamed the *Knock Nevis*, she is now permanently moored in the Persian Gulf where, needless to say, she is by far the largest FSO in the world.

BELOW: A sight unlikely to be repeated soon—the *Knock Nevis* at sea—as she is now moored as a storage facility.

THE LARGEST BULK CARGO SHIP, EVER

BERGE STAHL

When it comes to absolute bulk, few ships are able to give super tankers a run for their money. However, one that comes close is the MS *Berge Stahl*, the largest bulk carrier cargo ship of all time. This vessel is so huge there are only two ports in the world where she can dock.

SPECIFICATIONS

Country:	Norway
Year built:	1986
Dimensions:	1125ft (343m) long; 213ft (65m) wide
Weight:	402,087 tons (364,768,000kg)
Speed:	13.5 knots/ 15.5mph (25 km/h)
Power:	27,610hp (20,589kW) from one engine
Crew:	30
Cost:	N/A

ABOVE AND BELOW: Similar in design to supertankers, bulk cargo carriers sit much lower in the water. Gigantic, purpose-built loading facilities are required for ships of this size.

There isn't a lot of variety to being a member of the crew on the MS *Berge Stahl*. The name, which means "Steel Mountain," is very apt, because all this ship does is carry huge amounts of iron ore between the Terminal Maritimo de Ponta da Maderia in Brazil to the Europoort near Rotterdam in the Netherlands. She can't actually go anywhere else, because her size simply makes it impossible for her to tie up anywhere. Other commercial ports simply aren't deep enough for her depth of 75ft (23m).

Brazil to the Netherlands and back again

Built in 1986, the *Berge Stahl* travels between Brazil and the Netherlands about 10 times a year, or around one trip every five weeks. That may not sound like too much—until you take into account that on each journey she can carry 397,000 tons (360,000,000kg) of material.

Surprisingly, she makes do with just one diesel engine and propeller to move this burden—both enormous at 29ft 6in (9m). The main diesel engine is a Hyundai with an amazing 27610hp (2590kW)—it is also the same size as a three-storey building. Her screw and rudder measure the same in height as well. She's not fast (top speed is 13.5knots/15.5mph [25km/h]), and she's not that pretty either. But when it comes to getting her job done, no other bulk carrier can match her.

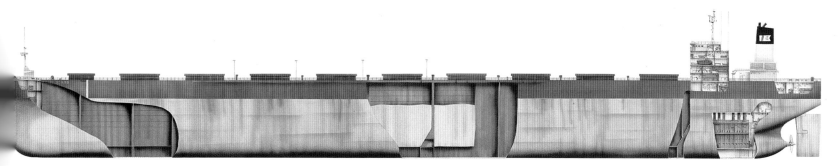

THE LARGEST CONTAINER SHIP, CURRENT

EMMA MAERSK

With the largest ship ever built— the *Knock Nevis* supertanker (see page 130)—now serving as a static storage facility, the *Emma Maersk* is now the largest container ship in the world, and the biggest oceangoing vessel still in current use. Yet she only has a crew of 13.

Compared to most of the other ships in this book, the *Emma Maersk* is a baby in age—she was only launched in August of 2006. But she's hardly a baby in size. With a length of 1305ft (398m), if she was to be laid upright beside the Empire State Building, she'd still be 52.5ft (16m) taller.

A load of containers

Named after the wife of the former CEO of the AP Moller-Maersk Group, which owns her, the *Emma Maersk* is able to transport 11,000 standard 20ft (6m) shipping containers. However, that figure is the estimation of Moller-Maersk, others put the total capacity of the ship at closer to 14,500 TEU (twenty-foot equivalent units). When fully loaded, the containers on the deck stretch 22 across and seven high, although there's room for an eighth layer if needed.

Such a ship obviously needs a big engine, and in the case of the *Emma Maersk*, she has the largest diesel engine ever manufactured. The 14-cylinder engine puts out around 107,389hp (80,080kW), and supplementary engines give an extra 40,000hp (53,641kW) for other ship functions. Usual speed should be around 25 knots, but it's likely that the ship will have a top speed considerably in excess of this. However, for commercial reasons, Moller-Maersk hasn't let on what it is.

The *Emma Maersk* has already been involved in one incident. While being built, a welding fire destroyed all her accommodation quarters, including the bridge. This added seven weeks onto her build time.

SPECIFICATIONS

Country: Denmark
Year built: 2005–06
Dimensions:
1305ft (398m) long;
185ft (56m) wide
Weight: 188,500 tons
(170,974,000kg)
Speed: In excess of
25.5 knots/29mph
(47.2 km/h)
Containers: Estimated
14,500
Crew: 13
Cost: $145 million

ABOVE: *Emma Maersk* in port. How many containers she can carry is a commercial secret, but 14,500 seems a reasonable estimate.

THE LARGEST OPEN DECK TRANSPORT SHIP
(USED FOR CARRYING OTHER SHIPS)

BLUE MARLIN

Think of the *Blue Marlin* as an aquatic pickup truck, and you won't be too far off the truth. This totally extraordinary vessel is semisubmersible, so its center section can be lowered beneath the water to allow loading of heavy floating items, often many times larger than itself.

SPECIFICATIONS

Country: Norway (built), Netherlands (owned)
Year built: 2000
Dimensions:
736ft 6in (225m) long;
207ft (63m) wide
Deadweight:
84,000 tons
(76,061,000kg)
Cruising speed: 14.5 knots/17mph (27km/h)
Power: 31,942hp (23,640kW)
Crew: Up to 55
Cost: Under £500 million, including modifications

Ships don't come much more amazing than the *Blue Marlin*. The largest heavy-lift transport ship in the world is almost a cross between a submarine and a dry-bulk carrier, with a long, flat, wide center section. The term "flo/flo" (for float on, float off) has been coined to describe the way this type of vessel works. Ballast tanks can be flooded to allow this "bed" to submerge, allowing anything from cargo to drilling rigs, and even whole ships to be floated onto it. The ballast tanks are then pumped out, and the ship rises and sets off to carry its load to its destination.

Getting bigger, getting better

When built, the *Marlin* had a load capacity of 30,000 tons (27,215,542kg), but work carried out over 2003 to 2004 increased her deck width and carrying abilities. Soon afterward, she transported the oil platform, *Thunder Horse*, to Texas. That weighed 60,000 tons (54,431,084kg) itself, so the modifications on her were obviously a total success.

However, the job that most caught the world's attention was when the *Blue Marlin* was hired by the US Navy to piggyback the crippled USS *Cole* from Yemen back to the United States after it was attacked by bombers. It was also responsible for moving the huge seabased X-Band Radar (see page 135) for the US Government in 2006.

TOP AND ABOVE:
The MV *Blue Marlin* has transported the X-Band Radar as well as the damaged USS *Cole* warship.

THE LARGEST PIPE LAYER

PIPE LAYER *SOLITAIRE*

Oceans are now no longer any barrier to major pipelines, thanks to ships like the *Solitaire*, a highly specialized pipelaying vessel operated by the Swiss-based Allseas Group. Effectively a floating factory—where steel pipes are welded together before being laid out—the *Solitaire* is an extraordinary example of man's maritime ingenuity.

BELOW: *Solitaire* in action, with its pipelaying cradle lowered beneath the surface of the sea by cables.

The Allseas Group operates a fleet of six highly specialized ships built for its business of offshore pipelaying and subsea construction. Pride of the fleet though is the *Solitaire*, the biggest pipelaying vessel in the world, and a simply astonishing-looking machine with its cranes, front boom, and helicopter landing pad.

How she works

At the aft of the *Solitaire* is a huge gantry—known as a stinger—from which the pipeline is gradually lowered to the bottom of the ocean. An automatic welding system onboard the vessel allows the ship to work at a fast rate. In the past, up to 5.6 miles (9km) have been achieved in one day using it. Thanks to her size and storage capacity, the *Solitaire* can carry up to 24,250 tons (22,000,000kg) of pipe, which allows her to operate far out in the ocean without having to return to port to replenish her stock or be supplied from support ships. In the often difficult conditions these ships operate in, this puts her at an advantage over her contemporaries.

A big ship should have some big achievements, and one such feat that the *Solitaire* has notched up is the deepwater laying record, having managed to place a pipeline at a depth of 9100ft (2775m).

SPECIFICATIONS

Country: Switzerland
Year built: 1998
Dimensions:
1302ft (397m) long
Weight: 104,560 tons
(75,684,000kg)
Speed: 13 knots/
15mph (24 km/h)
Pipe diameters: from
2in (5cm) to 60in
(152.4cm)
Crew: Up to 420
Cost: N/A

SEA-BASED X-BAND RADAR

Looking like some kind of bizarre oil platform, the US Government's Sea-based X-Band Radar is one of the more unusual—and gigantic—floating structures. It serves as part of America's ballistic missile defence system, and is thought to be able to detect objects as small as a baseball from 2900 miles (4667km) away.

ABOVE AND BELOW: Despite its oilrig resemblance, the X-Band Radar can move under its own power, although for longer trips a transporter ship like the *Blue Marlin* is quicker.

SPECIFICATIONS

Country:	USA
Year built:	2002
Dimensions:	
380ft (116m) long;	
280ft (85m) high	
Weight:	55,000 tons
(49,895,161kg)	
Speed:	Classified
Power:	Classified
Crew:	Up to 75
Cost:	$900 million

Built on a Russian-built semisubmersible oil-drilling platform, the USA's most unusual device for detecting incoming missiles isn't normally seen by the public. Based off a remote island in Alaska, but able to patrol the Pacific in its search for possible incoming attacks against the US, the Sea-Based X-Band Radar rarely comes close to populated areas. However, in 2006 it was carried from Texas to Pearl Harbor around South America (because it was too large to fit through the Panama Canal) on the back of the *Blue Marlin* heavy transport ship. When it arrived in Hawaii, large crowds turned out to see it.

Classified capabilities

It may be the last they see of the X-Band Radar for quite some time. Designed to be totally selfcontained, the floating installation has living quarters, workspaces, storage, power generators, and a bridge and control room on its main deck. It is be crewed by 75 personnel. It has its own propulsion system, although quite what speed the ungainly machine can manage is classified. It isn't likely to be fast though.

The main feature of the vessel is the X-Band radome, which weighs 1814 tons (1,645,633kg) and requires over a megawatt of power to operate.

WALLENIUS LINES *BOHEME* CLASS CAR CARRIERS

The carbuilding industry is big business—as is the job of simply getting the finished vehicles around the world so they can be sold. One of the leading companies in this field is Wallenius Lines, which operates the five biggest car carriers afloat.

BELOW: And you can't even see the join! Wallenius Lines' *Boheme* class of car carriers were initially slightly smaller, but had an extra length of section added to increase their capacity. A single ship like this can hold up to 7200 cars on its 13 decks, for transporting anywhere in the world.

The Wallenius Lines fleet is a noteworthy one, with its Pure Car/Truck Carriers (PCTCs) in service throughout the world transporting around two million cars and trucks a year. The current flagships of its fleet are the *Boheme* class, which can swallow up to 7200 cars, or a combination of 3700 cars and 600 trucks.

Soon to be surpassed

The five ships—*Mignon*, *Elektra*, *Boheme*, *Manon*, and *Undine*—didn't start their lives quite so large. Originally, they were capable of managing 5900 cars, but a lengthening program in 2005 and 2006 saw an extra 92ft (28m) added to their already not-inconsiderable 656ft (200m) length. However, they won't be the elite for too long, as the company will soon be taking delivery of three new PCTCs, which will be the largest car carriers in the world when complete. This pair shares the same length of 748ft (228m) as the *Boheme* Class, but will be able to hold an astounding 8000 cars.

The slablike Boheme carriers are fitted with 13 decks inside, three of which are moveable so that tall vehicles—up to 16ft (5m) high—can be accommodated. Another three decks are specially strengthened to accomodate extra heavy trucks. In order to allow the ships to load and unload at any dock, the two vehicle ramps are at the side, unlike on most passenger roll-on/roll-off ferries where they are at the front and rear, and thus require special loading/unloading facilities to be built.

SPECIFICATIONS

Country: Korea (built), Sweden (owned)
Year built: 1999–2003, modified 2005–06
Dimensions: 748ft (228m) long; 106ft (32m) wide
Weight: 74,146 tons (67,264,000kg)
Speed: 13 knots/ 24mph (24.1 km/h)
Power: 19,713hp (14,700kW) from one engine
Crew: 15
Cost: N/A

DISCOVERER ENTERPRISE DRILLSHIP

A drillship is a maritime vessel fitted with drilling apparatus to explore for new oil or gas wells, although they are used for scientific research as well. The biggest and most advanced one sailing the seas at the moment is the *Discoverer Enterprise*.

SPECIFICATIONS

Country: Spain (built), USA (owned)

Year built: 1999

Dimensions: 835ft (255m) long; 38ft (125m) wide

Weight: 45,000 tons (40,823,313kg)

Speed: 13 knots/ 15mph (24 km/h)

Power: 13,214hp (9854kW) from two engines

Crew: Up to 200

Cost: $300 million

ABOVE AND TOP: The *Discoverer Enterprise* (top) has a helicopter pad which means the ship can be easily re-supplied at sea. Above is a sister ship The *Discoverer Deep Seas*.

If the *Discoverer Enterprise* looks like a bizarre mating between an oil platform and a tanker, that's because, effectively, she is just that! Searching for oil and gas is an expensive and time-consuming business, so it makes sense to do it with something that can be moved around easily and react promptly to different conditions. The rig is 835ft (255m) long, nearly as long as three football fields, and 418ft (127m) high, more than a single football field.

Multitasking

Based on a twin-hulled tanker design, the *Discoverer Enterprise* can drill holes of 35,000ft (10,668m) in depth, in 10,000ft (3048m) of water, done by lowering a "marine riser" to the seabed onto which the drill bit is attached. Impressive enough, but what makes the *Enterprise* truly radical is that she has two derricks on her deck, with two drill strings, allowing her to do two jobs simultaneously. The deeper the water, the further apart the drilling can be. In 6000ft (1829m) of water, the wells can be as far as 150ft (46m) apart. If oil is found, the *Enterprise* can store up to 120,000 barrels-worth in her tanks.

Staying still

Even in a severe storm *Enterprise* is designed to only shift as much as 7ft (2.1m), with the help of six 7000hp (5220kW) thrusters.

THE LARGEST ICEBREAKER

SS *MANHATTAN*

The story of the SS *Manhattan* is an intriguing one. Built as an oil tanker, she was fitted out as an icebreaker to see if it was viable for a ship to bring oil from the ice-laden Alaskan oilfields rather than build a pipeline. The fascinating adventure was not without incident.

The SS *Manhattan* was already the biggest and most powerful of all US commercial vessels when it was decided to use her for an experimental voyage in 1969. The ship—as long as the Empire State Building is tall—was cut into four pieces. It was then put back together again but heavily reinforced, with a new heavy-duty icebreaking bow at her front. It easily made her the biggest icebreaker in the world by at least 15 times.

Trapped in ice

She set off from Pennsylvania for the Northwest Passage—the sea route connecting the Atlantic and the Pacific via the top of Canada—in August 1969, and encountered her first ice in September. At first, she was fine, managing to crack floes up to 60ft (18m) thick. However, as the ice got thicker, the challenges became tougher, and she became stuck. She was only able to escape when steam used for heating was diverted to her engines, adding an extra 7000hp (5220kW) to her 43,000hp (32,06kW) turbines. A Canadian icebreaker and a US Coastguard ship also assisted. After she had been extricated from the ice, she changed course and managed to reach the Prudhoe Bay Oil Field where she took on a single token barrel of oil before returning to New York. The trial had proved that navigation by ship was still too difficult to attempt, and the Transalaskan pipeline was constructed instead.

ABOVE AND RIGHT: These pictures illustrate the type of Arctic conditions the *Manhattan* was pitched against during its epic journey north.

SPECIFICATIONS

Country: USA
Year built: 1962, modified into icebreaker 1969
Dimensions: 1005ft (306m) long; 148ft (45m) wide
Weight: 115,000 tons (104,336,245kg)
Speed: N/A
Power: 43,000hp (32,065kW)
Crew: 45
Cost: $54 million conversion cost

THE LARGEST CATAMARAN

ASIA STAR
(RADISSON DIAMOND)

Yes, the *Asia Star* is a cruise ship. But no, she isn't like most other cruise ships around. She's actually the world's largest catamaran—where a ship has two hulls joined by a frame—or rather, a development of the concept known as a SWATH.

ABOVE AND BELOW: The twin-hulled design of the *Asia Star*—formerly the *Radisson Diamond*—was designed to eradicate seasickness! Much more of the hulls are below the waterline.

The *Asia Star* isn't the only twin-hulled cruise ship around, but she is by far the largest. Strictly speaking, she isn't a true catamaran, but a Small Waterplane Area Twin Hull (SWATH) ship—a design with very bulbous hulls beneath the waterline. This means that much of the ship's floatation comes from beneath the waves, where the hulls behave rather like submarines. The result is a vessel that gives a smooth ride even in rough seas.

Cruises for the seasick

The novel design of the ship, formerly known as *Radisson Diamond* but now the *Asia Star* after a change of ownership, was expressly intended to try and lure a new class of customer onto cruise ships: Those who might otherwise have been worried about seasickness ruining their holiday.

When launched in 1992, the *Radisson Diamond* was more than twice the length of the next-largest catamaran. It was also very wide for a ship of its length (430ft [131m] across by 105ft [32m] long), a feature necessitated by the twin hulls. With conventional single-hulled vessels, such a breadth would normally have to be accompanied by a hull stretching around 800ft (244m) long.

Despite the reputation of catamarans for being fast, the 12-deck, 175-cabin *Asia Star* is rather a sedate cruiser. Top speed is 12 knots/14mph (25.6km/h), although there is an engine in each hull, their size is limited by lack of space, you can't fit so much in two small hulls as you can one large one!

SPECIFICATIONS

Country: Finland (built), Hong Kong (owned)

Year built: 1992

Dimensions:
430ft (131m) long;
105ft (32m) wide

Weight: 22,371 tons (20,295,000kg)

Maximum speed:
12 knots/14mph (25.6km/h)

Passengers: 350 plus 290 crew

Cost: $125 million

THE LARGEST FLOATING HOTEL

RMS *QUEEN MARY*

The RMS *Queen Mary* is one of the most famous of the glamorous transatlantic liners introduced before World War II. In service until 1967, she went on to a second career as the world's biggest floating hotel, moored at Long Beach, California.

ABOVE: Old and new meet: In the foreground is the original *Queen Mary*, while the newly launched *Queen Mary II* sails in behind. The two great liners exchanged whistles in salute.

SPECIFICATIONS

Country: UK	
Year built: 1930–34, modified into hotel 1967–72	
Dimensions: 1,019ft 6in (311m) long; 118ft (36m) wide	
Weight: 81,240 tons (73,700,000kg)	
Cruising speed: 28.5 knots/33mph (55km/h)	
Power: 119,312kW (160,000hp)	
Capacity: 1957 passengers plus 1174 crew	
Number of hotel rooms: 365	
Cost: £5 million	

The career of the *Queen Mary* has been anything but dull. Her maiden voyage took place in 1936, when she proved to be the fastest ship to cross the Atlantic. During the war, she was a troopship. She was so prized by the Germans that a reward of $250,000 was offered to any U-boat commander that could sink her. After the conflict ended, she went back to being a UK–USA liner again.

From ship to building

When withdrawn from service in 1967, she sailed to Long Beach, California, where conversion work started to turn her into a hotel and museum. Most of her machinery was removed, and the interior completely revamped to turn her into luxury accommodation. Although she superficially retains her original looks, there is very little that hasn't been touched or altered in some way, and she is now classed by the Coastguard authorities as a building instead of a ship, because she is incapable of moving under her own power.

According to popular superstition, several ghosts haunt the *Queen Mary*, and the sound of splashing has been heard from the first-class pool, despite the fact that it has been drained for years. As one of the last remaining icons from the golden age of transatlantic sea travel, the *Queen Mary* has also featured in many films and television programs, including doubling for the SS *Titanic*.

SPECIFICATIONS
Country: USA
Year built: 1981
Dimensions:
310ft (94m) long;
69ft (21m) wide
Weight: 3335 tons
(3,025,460kg)
Service speed: 16
knots/18mph (30km/h)
Power: 7000hp
(5.2mW) from four
engines
Passengers: 6000
Cost: $25 million

THE LARGEST FERRIES BY PASSENGER CAPACITY

STATEN ISLAND FERRIES

Anything to do with New York is usually big. Think of the skyscrapers, statues, and Central Park, to name but a few. To be added to that list are the Staten Island Ferries that travel between Manhattan and the borough of Staten Island. Two of them—the *Andrew J. Barberi* and the *Samuel I. Newhouse*—are the largest passenger ferries, by capacity, in the world.

The bright orange Staten Island ferries are almost as much a landmark of New York harbor as the Statue of Liberty, the Big Apple icon they pass as they relentlessly shuttle back and forth on their 25-minute trips between Manhattan and Staten Island. Ferries have been operating the route since the 1700s. However, a rapidly rising population and increasing mobility has resulted in the ships constantly becoming bigger.

Barberi and *Newhouse* giants

Today 19 million passengers a year are carried on the 5.2 mile (8.4km) run, 24 hours a day, 365 days a year. The total, just for one day, is almost 65,000 passengers, during 104 boat trips. Many of these are carried on the two enormous Barberi Class vessels, the giants of the fleet of nine craft. Built in 1981, the *Andrew J. Barberi* and *Samuel I. Newhouse* can carry 6000 passengers each at a service speed of 16 knots/18mph (30km/h). The former was named after a long-serving school football coach, the latter after the publisher of the *Staten Island Advance* newspaper from 1922–79. Both of the vessels are identical in design and capabilities, and much of their capacity is a result of the fact that they are not equipped to carry vehicles, unlike other vessles in the fleet.

The service has been dubbed the biggest bargain in New York. It gives superb views and is free to travel on.

ABOVE: Two of the most familiar sights of New York harbor—the Statue of Liberty and the square-cut, bright orange bulk of a Staten Island ferry. No cars are carried, just passengers.

THE LARGEST LINER/CRUISESHIP, EVER

RMS *QUEEN MARY 2*

A worthy successor to her illustrious Cunard Queen predecessors, such as the original *Queen Mary* and the *Queen Elizabeth,* the *Queen Mary 2* was the longest, tallest, widest passenger ship ever when launched in 2003. Although since superseded in tonnage by the cruise ship *Freedom of the Seas*, she still retains the laurels of being the biggest transatlantic ocean liner.

BELOW: The RMS *Queen Mary 2* is the largest of all the Cunard Queens.

What's one of the last things you'd expect to find on board an ocean liner? How about a planetarium? Well, the *Queen Mary 2* has one, in addition to her 15 restaurants and bars, five swimming pools, casino, and ballroom. She also has many other modern amenities and entertainments that mark her out as probably the world's premier liner.

Not to be beaten

Conceived in 1998, it was always the intention for the *Queen Mary 2* to be the most impressive passenger ship in the world. Indeed, when it was found out that bigger ships were planned for construction soon after completion, her design was enlarged simply so she could beat them.

Around 20,000 people were involved in her construction, which resulted in just nine months between her keel being laid and her launch. In January 2004, she was named by Queen Elizabeth II of Great Britain. During one cruise in 2006, she passed by her spiritual mother, the first *Queen Mary*, in Long Beach, California, and, in a poignant moment, the two exchanged whistle salutes.

The dual diesel/gas turbine-powered QM2 has already joined the ranks of her glamorous ancestors as one of the greatest, most luxurious, and special ways of sailing the oceans ever conceived.

SPECIFICATIONS

Country: France (built), UK (operated)
Year built: 2002–03
Dimensions: 1132ft (345m) long; 147ft 6in (45m) wide
Weight: 167,000 tons (151,400,000kg)
Speed: 30 knots/ 35mph (56km/h)
Power: 157,000hp (117mW) from six engines
Passengers: 2620 plus 1253 crew
Cost: Approximately $800 million

THE LARGEST CRUISE SHIP (BY WIDTH)

FREEDOM OF THE SEAS

The new *Queen Mary 2* may be the largest liner around, but she was recently surpassed in size as the biggest passenger ship of them all by the *Freedom of the Seas*. With 18 decks and the sort of entertainment facilities that would more likely be found in a holiday resort than a ship, she is a prime example of how far modern technology has pushed the art of shipbuilding.

SPECIFICATIONS

Country: Turkey (built), USA/Norway (owned)
Year built: 2004–06
Dimensions: 1111ft 6in (339m) long; 184ft (56m)
Weight: 815,710 tons (740,000,000kg)
Speed: 21.6 knots/25 mph (40 km/h)
Power: 102,000hp (75.6mW) from two engines
Cost: Approximately $947,000,000

Imagine 37 double-decker buses parked end to end, or the Eiffel Tower laid flat on the ground (with another 54ft [16.5m] added to it). Now you have some idea of just how long the *Freedom of the Seas*—the current flagship of the Royal Caribbean Cruise Line—measures, stretching 1112ft (339m) from fore to aft.

Floating adventure

This mammoth ship is one of the latest leviathans to take to the oceans, and the first of three sisters—their size and cost suggesting much optimism about the future of luxury cruising. In addition to how much it cost to build, her operating costs, as of 2006, were around $1 million a day. But there's a lot to lure passengers to her. Aside from the experience of riding the biggest cruise ship afloat, she has a water park (including a wave generator), whirlpools, which extend over the ship's sides, a rock-climbing wall, all manner of shops and restaurants, and even an iceskating rink. It must almost be a disappointment having to get off when the ships calls at ports during its international trips.

BELOW: The sheer size of the *Freedom of the Seas* is such that it dwarfs all other vessels around it, as this view of the cruise ship entering port illustrates.

THE LARGEST YACHT, SINGLE MASTED AND TALLEST MAST

MIRABELLA V

The *Mirabella V* may look like other yachts with a single mast, but her scale is out of all proportion to anything that has gone before. This "super yacht" surpasses anything else of her type built, and cost an estimated $50 million. Which explains why she costs upward of $275,000 to hire.

This beautifully designed and utterly elegant yacht was created to be the largest and most luxurious sailing yacht in the world, offering a level of refinement and speed previously unheard of. She is one of a fleet of similar vessels used for luxury charters by millionaire Joe Vittoria. Unusually, in order to reduce maintenance and provide insulation against noise and temperature, she is built of composite materials rather than traditional wood or metal.

Tallest mast in the world

Mere pictures do not do her dimensions true justice, but comparisons give some idea of her magnitude. She has a lifting keel, to allow her to use the harbor in Palm Beach, California. However, she is unable to pass underneath any sea bridge in the world because her 292ft (88.5m) mast, the equivalent in height of two of London's Nelson's Column, is simply too tall. Still, it's likely that the old sea hero Nelson would have approved of such a feat of maritime engineering. In width, she's about the size of a midsized British Naval destroyer.

Sail power is her most graceful way of traveling. However, she is also equipped with two engines, with an output of 1056hp (788kW) each, just in case that mast isn't quite tall enough for the available wind.

BELOW AND LEFT: The size of the *Mirabella*'s mast confines her mainly to the open sea, as she is unable to fit underneath any sea or navigable water bridge, including the ones in New York harbor.

SPECIFICATIONS

Country: UK (built), USA (owned)

Year built: 2003

Dimensions:
247ft (75m) long;
48ft 6in (15m)

Weight: 815 tons (740,000kg)

Speed: Approximately 20 knots/23mph (37km/h)

Power: 2112hp (1576kW) from two engines

Cost: Over $50 million

THE LARGEST YACHT, TRIMARAN

GERONIMO TRIMARAN

The racing yacht *Geronimo* was specifically built to shatter open ocean speed records, something she has been doing very well since she was launched in 2002 as the world's largest trimaran.

Those who crewed or traveled on small ships during the glory days of sail would probably have trouble coming to terms with a boat like the *Geronimo*. Although trimarans—boats with one main hull and two outriggers either side for stability and to make capsizing very unlikely—have been around for almost 4000 years, it is only within the last 30 years or so that they've come into widespread use. And there's been nothing like the *Geronimo* before.

Never gave up

This largest of trimarans is built from carbon fiber—including the sails—to save weight, and also sports the world's tallest canted mast, at 141ft (43m) tall. It can be moved eight degrees left or right of center to give extra performance.

The *Geronimo* took one year and over 100,000 man hours to construct, but the care and attention obviously paid off, because she is capable of speeds in excess of 44 knots/ 50.6mph (81.5km/h). According to French skipper Olivier de Kersauson, the yacht was christened after the famous Native American leader "…because Geronimo never gave up."

Record breaker

Among the sail records set by *Geronimo* are the fastest time to circumnavigate Australia (17 days and 13 hours in 2005), and she scooped the Jules Verne Trophy in 2004 for the fastest around-the-world trip by any yacht. She managed the feat in 63 days and 14 hours.

RIGHT AND ABOVE: The main sail is made of lightweight carbon fiber. She gets even more speed from her trimaran design, which cuts down water drag.

THE LARGEST PRIVATE YACHT

DUBAI (*PLATINUM/GOLDEN STAR*)

Luxury motor yachts have always been one of the more popular perks among the rich and famous. However, when the yacht variously known as *Platinum*, *Golden Star*, and currently as *Dubai* is complete, she'll be the biggest perk of them all!

SPECIFICATIONS

Country: Germany/UAE (built), Dubai (owned)
Year built from: 1996
Dimensions:
525ft (160m) long;
72ft (22m) wide
Weight: N/A
Speed: N/A
Power: 38,500hp kW (51,629.3) from four engines
Cost: N/A

ABOVE: this is the view that most people have had of the *Dubai* over the last decade—the boat still being built. But when finished, she promises to be the most exclusive private yacht around.

Very little is known about the yacht *Dubai*, except that she will be the largest and most luxurious yacht in the world. But that is assuming she ever gets finished. Originally commissioned, as the *Platinum*, in 1996 by a brother of the Sultan of Brunei, work in Germany stopped in 1998 when Prince Jefri ran into financial difficulties.

The unfinished yacht remained at the shipyard until 2001 when the Crown Prince of Dubai, Sheikh Mohammed, took her over, and moved her to the United Arab Emirates for construction to continue. At the time of writing, she has been 10 years in the making, and still needs to be officially completed, although she has made some small trips.

Outdoing the other royals

But then again, the now-named *Dubai* is some quite vessel. At over 100ft (30.5m) longer than the British royal family's former yacht RY *Britannia*, she measures 525ft (160m) in total. That puts her up amid the ranks of some of the smaller ocean liners, yet the accommodation will run only to about 24 guests in addition to the royal entourage and crew.

Among the features the *Dubai* is thought to have are: Her own theater, cinema, gym, squash court, swimming pool, health spa, a helipad, room for vehicles—which can be taken ashore in their own landing craft—and even, believe it or not, her own submarine! But who knows what else will have been added when she finally goes to sea properly? Whenever that may be...

COLUMBUS

The world's largest raft? Yes, for although the *Colombus* may look like a conventional wooden ship with sails, she was classed as a raft. However, she was a raft with a tricky voyage to undertake, a journey across the Atlantic from Québec to London.

BELOW: The *Columbus*'s flat bottom classed it as a raft—and it was designed to be disposable, dismantled for wood at the end of the voyage.

As moneymaking schemes go, the *Columbus* must have been one of the best of the nineteenth century. Or at least she would have been if she hadn't sunk. Built in Québec in 1824, her sole purpose was to carry wood to Europe, with the intention that once she arrived she would be broken up to provide even more profit.

Canada to England by raft

Thus the flat-bottomed *Columbus* was built as simply as possible, and when she was launched the vessel was already loaded with 4,064,000kg (4480 tons) of timber. More was added to help secure her sail rig. Amazingly, this very basic craft would be the home to 60 men over the two months of September and October of 1824 that it took *Columbus* to reach England.

It didn't go well right from the start. She grounded on the St. Lawrence River after four days, and it took three days for her to be refloated. By the time she reached London, she was leaking so badly the only thing keeping her from sinking was the total 6945 tons (6,300,000kg) of wood she was carrying, and she had to be helped into port by other ships.

Against the advice of practically everybody, her owners decided not to dismantle her, but send her back to Canada for another load of timber. She promptly sank in the English Channel.

NANTUCKET LV-117

Lightships were once an essential part of the maritime scene, moored in waters that are too deep for a conventional lighthouse to be sited. The USA decommissioned its last one in 1985 after over 160 years of using such ships, but several still survive as museum pieces. One is the *Nantucket* WLV-535, the world's largest example of a lightship.

SPECIFICATIONS

Country: USA
Year built: 1936
Dimensions:
149ft (45.5m) long; 32ft (10m) wide
Weight: 1050 tons (952,544kg)
Best speed: 12 knots/14mph (22km/h)
Power: 900hp (671kW)
Crew: 7
Cost: $300,956

LEFT AND ABOVE: Masts of the LV-117 were fitted with powerful beacons, the rear one with lights from railroad locomotives! The name in large letters on the side was for recognition and location purposes, to aid nearby shipping.

Lightships are meant to be easily visible to other ships through their bright-red paint during the day, and their powerful beacons at night. But neither of those did the predecessor to the Nantucket LV-117 lightship too much good. While it was helping to protect the dangerous shoals off Massachusetts, the RMS *Olympic* (the sister ship to the *Titanic*) rammed it. The *Olympic* survived, but the *Nantucket* didn't and sank. Still, at least the British were good enough to stump up the money for a replacement in the form of the biggest lightship of the seas.

War and hurricane

The new *Nantucket* survived World War II, during which it was painted gray and fitted with guns, as well as Hurricane Edna in 1954, which ripped off part of its superstructure. It was retired in 1975, and eventually designated as an historic landmark.

At night, the *Nantucket* was difficult to miss, thanks to its superb illumination. Its foremast was fitted with a 20in (500mm) lens lantern, while on the main mast were 24 high-intensity lights from a railroad locomotive, six each mounted on the four sides of a revolving lamp. Also installed were radio beacons and radar, as well as a submarine oscillator, so that the *Nantucket* would be noticeable under the waves as well. This was soon removed though, as it was deemed obsolete.

PETRONIUS OIL PLATFORM

The tallest freestanding structure in the world happens to be an oil platform, but only just over 10 percent of it is actually above the water. By dint of its stature, the *Petronius* oil platform, off the coast of New Orleans, is also the largest floating structure in existence as well.

M any oil platforms, such as the *Hibernia* (see page 151), are securely attached to the seabed. However, where drilling and extraction takes place in very deep water, floating structures have to be used instead. None is more impressive than the Texaco/Marathon Oil *Petronius* in the Gulf of Mexico. At peak production, this lofty oil platform produces 50,000 barrels of oil per day, along with 70 million ft^3 (2 million m^3) of natural gas.

Tallest on Earth or water

It looks impressive enough from the surface of the sea, stretching 246ft (75m) into the air. But that's only part of the story. Underneath the waves lie another 1755ft (535m), making the full height of the Petronius 2001ft (610m). And that's taller than anything else made by man, save for a radio mast in the USA, which doesn't have anywhere near the same complexity to its design or engineering.

Still afloat

The design of the *Petronius*, with only a small part of it poking above the water, actually makes it very stable, and even in strong seas, there is very little pitch around the buildings. The platform is actually anchored to the ocean floor by giant "footers," but even with its considerable height, it still "floats" 1754ft (535m) above the seabed. It has proved capable of standing up to the many hurricanes that afflict the Gulf of Mexico, albeit with some damage caused, which has held up oil and gas extraction.

RIGHT: The visible part of the *Petronius* is massive enough, but the vast majority lies under the surface. Just 246ft (75m) is above the sea, most of which is drilling derrick.

SPECIFICATIONS

Country: USA	
Year built: 1997–2000	
Dimensions: 2,001ft (610m) high; 354ft (108m) base diameter	
Weight: 43,000 tons (39,008,944kg)	
Processing capacity: 50,000 barrels of oil and 70millionft³ (2,000,000m³) natural gas per day	
Crew: N/A	
Cost: $500 million	

SPECIFICATIONS

Country: Canada
Year built: 1990–93
Dimensions: 346ft
(105.5m) high; 108m
(354ft) base diameter
Weight: 1,200,000 tons
(1,088,621,688kg)
Processing capacity:
150,000 barrels per day
Crew: Up to 185
Cost: $5.8 billion

LEFT: The *Hibernia*
platform sits on a
concrete island in
the shape of a star -
the edges designed
to ward off any
passing icebergs.
The structure is filled
with ballast and
storage tanks.

THE LARGEST OIL/GAS PLATFORM,
SECURED TO SEABED

HIBERNIA OIL PLATFORM

The world's largest oil platform sits about 196 miles (315km) east of Newfoundland in Canada. It is home to around 100 people in an inhospitable climate that sometimes sees stray icebergs crashing into the structure.

The production platform *Hibernia* isn't just a massive structure in its own right. It's was—and is—a mammoth undertaking just to build it, and keep it safe and sound where it is. The main facility weighs 37,000 tons (33,565,835kg), but in addition to this, it has a gravity base weighing 600,000 tons (544,310,844kg) that secures it to the ocean floor. That's a lot of engineering.

Rising 164ft (50m) out of the water, the *Hibernia* sits in 262ft (80m) of deep ocean. It weighs in at an awesome 1,200,000 tons (1,088,621,688kg) in total, but is considerably heavier when its tanks are full, as it is able to store 1.3 million barrels of crude oil. However, thanks to the dedicated fleet of tankers that continuously shuttle back and forth between it and the mainland, the *Hibernia* rarely has to make use of all this space, although very bad weather can hold up loading operations.

Crucial to the long-term future of the platform is its iceberg protection, as this part of the world is very prone to such maritime hazards. The 16 serrated outer edges of the concrete island are designed to withstand any icebergs that drift into it. Just to be on the safe side, though, support vehicles are permanently moored there, with one of their main purposes being to tow away any icebergs that get a little too close.

THE LARGEST DIESEL-POWERED FAST CRAFT

EVOLUTION ONE12 CATAMARAN

The *Evolution One12*, so called because it is 367ft 6in (112m) long, is a new series of catamarans built by the Australian firm of Incat. They are the largest diesel-powered fast craft in the world, and capable of carrying passengers and vehicles for commercial activities, or being outfitted as military vessels.

SPECIFICATIONS

Country: Australia
Year built from: 2003
Dimensions:
369ft 6in (113m) long;
99ft 6in (30m) wide
Weight: Varies
Speed: Up to 50 knots/58mph (93km/h)
Power: 48,276hp (36,000kW) from four engines
Crew: Varies
Cost: Varies

A more accurate description of the *Evolution One12* type would be as a "seaframe," rather than a complete craft. The aluminum-hulled craft is available as a base structure, onto which different equipment can be fitted, depending on the completed purpose of the ship, whether passenger, freight, or military orientated.

Options for versatility

Whatever the finished configuration, the four 20-cylinder diesel engines providing a total of 48,276hp (36,000kW) of power should be enough to drive more lightly equipped models to around 50 knots/58mph (93km/h). The concept was introduced in 2003, since when the wave-piercing catamarans have been a success for Incat, being constructed for customers all over the world. Options include the ability to carry 312 cars, although more are possible with the fitment of extra decks. In fact, the *One12* can be outfitted purely as a car or truck transporter, with the generous breadth allowing even the biggest trucks to turn around inside her. However, there is a general cargo limit of around 1500 tons (1,360,800kg), at which point the *One12* would have to operate at a reduced speed. If a customer is going for sheer passenger numbers, then up to 1200 can be accommodated. And as for military applications, well, they're merely limited by imagination and budget.

ABOVE: The *Evolution One12* can be designed around a customer's needs—the catamaran itself is a basic shell, available in different configurations. Computer modeling is used to show what the finished craft will look like.

THE LARGEST FLOATING MANMADE ISLAND

MEGA-FLOAT ISLAND, YOKUSUKA PORT, TOKYO BAY

Out in Tokyo Bay sits one of the more extraordinary maritime engineering achievements of recent times. The Mega-Float island airport, opened in 1999, is in *The Guinness Book of Records* as the largest artificial island ever built.

Reclaiming land from the sea to build upon has been going on for centuries, however, it has become more widespread recently, especially in coastal areas with high populations. However, the Mega-Float island in Japan is a new and experimental approach. It eschews conventional landfill techniques, and is instead a floating structure 0.6 miles (1km) long, made up of four interconnected steel boxes, each one each about 10ft (3m) deep with the largest one 1312ft (400m) long. The 30 "dolphin" tethers that moor it to the seabed are intended to keep it from drifting, even if several become detached, and the watertight compartments in the boxes that make up the "hull" of the island should make sinking practically impossible too.

ABOVE: The prototype Mega-Float currently serves as an airport, but potential uses for future manmade islands are practically unlimited—they could even be used as the basis for permanent floating communities.

Future ideas

There are several benefits to the Mega-Float concept when compared to a traditional island, according to those behind it. It's less destructive to the environment, can be expanded easily, and should cope better with natural disasters such as earthquakes.

Future applications for Mega-Float include airports and disaster-relief areas, with the island at Yokosuka built as an airport so that it's behavior with planes landing and taking off from it could be thoroughly tested. The results have proved promising, and it is now envisaged that future Mega-Floats could be as long as 2.5 miles (4km), allowing giant international airports to be built, as well as hotels, leisure parks, and even whole towns and communities.

5 FLIGHT

It's only recently that powered flight has celebrated its one-hundredth birthday, but mankind's century in the air has resulted in some remarkable machines. We're now very used to the huge aircraft of today—although a large plane overhead can still draw attention—and think nothing of hundreds of passengers or major freight loads routinely jetting around the globe. But such creations would have been sheer fantasy to the aviation pioneers of the early twentieth century.

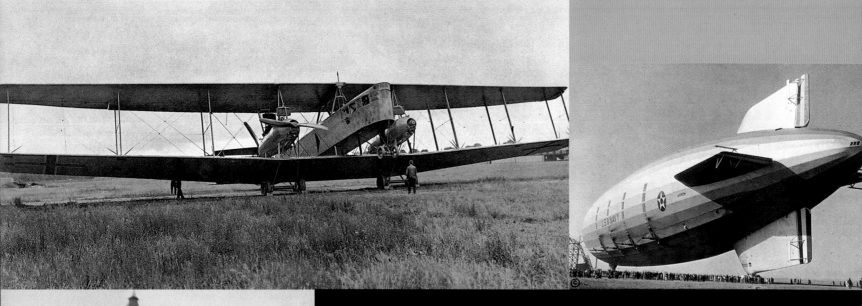

ABOVE: For their era, the Staaken R bombers were enormous—and terrifying war machines.

LEFT: The V2 rocket introduced modern rocket warfare but also made the first steps toward space travel.

Flight has always been one of the loftier human dreams. But it wasn't until 1783 it was actually achieved—for a reasonable length of time and in a manner that didn't usually end in an unpleasant injury or death—by the Montgolfier brothers with their hot air balloon.

But balloons had limited potential. Mastering speed and directional control proved trickier, and even the Victorians, who achieved so much else with steam power and engineering genius, failed to properly beat gravity and nature. It wasn't until December 1903 that the Wright brothers of Ohio mastered controlled and powered flight—even if it was just for 12 seconds initially. It was enough to open the floodgates to a new era of inventiveness and achievement.

As is usually the unfortunate way, war was the reason for much of the airplane's early development. Only a decade after that initial takeoff, military machines, such as the Zeppelin Staaken R planes, enormous bombers with six engines and a wingspan of 138ft 6in (42.2m), were being built that were both incredibly sophisticated and massive when compared with their forebears a few years earlier.

The Zeppelin name was—and remains—more associated with airships, and although it was the Germans who were building the

LEFT: USS *Akron* was huge enough to carry aircraft, but its short life also demonstrated how vulnerable airships were.

LEFT: Lockheed's Constellation was a graceful and glamorous propeller airliner design, distinguished by its unusual triple tail design.

ABOVE: Superfortress by name and nature: The B-29 was the biggest, most advanced bomber of World War II.

largest machines in the air, during the dirigible's golden age in the 1920s and 1930s, other countries were coming close. America was responsible for the USS *Akron*, an aerial aircraft carrier capable of carrying, launching, and retrieving four aircraft using a "trapeze" system. It was an innovative idea, but ultimately led nowhere—especially not after the enormous *Akron*, built in 1931, crashed in 1933—but was an indicator of just how innovative and daring aeronautical engineers were now being.

The only true rivals to the passenger-carrying Zeppelin planes were glamorous

flying boats, the largest aircraft of the first half of the twentieth century. Their ability to land and take off on water allowed them greater dimensions, and examples like the Boeing 314 Clipper were the jumbo jets of their day, albeit far more luxurious.

World War II saw aircraft come into their own as major weapons that became vital to an Allied victory. Had the British RAF not overcome the Germans during the Battle of Britain in 1940, there would have been little to stand in the way of an invasion. Bomber aircraft took on massive scale (the enormous B29 *Superfortress* lived up to its name in every

way) and postwar, graceful propeller-driven airliners, like Lockheed Constellation, benefited from the lessons learnt in conflict. When Orville Wright took his last flight, on a Constellation, in 1944, he commented that the wingspan alone was longer than the *Wright Flyer*, initially flown 40 years before.

However, propeller planes, as the giants of the sky, were on their way out. The final days of World War II saw jet aircraft become operational, alongside the German V1 and V2 rockets—the latter capable of reaching space. They foretold of a future where the jet engine would rule the skies.

THE LARGEST MANNED HOT AIR BALLOON

VIRGIN PACIFIC FLYER

The Virgin Pacific Flyer balloon wasn't just the biggest manned hot-air balloon ever to fly. It set a number of records back in 1991, carrying entrepreneur Richard Branson and adventurer Per Lindstrand on the longest lighter-than-air flight in history.

There were some who dismissed Richard Branson and Per Lindstrand's balloon flight from Japan to northern Canada as little more than an oversized publicity stunt for Branson's Virgin group of companies. They may have had a point. But as marketing ideas go, the Virgin Pacific Flyer was more epic than most, and its flight was a genuinely significant event in the history of aeronautics.

Space capsule

With a total inflatable volume of 2,600,300ft³ (74,000m³), the Virgin Pacific Flyer dwarfed any previous manned hot-air vessel. Built entirely to break the long-distance balloon record, as well as gain a little bit of corporate advertising on the side, it took off from Japan on January 15. It came down, albeit rather inelegantly, two days and 6761 miles (10,889km) later in northern Canada. The secret of the Flyer's success was the way it was designed to make use of the swift trans-oceanic jetstreams. During the flight, it managed to reach 245mph (395km/h), an extraordinary speed for a balloon with no real form of linear propulsion, and still a record. Throughout the trip, Branson and Lindstrand survived in a pressurized pod, dubbed a "space capsule" by some, because of the height at which the Flyer traveled.

Branson and Lindstrand teamed up again in 1998 to try to circumnavigate the world in another hot-air balloon. This attempt was less triumphant, however. They crashed in the Pacific Ocean and had to be rescued. Nothing of the size of the Virgin Pacific Flyer had ever been seen in the balloon world before.

SPECIFICATIONS	
Country:	UK
Year built:	1991
Maximum speed:	
245mph (395km/h)	
Envelope size:	
26,000,300ft³	
(74,000m³)	
Total distance flown:	
6761 miles (10,889km)	
Cost:	N/A

LEFT AND ABOVE: The small "space capsule" suspended below the Virgin Pacific Flyer gave Branson and Lindstrand little room inside.

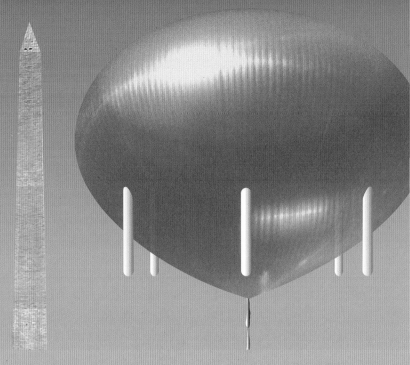

LEFT AND RIGHT:
Inflated or deflated,
the balloon was
still taller than
the Washington
Monument.

SPECIFICATIONS

Country: USA

Year built from: 1975

Dimensions:
786ft (239m) long; 64ft
(19.5m) wide

Capacity: N/A

Inflatable volume:
70,732,718ft^3
(2,003,192m^3)

Cost: N/A

THE WORLD'S LARGEST UNMANNED BALLOON

WINZEN BALLOONS

Used for scientific research at high altitudes, the largest balloons flying regularly today don't carry humans but instruments to study the upper levels of Earth's atmosphere, and look beyond into space. From altitudes as high as 30 miles (48km) such balloons get clearer readings than any ground-based instrument.

Winzen Research was started in 1949 with the company specializing in high-altitude balloons for scientific study. The firm was a pioneer in constructing balloons out of polyethylene plastic, which allowed its creations to travel far higher than other comparable balloons thanks to less stretch within the material.

An unsuccessful launch

Its most ambitious project was in 1975, when it was behind for the largest balloon ever manufactured. Rather inelegantly christened SF3-579.49-035-NSC 01, the inflatable volume was 70,732,718ft^3 (2,003,192m^3), which made it 10 times the size of the mammoth Hindenberg and Graf Zeppelin II airships of 1930s. Had it taken off, it would have been more than 785.78ft (239.49m) in height. Unfortunately though, at its launch from the National Scientific Balloon facility in Palestine, Texas, the balloon developed rips and never left the ground. However, Winzen was more fortunate with a marginally smaller 60,000,000ft^3 (1,699,012m^3) balloon, built at its base in Sulphur Springs, Texas. This did take off successfully, becoming the largest balloon ever to fly properly.

As the illustration shows, high-altitude balloons, such as the ones built by Winzen, start their ascent partially deflated—when they are at their maximum length. Filled with just enough helium to lift off with payload, the gas inside expands as the balloon gets higher.

THE LARGEST AIRSHIPS EVER

HINDENBURG/GRAF ZEPPELIN II

Prior to World War II, Germany's Zeppelin airships were the kings of the sky, and none was greater than the *Hindenburg* and the *Graf Zeppelin II*. Even 60 years after they were destroyed, they still remain the largest manmade objects ever to fly.

During the Franco-Prussian War of 1870–71, Count Ferdinand von Zeppelin became intrigued by the idea of using "dirigible" balloons for military purposes. But even his vision could hardly have foretold the ultimate, yet tragic, realization of his dreams 60 years later.

In 1935, Zeppelin's company completed the LZ129 *Hindenburg* airship, the largest aircraft built at that time. It was subsequently only equalled by its twin-sister ship, the LZ130 *Graf Zeppelin II*, work on which started in 1936, after the *Hindenburg* went into service.

Monumental undertaking

Even in today's era of huge machines, the Zeppelins were monumental undertakings. Constructed primarily to provide scheduled flights between Germany and the USA, the *Hindenburg* was as tall as the Statue of Liberty. It was longer than three jumbo jets, but could carry just 133 people (72 passengers and 61 crew). However, this was well beyond the capacity of the biggest planes of the time, and its speed of 84mph (135km/h) meant it was able to cross the Atlantic far faster than a ship. It was simply the latest word in high-tech, luxury travel.

The *Hindenburg* was in service for just over a year before it was destroyed by fire while landing in New Jersey, USA, on May 6, 1937. The cause has never been established, but the hydrogen-filled *Hindenburg* was totally consumed in just 34 seconds, killing 36 people.

ABOVE AND TOP: The hangars required to house the *Hindenburg* and *Graf Zeppelin II* were huge. Swastikas on the tailfins were aerial propaganda, broadcasting to the world what regime was behind these (then) greatest of flying machines.

SPECIFICATIONS

(for LZ129 *Hindenburg*)
Country: Germany
Year built: 1935
Dimensions: 804ft (245m) long; 135ft (41m) diameter
Capacity: 133 people
Power: 4800hp (3560kW) from four engines
Lifting ability: 1.099 MN (112.1 metric tons force)
Cost: £500,000

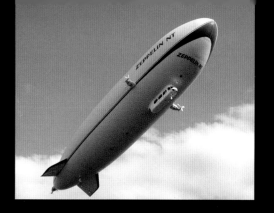

ZEPPELIN NT

The Zeppelin story didn't ultimately end with the *Hindenburg* and the *Graf Zeppelin II*. In the 1990s, the successor to the original Zeppelin Company started building and selling airships again. The current version is the NT, and although it is nowhere near the size of its ancestors, it is still the biggest airship around today.

Modern airplanes are too advanced for Zeppelins to be more than novelties. However, these graceful craft are still fascinating machines.

Size matters

Zeppelin Luftschifftechnik GmbH restarted airship production in 1997, although the craft of today differ somewhat from the Zeppelins of old. The size is the obvious distinction. An NT is 230ft (70m) long, approximately one-quarter the size of the *Hindenburg*. However, an NT is inflated with helium, which is flammable. While original Zeppelins had a full skeleton inside, the framework of the modern NT is semirigid. But, compared to the more common, nonrigid blimp-type airships, an NT is still considerably bigger in scale.

Only four Zeppelin NT models, have been built so far, all to the same design. The media primarily uses them for covering major events from the air, where the NT's lack of vibration and speed is a bonus. They are also used for advertising, joyrides, and environmental research. However, the company has plans to build a bigger version, the NT14, to go into service in 2008. It will be able to carry 19 people—just one-seventh the number that its great-grandmother, the *Hindenburg*, could manage.

ABOVE AND BELOW: Modern Zeppelins are similar in design to their more famous predecessors, albeit built to a smaller scale. There is less rigid framework inside the envelope as well, aiding lightness.

SPECIFICATIONS

Country: Germany
Year built from: 1997
Dimensions:
230ft (70m) long; 64ft (19.5m) wide
Capacity: 14 people
Power: 600hp (441kW) from three engines
Lifting ability: 21 tons (19,000kg)
Cost: N/A

ABOVE: The *Soaring Dreams* airship makes a lively addition to an American city skyline as it flies over. The artistic exterior design is the work of 5000 children.

THE LARGEST BLIMP, CURRENT

AMERIQUEST *SOARING DREAMS* BLIMP

It must be pretty hard to miss Ameriquest's *Soaring Dreams* passenger blimp when it flies overhead. This brightly colored airship was decorated by almost 5000 children from 50 American cities, making it the world's largest airborne piece of art, as well as the biggest blimp around.

The "official" term for this kind of craft is "non-rigid," as it doesn't have an internal framework like other airships. Prior to 2005, Ameriquest's airship *Liberty* was purely used for advertising the US lending company, so it was patriotically finished in the Stars and Stripes livery, along with the firm's logo. An idea called the Soaring Dreams Project saw American children paint different parts of a 40,000ft (12,192m) canvas during that year, which was then fixed to the airship. A colossal 450 gallons (1703.5 liters) of paint were used, and the covering added 1400lb (635kg) to the blimp's overall weight. The result is probably the most flamboyant aircraft ever to fly.

With a capacity of 10 people, including the pilot and copilot, the *Soaring Dreams* passenger blimp has become a familiar sight, turning up at major outdoor events. Its length when fully inflated is 206ft (69m), and the craft has a cruising speed of 45mph (72km/h), which means that it can take up to three weeks for it to cross America from coast to coast. One of its more unusual features is that it has the ability to hover, making it one of only two airships in the US with this feature.

THE LARGEST BIPLANE, STILL FLYING

REPLICA VICKERS VIMY

The original Vickers Vimy was a heavy British bomber aircraft. It entered service right at the end of World War I, and when peace arrived, it became a long-distance commercial plane instead. A modern replica built in the 1990s is now the largest biplane still in operation.

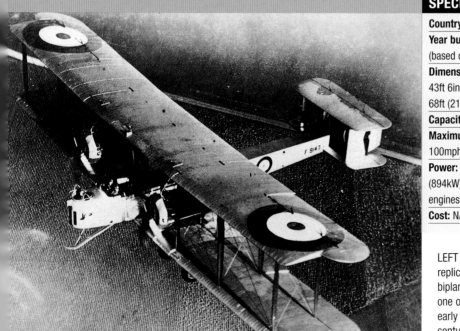

SPECIFICATIONS

Country: Australia/USA
Year built: 1992–94
(based on 1917 design)
Dimensions:
43ft 6in (13.3m) long;
68ft (21m) wingspan
Capacity: 2 people
Maximum speed:
100mph (165km/h)
Power: 1200hp
(894kW) from two
engines
Cost: N/A

LEFT AND ABOVE: The replica Vickers Vimy biplane is a tribute to one of the greatest of early twentieth-century aircraft.

Why build a "new" version of a plane that went out of production almost 80 years ago? Well, the ponderous but powerful Vickers Vimy epitomized cutting-edge technology back at the end of World War I, and achieved a number of firsts. In 1919, for example, a Vickers Vimy became the first airplane to cross the Atlantic nonstop, and this was soon followed by a flight from London to Darwin in Australia. And in 1922, one set off from London to fly to South Africa, although it crashed en route.

Something old, something new

An Australian/American team felt that the achievements of the Vimy shouldn't be forgotten, and so decided to construct a replica to re-enact these three pioneering flights. Taking 17 months to build, the result was a biplane that stayed as true as possible to the original blueprints, albeit with some modern concessions. For example, the two Rolls-Royce engines used originally gave way to Chevrolet V8 car engines, and instead of a wooden frame, the new Vickers has steel tubing.

The 1990s version proved just as capable of coping with long distances as the real thing. In 1994, the flight from England to Australia was achieved. The year 2000 saw London to South Africa conquered, which is more than a real Vimy managed. In 2005, the reborn Vickers crossed the Atlantic. It continues to fly at displays as a testament to the great early aircraft.

THE LARGEST BIPLANE, NORMAL USE

ANTONOV AN-2

The era of the biplane largely ended with World War II. But some of the more versatile and useful designs continued to be built well into the postwar era and are still in service today. The world's largest biplane still in normal service is the Russian Antonov An-2.

ABOVE: Despite its historic appearance, the AN-2 was produced up until 1992. The classic looks are part of its appeal to enthusiasts.

SPECIFICATIONS

Country: Russia
Year built: 1947–92
Dimensions: 41ft (12.4m) long; 59ft 8in (18.2m) wingspan
Weight: 12,000lb (5500kg)
Capacity: 12 people or 4718lb (2140kg)
Maximum speed: 160mph (258km/h)
Power: 1000hp (750kw)
Cost: From $30,000

Of course, compared to some of the enormous biplanes from past eras, Antonov's An-2 is small fry. But the difference is that those planes are now museum pieces or gone completely. The Antonov An-2, nicknamed "The Worker" or Annushka in its homeland (and known in the West as "The Colt"), is still very active. Despite the first one appearing in 1947, the craft continued to be built right up until 1992.

Slow motion

It is the simplicity of the An-2 that has ensured its long life. It is capable of flying extremely slowly and can take off and land in short distances on unmade surfaces. China also

manufactures just such a craft, albeit by a different name. However, the An-2 was the biggest single-engined biplane when it appeared just after the end of the war. The passing of time and the demise of its rivals have now awarded it the status of the biggest biplane still operating.

Used for practically anything from passenger work (it can take 12 people) to carrying cargo, agricultural work, fighting fires, air ambulance, and military work, the An-2 can fly as low as 30mph (48km/h) without stalling. In a strong headwind, it can even fly backward. In the West, it has become a popular collector's machine for air displays because of its blend of classic looks and reasonably modern technology.

THE LARGEST TRIPLANE, EVER

CAPRONI CA-42

Attempts to squeeze long distances out of early aircraft saw some extraordinary-looking machines, such as the Caproni Ca-42, take to the sky. The Caproni Ca-42 was a bomber from the era of World War I, and it was fitted with three large wings. No other triplane could equal this destructive giant in stature.

SPECIFICATIONS

Country: Italy
Year built: 1917–19
Dimensions:
42ft (13m) long;
98ft (30m) wingspan
Weight: 8818lb
(6709kg)
Capacity: 3913lb
(1450kg)
Maximum speed:
87mph (140km/h)
Power: 1200hp
(894kW) from three
engines
Cost: N/A

ABOVE: The Ca-42's three-wing construction made the plane look delicate and precarious to fly, but combined with the power from its three engines, gave it enough lift to carry a reasonable load.

The company founded by Gianni Caproni was Italy's foremost aircraft manufacturer during World War I, specializing in huge bomber aircraft. In 1917, the Caproni triplane series—the Ca-4—was first tested by the Italian Air Force, and introduced into service in 1918.

Three wings, three engines

Bomber technology was still in its infancy, and only a few of these gigantic aircraft were built (some sources quote just 38 manufactured) of which the Ca-42 was the ultimate military variant. Powered by three engines (two at the front, one at the rear) the very tall Ca-42 looked cumbersome, ungainly, and fragile. However, despite its three wood-and-

fabric wings looking barely supported, its design was inherently sound. And it was fast—for the time—and could deliver a large load of bombs. Standard armament was four machine guns, although the Ca-42's size meant that it could be fitted with up to eight.

The Ca-42's career was shortlived. At the end of the war, it was replaced by more conventional designs, aircraft technology having progressed to such an extent that biplanes were capable of doing all that a Ca-42 could, and more besides. However, some of the bombers forged a second career for themselves and were converted to passenger aircraft that were capable of carrying 23 passengers after adaptation.

CAPRONI CA-60 TRANSAERO

The history of aviation is littered with fantastic one-offs that promised much, but ultimately delivered little. One of the most extraordinary was Caproni's Ca-60 seaplane. This amazing creation was the product of a theory that the more wings a plane had, the better it would fly. This turned out not to be the case, however.

BELOW: The Transaero was an extraordinary-looking contraption, and it wasn't a surprise that this imaginative design was inherently un-airworthy. Its test flight ended in total disaster in the middle of a lake.

The idea behind the Caproni Ca-60 was that it would provide a transatlantic passenger service for between 100 and 150 passengers, something that, at the time, no other aircraft could offer. The thinking was sound enough, but the aircraft that subsequently materialized was little short of crazy, although remarkable to look at. Its designers reasoned that the more wings and engines it was fitted with, the better able it would be to fly long distances.

Slowly up, quickly down

Or rather not, as things turned out. In 1920, one experimental model was built. It had three banks of three wings (left over from bombers that took part in World War I) and eight engines. Its first test flight was in March 1921 from Lake Maggiore, in Italy. The ungainly machine managed to struggle to a height of 60ft (18m) before it simply collapsed and took a nosedive into the lake, killing both pilots. Although it was obvious to most people that the whole thing was simply too ambitious to fly, an attempt was made to repair it. Then a mysterious fire completely destroyed it for good.

Despite its failure, the Triple Hydro-triplane, as the Ca-60 was dubbed, was fascinating. No one before, or since, has attempted to build an airplane with so many wings.

THE LARGEST WOODEN AIRCRAFT/THE LARGEST WINGSPAN EVER

HUGHES H-4 "SPRUCE GOOSE"

Contrary to popular belief, Howard Hughes's gigantic H4 Hercules flying boat wasn't the largest aircraft of all time. However, it does still hold the record for having been the biggest wooden airplane and flying boat, as well as having the largest wingspan ever.

TOP, ABOVE RIGHT, AND BACKGROUND: It traveled on water, it traveled on the ground … but flying proved more tricky for the Spruce Goose.

In the annals of aviation, no plane has ever inspired so much controversy and notoriety as the Spruce Goose— a derogatory nickname that Howard Hughes, the man behind it, hated. But cut through all the intrigue and scandal surrounding the Spruce Goose, and you are left with one of the world's most astonishing flying machines ever built.

Herculean task

The inspiration behind the H-4 Hercules was to provide wartime transport for troops and cargo across the Atlantic. From the start, the intention had always been to build it from wood to save metal for the military effort. However, by the time the huge craft was complete, World War II had been over for two years, and Hughes was called to account for the massive amount of money that had been spent. As if to prove a point, during engine tests, he decided to try and get the H-4 airborne. In November 1947, the Spruce Goose managed to fly 1 mile (1.6km) at an altitude of 70ft (20m), attaining a speed of 80mph (130km/h) before landing again on the waters of Long Beach, California. The H-4 never flew again, although it was maintained in flying condition until Hughes died in 1976, after which the Spruce Goose became a museum piece. It still remains on display today, a monument both to engineering folly and audacious farsightedness.

THE LARGEST AMPHIBIOUS AIRCRAFT, CURRENT

BERIEV BE-42 "MERMAID"

Although much less numerous than their wheeled counterparts, amphibious aircraft—

flying boats—are still being built today. The biggest in production is the Beriev Be-42

"Mermaid," which is also capable of landing on the ground when there isn't a handy

stretch of water nearby.

SPECIFICATIONS

Country: Russia (USSR)
Year built from: 1986
Dimensions: 144ft (44m) long; 135ft (42m) wingspan
Weight: 95 tons (86,000kg)
Maximum speed: 470mph (760km/h)
Power: 209,763lbf (284.4kN) from four jet engines
Cost: N/A

The Beriev Aircraft Company of Russia was formed in 1934 and developed a niche for itself building amphibious aircraft. In 1986, it was responsible for the Be-42 "Mermaid," which became the largest amphibian plane in existence, once the rest of the world found out about this military patrol and surveillance craft in 1988.

Land or water

The design of the Be-42 is so highly individualistic that there's little else around it could be mistaken for. The two main engines sit atop the swept-back wings, while directly underneath are booster engines to give extra thrust during takeoff. One of the more innovative—and certainly useful—features of the Mermaid is that it is also fitted with retractable wheels, giving it the ability to land conventionally if necessary. Combine this with the front probe to allow inflight refueling, the Be-42 has to be one of the most versatile aircraft around today, with a true capability to go anywhere and land anywhere. In military trim, the Be-42 is capable of carrying 14,330lb (6500kg) of bombs, torpedoes, or mines, but the fall of the Soviet Union has rendered most of the aircraft obsolete. However, Beriev is currently trying to interest commercial customers in a smaller-scale civilian version.

ABOVE: The Be-42's hull is watertight and capable of operating on water or —as here—on land. Each wing has a float on the end for extra stability in the water.

THE LARGEST BOMBER EVER

CONVAIR B-36 BOMBER

As a statement of total aerial military might, no aircraft has ever topped the Consolidated B-36 bomber. It was an elephantine plane and was compared by one pilot to "flying an apartment house." It was so vast that it required 10 engines to get airborne.

The first test flight of a Convair B-36 took place only a year after the end of World War II, yet the aircraft, nicknamed the "Peacemaker," was an enormous technological step forward compared to the bombers that had flown during that conflict. Its wingspan was twice that of a World War II B-17, and it was powered by both jet and propeller engines. It was capable of reaching the Soviet Union from the USA, and, most deadly of all, it carried a nuclear payload as standard.

Supersized wings

It was the size of the B-36's wings that enabled it to fly so far. Not only could long-range fuel tanks be fitted, but there was also room for 10 engines. Six were backward-facing propeller engines, known as a pusher configuration. They had blades of 19ft (5.8m) in length, backed up by four jet engines, two on each wingtip. The propeller engines put out 3800hp (2500kW) each, and the jets managed 23kN (5200lbf) of thrust. This made the B-36 immensely powerful and capable of flying more than 40,000ft (12,000m) higher than any aircraft sent to intercept it.

However, the B-36 was difficult to pilot. It required a lot of maintenance, and worst of all, was unreliable, with engines that often caught fire in flight. But its biggest failing was that it used propellers, which were fast becoming obsolete. The last example was built in 1954, and by 1959 all were superseded by the advent of the fully jet-powered B-52 Stratofortress.

SPECIFICATIONS	
Country: USA	
Year built: 1946–54	
Dimensions: 162ft (49.5m) long; 230ft (70m) wingspan	
Weight (loaded): 133 tons (120,700kg)	
Maximum speed: 420mph (685km/h)	
Power: 20,800lbf (92kN) from four jet engines; 22,800hp (10,000kW) from six propellers	
Cost: $4.1 million	

ABOVE AND BACKGROUND: So massive was the B-36 that it combined propeller and jet power to get into the air and stay there. The six props faced backward, while the four jets were suspended in pods below the wings.

BOEING B-52 STRATOFORTRESS

It seems a little chilling referring to an immensely destructive aircraft as "successful," but the B-52 Stratofortress deserves the accolade for its longevity as well as abilities. It has been in service with the US Air Force since 1954, and still plays a frontline role as the largest bomber in existance.

The career of the B-52 Stratofortress has been little short of extraordinary. It was introduced in 1955, yet still flies (and fights) today, and the plan is that it will remain on duty until around 2050. That a century-old design will still be regarded as a valid military force speaks volumes about how inherently good the B-52 is at its job. And with the last example built in 1962, those planes still in action in the middle of the twenty-first century will be around 90 years old.

Big and Buff

Nicknamed the "Buff," the B-52's original raison d'être was to fly long-distance nuclear missions to Russia, if required. Squadrons were kept at a constant state of readiness, able to take off with a few minutes' notice. But the B-52 has since proved itself capable of functioning just as easily as a conventional bomber at any altitude. However, of the 744 models built, only 85 remain on the Air Force's books. These have been constantly updated with the latest technology.

The most recognizable feature of the B-52—apart from its substantial dimensions—is its set of eight turbojet engines slung out in groups of two below the wings. Each one is capable of developing a thrust of 17,000lbf (76kN).

ABOVE AND BELOW: Eight jet engines power the enormous B-52. This deadly but chilling shape should still be in the skies over 40 years from now.

SPECIFICATIONS

Country: USA	
Year built: 1952–62	
Dimensions: 159ft 6in (48.5m) long; 185ft (56.5m) wingspan	
Weight (loaded): 132 tons (120,000kg)	
Maximum speed: 650mph (1000km/h)	
Power: 136,000lbf (608kN) from eight jet engines	
Cost: $9.28 million (1962)	

THE LARGEST SUPERSONIC AIRCRAFT

CONCORDE

Rarely does mankind take a technological step backward, but when Concorde stopped flying in 2003, the era of supersonic commercial jet travel came to an end. More than just a very fast airline, Concorde was one of the most striking machines ever created. She was an icon to all those who traveled on her, and the many more who longed to.

TOP AND ABOVE: From any angle, Concorde was—and is—an extraordinarily handsome aircraft, and its looks never seemed to age.

Like many of the world's most inspirational machines, Concorde wasn't actually a success. Conceived in the optimistic 1960s, the graceful delta-winged aircraft was intended to introduce the masses to air travel at faster than the speed of sound. However, by the time the aircraft went into service in 1973 orders had fallen through, development costs were 600 pecent over estimate, and pollution and noise worries meant that the aircraft was banned from many of the world's airports. Thus, only 20 (including prototypes) were built. British Airways and Air France put them in to service.

Elegance

However, few white elephants have been so beautiful as Concorde. Despite being conceived over 40 years ago, the design still looks futuristic and elegant. And it did, eventually, become a success, establishing itself as the ultimate, if expensive, way to fly the Atlantic. Concorde embodied luxury, power, and speed blended together in an engineering aviation miracle, capable of moving at a mile every 2.7 seconds. When it was finally withdrawn from service, millions, particularly in France and the UK, watched the final flights on TV. It remains one of the most famous airplanes in the world. Its profile, with "droop nose" used for takeoff and landing, has made it the most recognizable.

BOEING 747

No book on mega machines could be truly complete without mentioning the Boeing 747. Although recently superseded as the biggest airliner, for over 35 years there was simply nothing bigger an ordinary passenger could fly on. The Boeing 747 revolutionized air travel for the masses.

BELOW: The Jumbo shape is familiar to millions, and a common sight at major airports.

When the 747 was jointly conceived by Pan Am and Boeing in 1965, it was like nothing that had been dreamt up before. They envisioned a giant jet aircraft capable of carrying up to 524 passengers in spacious comfort. The project could have been a financial disaster, but from the moment the 747, nicknamed the jumbo jet, entered service in 1970 it was a resounding success, and has since become the mainstay of long-distance, popular air routes. When a lot of people want to go a long way, it's invariably a Jumbo Jet that will take them there.

The Jumbo's hump

Operated by practically every major airline across the world, over 1430 Jumbos have been built.

Production of the 747-400 continues to this day, demonstrating just how inherently "right" the original design was. Only the Hughes H-4 Spruce Goose (see page 167) could boast a wingspan that was greater than that of a 747. But one of the 747's other radical features, which soon became the Jumbo's most recognizable trademark, was the second short deck above the main deck. The "hump" was added in case the 747 failed to become successful as a passenger aircraft. By moving the cockpit, and some of the passenger accommodation, to a higher level, a loading door in the nose could be incorporated so the Jumbo could easily be converted into a cargo transporter.

SPECIFICATIONS

Country: USA
Year built from: 1969
Dimensions: 232ft (70.5m) long; 211ft 6in (64.5m) wingspan
Weight: 400 tons (362,880kg)
Capacity: Up to 524 passengers, depending on configuration
Maximum speed: 700mph (Mach 0.92/1127km/h)
Power: 245,997lbf (1096kN) from four engines
Cost: $275 million (2005)

THE LARGEST COMMERCIAL JET, IMPENDING

AIRBUS A380

Once it was the Jumbo that was the king of the commercial passenger skies. Now the crown has been taken by the Superjumbo, the nickname the Airbus A380 has already been christened with, despite the fact that it has only just entered service.

SPECIFICATIONS

Country: Europe
Year built from: 2002
Dimensions: 239ft 6in (73m) long; 261ft (80m) wingspan
Weight (empty): 305 tons (276,800kg)
Capacity: Up to 853 passengers, depending on configuration
Maximum speed: 602.6mph (0.89 Mach/977.04km/h)
Power: 306,000lbf (1360kN) from four engines
Cost: $296–316 million (as of 2006)

Even a substantial Boeing 747 looks humble sitting next to a new Airbus A380. This is the world's only double-decker airliner, and it has over 50 percent more floor space than a 747. It is capable of seating a maximum of 853 people, which is over 300 more than a Jumbo can manage at full stretch.

Boeing breaker

The A380 was developed to break Boeing's dominance of the high-capacity aircraft market. Expanding significantly larger in terms of length wasn't a viable option. Instead, the A380 went taller, with an extra full-length deck added along its top. Building started in 2002, with various components constructed throughout Europe. The first prototype was unveiled in 2005, with deliveries in 2006.

The A380 surpasses the 747 in practically every way. It is longer, taller, and has a bigger wingspan, although this still falls 24ft 6in (7.5m) short of the wingspan of Hughes' H-4 Spruce Goose of 60 years earlier. Despite having extra power, it's more economical, and the "fly-by-wire" technology (whereby it uses electronic systems rather than hydraulic and mechanical parts) makes it easier to pilot and more maneuverable. However, it's not quite as fast as a 747, but the difference only adds up to about 62mph (100km/h).

LEFT AND ABOVE: Up to 853 people can be carried by the new Airbus A380.

A Beluga is a type of whale, and it's a fitting moniker to be applied to the bulbous A300 Super Transporter. There are only five of these, far from elegant, aircraft in existence, but what they lack in looks, they make up for in their carrying capacity.

SPECIFICATIONS

Country: Europe	
Year built: 1992–99	
Dimensions: 184ft (56m) long; 147ft (45m) wingspan	
Weight (loaded): 169 tons (153,900kg)	
Capacity: 125ft (38m) long; 24ft (7.5m) diameter	
Cruising speed: 557mph (897km/h)	
Power: 123,000lbf (548kN) from two engines	
Cost: N/A	

THE LARGEST CARGO AIRCRAFT, CURRENT

AIRBUS A300 "BELUGA" SUPER TRANSPORTER

What do you get if you cross the bottom half of an A300-wide body airliner with an impressive amount of space added on top? The answer is the Airbus Beluga, the largest transport aircraft in the world by volume. It might not be attractive, but it can certainly carry a lot.

Multinational carrier

Airbus is a company formed of European companies with manufacturing plants in Britain, France, Spain, and Germany. This means a lot of big items have to be carried between these nations. Originally, planes by rival manufacturer Boeing were used for this, until the joke that "every Airbus is delivered on the wings of a Boeing" wore too thin. So, Airbus simply built its own enormous transporter, using its A300 as the basis. A rounded load area was grafted on top, measuring 25ft (8m) in diameter. The cockpit was moved downward to allow a 56ft (17m) high loading door to be installed. This gives the A300 Beluga unprecedented large cargo ability. It can fit in entire items up to 24ft 6in (7.5m) tall/wide, and 125ft (38m) long.

Such practicality means that the five Belugas are often hired out, and have carried space station parts, other complete aircraft, big machinery, and even large but delicate artworks all over the world.

THE LARGEST PURELY MILITARY TRANSPORT AIRCRAFT

LOCKHEED C-5 GALAXY

When it comes to getting bulky items of military equipment anywhere in the world at short notice, the United States Air Force turns to its fleet of enormous Lockheed C-5 Galaxies, the biggest transport aircraft on its books.

SPECIFICATIONS	
Country: USA	
Year built: 1968–89	
Dimensions: 247ft (75m) long; 222ft 6in (68m) wingspan	
Weight (loaded): 384 tons (349,000kg)	
Capacity: 31,000ft^3 (880m^3)	
Cruising speed: 570mph (920km/h)	
Power: 172,000lbf (760kN) from four engines	
Cost: $167.7 million	

ABOVE: A member of the military ground crew guides a Galaxy during taxiing, its bulky looks hinting at the large carrying capacity.

Watching a Lockheed C-5 Galaxy being loaded is a bizarre sight. The whole width and height of the nose and tail of this squat and bulging aircraft can open to allow entry to the 121ft (37m) long and 19ft (6m) wide interior bay. It looks like the vast machine is literally gobbling up whatever has been placed in front of it.

Fast and adaptable

It has been the foremost heavy air transporter of the United States Air Force since 1970, and there's not much a Galaxy can't consume, being able to swallow up to 132 tons (120,000kg). If there's anything the US military needs carrying in a hurry, such as tanks, troops, machinery, and engineering equipmen such as the 74 ton (67,130kg) mobile scissors bridge, the Galaxy can take it. Its large volume isn't the only thing it has going for it either. It's also easy to load and unload quickly. Because it is so wide, two rows of vehicles can be driven side by side into its belly, and the suspension can be lowered so that the aircraft "kneels down" to truck-bed height so things can be passed directly to and from vehicles.

In addition to the payload space, there are an additional 73 seats for personnel, behind the cockpit, to make the C-5 even more useful.

THE LARGEST AIRCRAFT, MASS PRODUCTION

ANTONOV AN-124

Nothing in aviation mass production is bigger than the Antonov An-124, a civilian and military cargo aircraft built in Russia in the 1980s and 1990s. Production originally only stopped because of the fall of the Soviet Union but is due to resume up until 2020, meaning that the An-124 will remain the ultimate series of aerial load-luggers.

TOP AND ABOVE: As with other cargo aircraft, a whole section of the An-124's nose can hinge upward for loading, but this Russian aircraft can carry more inside its body than any other production airplane.

Known as the Condor in the West and the Ruslan in its homeland, the An-124's size makes every other aircraft look puny by comparison. It is a gigantic machine, with an awe-inspiring payload capability. Among the items that An-124s have carried are railroad locomotives, boats, aircraft, elephants, and whales. It even carried an ancient obelisk back to its native Ethiopia, though the 78ft (24m) long monument had to be cut into three pieces to get it all there.

Russia's Galaxy?

Similar in appearance to the Lockheed C-5 Galaxy but even bigger still (with 10 percent more space inside), the An-124's conceived role was as a military transport. However, the disintegration of the USSR changed this, and many Condors ended up in commercial use instead, where there was much demand for their incredible abilities. The similarities to the earlier American C-5 Galaxy aren't just skin deep, as the An-124 also has vast front and aft loading doors (the latter hinged upward like the C-5) and the ability to "kneel down" using its landing gear. There's also space for 88 passengers on the upper deck.

However, when it comes to flying, the An-124 is beyond comparison. Its 165 ton (150,000kg) lift capability has yet to be beaten by another mass-produced aircraft.

THE LARGEST PLANE, CURRENT

ANTONOV AN-225 MRIYA

This is the big one—the largest aircraft in the world. Its Russian name is Mriya, which means "dream," and ultimately, that's what the An-225 was. Built to carry the Russian Space Shuttle, only two were built before the shuttle project was canceled.

SPECIFICATIONS

Country:	USSR/Russia
Year built:	1988
Dimensions:	276ft (84m) long; 291ft (88.5m) wingspan
Weight (empty):	193 tons (175,000kg)
Payload:	275 tons (250,000kg)
Maximum speed:	530mph (850km/h)
Power:	309,600lbf (1374kN) from six engines
Cost:	N/A

As if the Antonov-124 wasn't huge enough already, a proposal was made in the 1980s to make it even bigger so it could transport Russian space technology, including the forthcoming Buran Shuttle. What materialized was the An-225, complete with extended fuselage and wings, another two engines added to the existing four, landing gear upgraded to 32 wheels, and the rear loading door deleted. Completed in 1988, the An-225 immediately entered the record books as the largest and heaviest plane ever to fly more than once.

Super dimensions

Dimensionally, it is almost 26ft (8m) longer than a "stretched" Boeing 747–8. Only the Hughes H-4 Spruce Goose (see page 167) exceeded the 225's wingspan. The next-longest wingspan is the new Airbus A380 (see page 173), and that is some 29ft 6in (9m) shorter.

The An-225's career was nearly shortlived though. When the Soviet Union broke up, only two An-225s had been constructed. Both were mothballed and robbed for spares, and it wasn't until the end of the 1990s that just one was recommissioned as a heavy transport plane, with plans to bring the other one back at a later date. There is some prospect of using the An-225 as a high-altitude space-vehicle launcher in the future, which would at least be similar to the role it was originally intended for.

LEFT AND BELOW: Originally built to transport Space Shuttles, the An-225 has been reborn as a heavy transport aircraft. This shot illustrates the heavy duty landing gear.

THE LARGEST EXPERIMENTAL AIRCRAFT

XB-70 VALKYRIE

Startling in appearance, and startling in what it was meant to do, the XB-70 was a bold attempt to build an advanced bomber. Had any more than two experimental aircraft been built, it would have been—and would most likely have remained until this day—the largest supersonic bomber in existence.

SPECIFICATIONS

Country: USA
Year built: 1964
Dimensions: 186ft (56.5m) long; 105ft (32m) wingspan
Weight: 267 tons (242,500kg)
Maximum speed: 2360mph (Mach 3.1/3800km/h)
Power: 168,000lbf (798kN) from six engines
Cost: $1.5 billion

ABOVE AND FAR LEFT: Despite the immense amount of money that went into developing the purposeful-looking XB-70, this proposed supersonic bomber ended as a museum piece.

When the XB-70 Valkyrie was conceived in the 1950s, its specifications must have sounded like something straight out of science fiction. It was to be capable of flying at three times the speed of sound. It was to be built out of stainless steel and titanium. And it was to have a delta-wing configuration with drooping wingtips to offer more stability at high speeds. So, when flying supersonic, the wing ends could bow to an angle of 65 degrees.

Beyond Mach 3

As futuristic as it was, two experimental models were completed by the middle of the 1960s, and testing began. Both managed to go beyond Mach 3, but, in 1966, during a photographic flight, the second prototype was hit by a fighter plane following it and crashed. The original example continued flying, but by now its role was reduced to a test mule to examine the effects of supersonic travel on large planes. It was retired in 1969, and is now a museum piece.

Interestingly, although the two aircraft were developed completely independently of each other, the shape of the XB-70 bears a close resemblance to that of the later Concorde, with the long, slim fuselage, delta-wing configuration, and rectangular engine intakes being common characteristics of both. On the XB-70 though, it was the wings that drooped, and not the nose, as on Concorde.

THE LARGEST TANKER (IN-FLIGHT FUELING) AIRCRAFT

McDONNELL DOUGLAS KC-10 EXTENDER

One of the key components of an aircraft in modern aerial warfare is the ability to be refueled in the air, to achieve far greater range. Such a job is carried out by air-to-air tankers, of which the McDonnell Douglas KC-10 is the largest type currently in use by the United States Air Force.

BELOW: An F-15 Eagle demonstrates just how intricate an operation inflight refueling from a KC-10 Extender is.

SPECIFICATIONS

Country: USA
Year built from: 1981
Dimensions: 181ft (55.35m) long; 165ft 6in (50.5m) wingspan
Weight (empty): 120 tons (109,328kg)
Maximum speed: 610mph (982km/h)
Power: 157,500lbf (702kN) from three engines
Cost: $88.4 million (1998)

If the KC-10 Extender looks familiar, it is because it is based on the DC-10 civilian airliner. However, in place of passengers, the KC-10 carries aviation fuel, which is dispensed by a line—either a boom or drogue (the KC-10 has both)—trailing from the back. Refueling involves precision flying between the two aircraft, one of which can be as large as a C-5 Galaxy. The course and speed of the two craft must be matched until the retractable probe of the KC-10 fits into the trailing line. Only then can transfer take place. An operator in the KC-10 helps guide the line using "fly-by-wire" technology, but the operation still takes a lot of skill.

No need to land

In total, the KC-10's six large tanks hold 179 tons (162,200kg) of fuel, more than twice the capacity of the next-largest USAF tanker, the KC-135. This can be dispensed at the rate of 1100 gallons (4180 liters) per minute. Because of the need to stay in the air for long periods, the KC-10 can itself be refueled in midair, although it already has the longest range of any production aircraft. It is capable of flying from America to Europe, dispensing fuel, and then returning to the USA, without having to land once.

THE LARGEST SOLAR-POWERED AIRCRAFT

NASA HELIOS

With ever-increasing concern about the future of the environment, some alternative to fossil fuels needs to be found. So, what impact will this have on the future of air transport? Until it met with disaster, one of the goals behind NASA's Helios project was to explore this very question.

ABOVE AND BELOW: The flexible design of the solar-powered Helios allowed it to bend while in flight.

Radical in concept and looks, NASA's Helios electrically powered aircraft could have offered an alternative to environmentally damaging air travel. It was a unique aircraft, taking its power from the sun by day, and from regenerative fuel cells at night, making possible flights lasting for weeks or even months without the need to land. And this would be accomplished without pollution, because no consumable fuel was used.

Ocean failure

Although unmanned and controlled by remote, Helios was able to carry a 600lb (272kg) payload—the equivalent of over 40 average humans—up to 70,000ft (21km). During one flight, it reached 96,863ft (29.5km), where the atmosphere is similar to that of Mars. This enabled scientists to collect useful data for potential missions to this planet. There was also an intention to fly the craft, uninterrupted, for 96 hours during another test. Unfortunately, Helios never had the opportunity to attempt this. In June 2003, while flying over the Pacific near Hawaii, it broke up and fell into the sea, and all its experimental technology was completely lost.

However, so promising were the results from Helios that NASA intends to continue its research into so-called "atmospheric satellites." It is likely then, that before too long, the offspring of Helios will once again soar to high altitudes in the name of environmental and space research.

SPECIFICATIONS

Country: USA
Year built: 1999
Dimensions:
12ft (3.6m) long;
247ft (75m) wingspan
Weight: (loaded):
2048lb (929kg)
Maximum speed:
170mph (273.5km/h)
Power: 28hp (21kW)
from 14 propeller
engines
Cost: $1 million

LOCKHEED SR-71 BLACKBIRD

It's somewhat ironic that one of the first "stealth" aircraft—the SR-71 Blackbird—should eventually become one of the world's most famous military planes, thanks to its futuristic design and astounding performance.

The world's largest stealth reconnaissance aircraft sounds rather like contradiction in terms. After all, if you want something not to be noticed, surely it's best to make it as small as possible? In fact, by general military aircraft standards, the SR-71 Blackbird is a compact aircraft, especially considering its flight capabilities. And its shape was designed to make it more difficult for radar to pick up—although in truth, as radar technology progressed, the Blackbird soon became highly noticeable on hostile screens. However, so high and so fast did the SR-71 fly that no missile could ever catch it.

Ironing out the wrinkles

The SR-71 first took to the skies in 1966, and was an extraordinary-looking machine for the time. Indeed, it remains so to this day, despite the fact that the last one was retired in 1998. Able to fly at three times the speed of sound, and at altitudes of up to 100,000ft (30,000m), the Blackbird was painted in a menacing matt radar-absorbent black paint and skinned in titanium alloy. The latter is very resistant to the heat encountered at high altitudes, though it was still common for the aircraft's nose to be wrinkled after landing. Ground crews would have to smooth it out again using a blowtorch!

The SR-71 still holds the record for the quickest flight between New York and London, achieving the feat in just one hour and 55 minutes. By comparison, a Jumbo jet takes around six hours, and Concorde could do the same distance in around three hours and 20 minutes.

ABOVE: From any angle, but especially above, the SR-71 looked utterly intimidating. Sleek lines and two enormous jet engines were the secret to its ability to fly higher and faster than anything else in its day.

SPECIFICATIONS

Country: USA
Year built: 1964–69
Dimensions: 107ft 6in (33m) long; 55ft 6in (17m) wingspan
Weight (loaded): 85 tons (77,000kg)
Maximum speed: 2190mph (Mach 3.3 plus/3530km/h)
Power: 65,000lbf (290kN) from two engines
Cost: $34 million

NORTHROP B-2 SPIRIT BOMBER

The B-2 "Spirit" bomber isn't just the largest stealth bomber to take to the skies, it's also the single most expensive aircraft ever built. Intended to drop both conventional and nuclear weapons without even being seen by the enemy, it is probably the deadliest plane ever built, and still one of the most secretive.

SPECIFICATIONS

Country: USA
Yea built: 1988–98
Dimensions:
69ft (21m) long;
172ft (52m) wingspan
Weight (loaded): 168 tons (152,600kg)
Maximum speed: 475mph (764 km/h)
Power: 69,200lbf (308kN) from four engines
Cost: $2.2 billion

It's probably best to keep your fingers crossed that you are never on the receiving end of an attack from a B-2 Spirit. It can bomb 16 targets in a single pass, and it's more than likely you won't even see it coming, however sophisticated your technology. Using a combination of flat and angular surfaces, radar-absorbent material, speed, and height, the B-2 is almost undetectable even to the most sophisticated radars. And that makes it very difficult to defend against.

Worth double its weight in gold

Introduced in 1997—although first flown under conditions of utmost secrecy in 1989—a mere 21 B-2s have been built,

despite the original plan being to construct 135. However, at an estimated cost of $2.2 billion each, a B-2 doesn't come cheap. In fact, its value is approximately double what it would be if it was made of gold. It's expensive to fly and maintain, too. For example, the radar-absorbent covering is so sensitive that all the aircraft have to be kept in spotlessly clean, humidity-controlled hangers.

Capable of flying 6000 miles (9650km) without refueling, most of the capabilities of the B-2 are still classified. They are likely to remain that way into the future, as it is envisaged that the aircraft will remain in operation well in to this century.

TOP AND ABOVE: The special black coating of the B-2 Spirit is one of the measures it uses to avoid radar, as it's the very flat, very angular "flying wing" design.

BOEING E-3 SENTRY (AWACS)

Whether or not UFOs actually exist is still the subject of fierce debate. However, one flying saucer that is definitely real and up in the skies above us is that carried on the back of the Boeing E-3 reconnaissance aircraft, in the form of its large rotating radar dome.

U p to a point, the E-3 Sentry looks remarkably similar to the Boeing 707-320 civil airliner upon which it is based. Then you notice the 14ft (4m) struts emerging from the rear fuselage, onto which is attached a 30ft (9m) radar dish, slowly turning as the plane flies. Suddenly, the E-3 Sentry doesn't seem quite so ordinary anymore.

The Seven Dwarfs

The E-3 is an airborne warning and control system (AWACS). In other words, it patrols the skies monitoring other air traffic, and providing communications, data, and battle information for friendly forces. It is also used to support missions combating drugs as well. In addition to its main user (the United States), examples also fly with several European NATO forces. The British RAF has nicknamed its collection of E-3s the Seven Dwarfs.

With the ability to operate at heights of up to 29,000ft (9000m), the E-3 can "see" for approximately 400 miles (644km), although for low-flying subjects, its range is reduced to 250 miles (375km). However, because of its height, this is still significantly better than many ground-based radars, and the mobility gives the E-3 more chance of survival, as well as allowing it to react more quickly to changing situations. It can stay in the air for up to eight hours, or a lot longer if refueled in flight.

SPECIFICATIONS	
Country: USA	
Year built: 1975–92	
Dimensions: 153ft (47m) long; 146ft (44.5m) wingspan	
Weight (loaded): 162 tons (147,400kg)	
Maximum speed: 530mph (855km/h)	
Power: 84,000lbf (374.2kN) from four engines	
Cost: $270 million (1998)	

LEFT AND ABOVE: From below, maybe it's possible to confuse the E-3 with an "ordinary" airliner. From the side or above though, the huge, constantly revolving radar dish makes it clear what its true purpose is.

THE LARGEST TANDEM ROTOR HELICOPTER, CURRENT

BOEING CH-47 CHINOOK

Helicopters aren't best known for their lifting abilities. They're usually lightweight machines where the emphasis is on speed and maneuverability rather than carrying heavy weights. However, the CH-47 Chinook, currently the world's biggest tandem-rotor helicopter, is capable of transporting quite significant loads.

SPECIFICATIONS

Country: USA

Year built from: 1961

Dimensions: 90ft (30m) long; 60ft (18m) rotor diameter

Weight (loaded): 13 tons (12,100kg)

Maximum speed: 196mph (315km/h)

Power: 10,138hp (5600kW) from two engines

Cost: Approximately $32 million (1995)

LEFT: Long-bladed tandem rotors and two powerful engines give the CH-47 Chinook the ability to transport aircraft and tanks, making it a useful tool during battle conditions.

What makes the CH-47 Chinook so adept at heavy transport? Unlike conventional helicopters, both of its rotors are horizontally mounted, and rotate in opposite directions to each other. That eliminates the need for a vertical motor at the rear (as most other helicopters have), to counteract the twist effects of the main rotor. This means all its power can be used for lift and thrust. Under battlefield conditions, the CH-47 can carry up to 33 troops and/or items of artillery more quickly than a land vehicle could manage and with more versatility than a fixed-wing aircraft is capable of. Its underslung payload maximum is up to 13 tons (11,793kg), meaning it can even manage bulldozers and loaded shipping containers.

Military and civilian

One of the most successful helicopter designs ever, over 1000 Chinooks have been built and sold to 16 countries. Their use isn't just military either. The civilian version is commonly used for construction and logging, and, with a water dispenser slung below it, for fighting fires.

First flown in 1961, the Chinook has proved its value in most major US conflicts since Vietnam, where one of its key roles was the recovery of downed aircraft. During that war, Chinooks managed to retrieve over 12,000 planes. The CH-47 may be approaching its fiftieth birthday, but to users like the US Army and the Royal Air Force, and others around the world, it's still a vital piece of military equipment.

Nothing like the Mil Mi-12 had been constructed before production of the first prototype was begun in 1965. And since the cancelation of the project in the early 1970s, no company has attempted to build anything else quite so huge and complicated.

The Mi-12's design brief was that it had to be capable of lifting up to 33 tons (30,000kg), more than any other helicopter had ever managed. In fact, thanks to its ingenious but somewhat eccentric design, the "Homer" (as NATO dubbed the craft) proved itself more than capable of this feat, hauling a payload of 49 tons (44,205kg) up to a height of 7400ft (2255m), a record that still stands today.

Four rotors and engines

The Mi-12 gained such a superb ability from its four rotors, with contrarotating pairs mounted facing upward on each wing, in an arrangement known as a two-rotor transverse system. Four gas-turbine engines, which were also mounted on the wings, powered the rotors. Yet despite the Mi-12 proving its worth, only two models were built before it was decided to end production. Rumor has it that a third experimental helicopter was constructed, but crashed during testing. If this is true, it may have been the reason for the end of the scheme. The original two Mi-12s are now museum pieces, and are unlikely to ever fly again.

BELOW AND ABOVE: The Mi-12's innovative design—two contrarotating rotors to each wing—allowed it to lift more than any other helicopter.

SPECIFICATIONS

Country: Russia (USSR)
Year built: 1965–70
Dimensions: 121ft 6in (37m) with two 115ft (35m) diameter rotors
Weight (loaded): 107 tons (97,000kg)
Maximum speed: 163mph (270km/h)
Power: 12,994hp (16,192kW) from four engines
Cost: N/A

THE LARGEST HELICOPTER, EVER

MIL MI-12 "HOMER"

Looking like a cross between a fixed-wing aircraft and a tandem-rotor helicopter, the Mil Mi-24 may have been one of the world's more bizarre aircraft designs, but its lifting capabilities were very impressive. And it still holds the record as the biggest helicopter ever built.

THE LARGEST GUNSHIP HELICOPTER

MIL MI-24 HIND

"Large and lethal" accurately sums up the Mil Mi-24, Russia's (and the world's) biggest attack helicopter. Pilots nicknamed it the "flying tank." This isn't far from the truth, because this combined gunship and troop transporter bristles with offensive weaponry.

D uring the Soviet war in Afghanistan from 1979 to 1989, the Mujahideen dubbed the Mil Mi-24 Hind the "Devil's Chariot." One rebel was quoted as saying, "We do not fear the Soviets. We fear their helicopters."

Attacker or ambulance

Such trepidation was justified, given the destructive capabilities of the helicopter, with its three equipment hardpoints on each of its midmounted wings. These can be fitted with a variety of different weapons depending on the mission being undertaken—from troop, tank, and building attack to air-to-air combat—in addition to the 0.5in (12.7mm) multibarrel machine gun projecting from the front. However, the Mi-24's role is not purely that of an attacker. The heavily armored machine can also carry up to eight troops or be fitted with four stretchers for use as an air ambulance.

The first Mi-24 Hinds entered service in 1970 after a very short 18-month development time. Around 2500 have since been produced, and constant upgrades have kept them up to date with current technology. A pilot and a weapons operator normally operate the two-engined chopper, with its distinctive double-bubble canopy. Over 30 countries operate the Mi-24, including the United States, although its versions are used as adversaries during helicopter training sessions.

SPECIFICATIONS

Country: Russia (USSR)
Year built from: 1970 (upgrades)
Dimensions: 57ft 6in (17.5m) long; 56ft 6in (17m) rotor diameter
Weight (empty): 12 tons (11,100kg)
Maximum speed: 208mph (335km/h)
Power: 4400hp (3200kW) from two engines
Cost: N/A

TOP AND ABOVE: The Mi-24 bristles with weaponry, and is a formidable foe against any opponent, either on the ground or in the air.

THE LARGEST HELICOPTER, CURRENT

MIL MI-26 HALO

Currently the heaviest and most powerful helicopter in production, the Mi-26 is also capable of carrying more than any other chopper around today. Its personnel capacity—90 soldiers (although some have carried up to 150)—puts it on a par with the C-130 Hercules transport plane, a much bigger, propeller-driven, fixed-wing craft. Beneath its conventional looks, it is an extraordinary helicopter

When the Mi-26 Halo was being developed in the 1970s, one major requirement was that it could lift up to one-and-a-half times more than any other helicopter. However, after its introduction in 1977, it achieved a maximum takeoff payload of over twice that of the Boeing Chinook (see page 184).

Eight-blade rotor

Because of its size and potential loads, the Mi-26 needs some pretty hefty mechanics to get it into the air. It was the first helicopter to have an eight-blade main rotor—the diameter of which is 105ft (32m). Two very powerful engines of 11,240hp (8380kW) each provide the brute strength. In addition to the main military version, several civilian models have also been offered, including a straight passenger version, a freighter, fuel tanker, flying ambulance, and a "flying crane," which is equipped with a gondola underneath its nose for sling operations.

However, despite its impressive performance, a new version is in development, intended to take the Mi-26 to even greater extremes. New engines are intended (each offering 10,000hp [7457kW] in power), and that will be coupled with an even more substantial payload capability. Clearly, some people are just never satisfied.

...ot (Russian Airlines) is ...ly commercial civilian ...nger operator of the Mi-26.

SPECIFICATIONS

Country: Russia (USSR)
Year built from: 1977
Dimensions: 131ft 6in (40m); 105ft (32m) rotor diameter
Weight (empty): 31 tons (28,200kg)
Maximum speed: 183mph (295km/h)
Power: 11,240hp (8380kW) from two engines
Cost: $12–15 million

HARRIER "JUMP JET"

Unique is a word that is often misused, but in the case of the Harrier "jump jet," the appellation is an apt one. The Harrier is the only successful Vertical/Short Take-Off and Landing (V/STOL) jet design to emerge from many attempts to perfect this novel and versatile type of aircraft. It plays a key role as a sea-based fighter with both Britain and America.

A jet fighter that can take off and land without a runway? When work started on the Harrier project in the 1950s, such ideas must have seemed in the realms of comic-book fantasy. Yet by October 1960, the first prototype had performed its first VTOL.

Forward, backward, or straight up

Further tests followed until the Harrier finally went into service in 1969, quickly establishing itself as one of the more versatile military aircraft around, with the ability to fly and fight like a conventional jet, but also able to land, take off, and hover like a helicopter. It achieves this by having four engine nozzles, which can be angled between zero degrees, for straight flight, and 98 degrees, which allows the Harrier to fly slightly backward. At the 90-degree setting, the plane can take off straight up. From the outside, the jet looks simple and graceful, but flying a Harrier successfully takes immense competence and concentration. Pilots are often recruited from the ranks of the helicopter elite because the Harrier's controls are similar to a helicopter when in hover mode.

The Harrier has a number of advantages over a traditional aircraft. If it stalls, it can be recovered by changing the direction of the thrust. And in an air battle, it has amazing maneuverability that no other aircraft can match.

SPECIFICATIONS
Country: UK
Year built: 1967–90s
Dimensions: 56ft 6in (14m) long; 30ft 6in (9m) wingspan
Weight (empty): 6 tons (5700kg)
Maximum speed: 629mph (1012km/h)
Power: 23,500lbf (104.7kN) from one engine
Cost: $32–40 million (Sea Harrier)

TOP AND ABOVE: In action, the Harrier operates like a conventional jet, but its ability to take off, land, and hover (for short periods) like a helicopter gives it a versatility that no other fighter plane can offer.

AIRSPEED HORSA MILITARY GLIDER

Gliders today are usually small, one- or two-person affairs, intended primarily for pleasure. But during World War II, this aircraft had a much more serious role to play. The Airspeed Horsa was the largest glider the world had ever seen, and its finest hour was as a vanguard for the 1944 liberation of Europe.

SPECIFICATIONS

Country:	UK
Year built:	1942–45
Dimensions:	67ft (20.4m) long; 88ft (26.8m) wingspan
Weight (loaded):	7.6 tons (6920kg)
Maximum speed:	127mph (204km/h) when towed; 100mph (160km/h) when gliding
Power:	None
Cost:	$12–15 million

ABOVE RIGHT AND BELOW: The Horsa could carry heavy military vehicles as well as personnel. Horsas were vital in the 1944 liberation of Europe, carrying troops and equipment silently behind enemy lines.

In size and appearance, the Airspeed Horsa seems more like a conventionally powered craft than a machine with no propulsion of its own. However, amazingly, these chunky gliders were able to get off the ground under tow, with loads of up to 28 troops and all their equipment aboard. Usual tow aircraft were Stirling, Halifax, and Whitley bombers, as well as Albermarle and Dakota transport planes.

Belly-flop landing

Made entirely out of wood (in order to save on weight and material), the Horsa was introduced in 1942. It could also carry a Jeep or antitank gun if required, and had a hinged nose to allow for loading vehicles, as well as a dispensable undercarriage, which could be jettisoned in flight. The Horsa's method of landing was to rather inelegantly flop down on a skid under its main fuselage. It was a dangerous operation that often went wrong, but its robust construction gave it a better survivability than many of its contemporaries.

In total, 3665 Horsas were built, and they were the main type used in the 1944 invasion of Europe, carrying thousands of troops silently behind enemy lines, almost undetected by the Axis powers. Out of 2596 gliders of all types sent on Operation Market Garden (to secure bridges across the Rhine in the Netherlands), 2239 landed successfully. The majority of these were Horsas.

THE LARGEST (UNMANNED) AERIAL VEHICLE, IN DEVELOPMENT

DASSAULT NEURON

The Dassault Neuron has yet to be built, but if the concept comes to fruition, it will be the largest and most advanced unmanned combat aircraft around. However, the plans have a long way to go yet, with the first flight of the Neuron not envisaged until at least 2011.

BELOW: The Neuron will do everything a modern combat aircraft can do now, plus more besides, but will be flown from many miles away.

SPECIFICATIONS

Country: France	
Year built: In development	
Dimensions: 33ft (10m) long; 39ft (12m) wingspan	
Weight: Approximately 5.5 tons (5000kg)	
Maximum speed: N/A	
Power: N/A	
Cost: $480 million (current development cost)	

Unmanned fighters and bombers are seen as the future of military aircraft, putting valuable personnel out of harm's way by having them at a ground-control stations rather than in the cockpit. Several countries are currently developing UCAVs (Unmanned Combat Air Vehicles), or already have them in operation. None, however, is as ambitious as the Dassault Neuron aerial vehicle.

Stealth-bomber looks

The Neuron's size is almost the same as that of a manned jet like the Dassault Mirage 2000 fighter, and the intention is that the production versions will have the same range, armament, and abilities as a plane with a human pilot in the cockpit. With its flying-wing design, the Neuron bears a distinct resemblance to the B-2 bomber and will have similar stealth potential. It will also be able to behave in a way that is completely different to traditional aircraft. One proposed feature is that Neurons can be grouped together and controlled automatically, so they attack en masse rather than independently of one another.

France is the major partner in the Neuron venture, but the project is a truly pan-European affair, with companies in Sweden, Spain, Italy, Switzerland, and Greece also collaborating. So far, a few static mockups of the Neuron have been completed for display and evaluation purposes. But keep watching.

The original version of the MQ-9, known as the MQ-1 Predator, has been in use since 1995. It is intended to be flown in risky environments where chemical or biological hazards may exist, enemy air superiority is too great, or over oceans. It has proved extremely adept in a number of different environments. In 2002, for example, one even engaged an Iraqi MiG-25 in combat, although the unmanned drone lost the engagement.

Bigger, better, and bolder

Given the accomplishments of the MQ-1, it was only a matter of time before an attempt was made to improve upon the original. The resultant machine was the MQ-9 (and its nonaggressive surveillance sibling, the RQ-9), currently the largest attack drone in operation. It is bigger, weightier and more powerful, better equipped, and can fly for longer—up to 30 hours plus—than its predecessor. With a ceiling of 50,000ft (15km), it can reach double the height of its ancestor, too. Typical armaments include Stinger air-to-air missiles, Hellfire ground missiles, and JDAM bombs.

In design, apart from the lack of a cockpit, the Reaper looks very strange with its Honeywell turboprop engine and propeller at the back flanked by three stabilizing fins. It's quite a user-intensive machine to fly as well, requiring a team of 55 dedicated people back at base.

SPECIFICATIONS

Country: USA
Year built from: 2002
Dimensions:
36ft (11m) long;
66ft (20m) wingspan
Weight (empty): 1.9 tons (1700kg)
Maximum speed: 250mph (400km/h)
Power: 898.5hp (670kW)
Cost: $8 million

THE LARGEST (UNMANNED) AERIAL ATTACK VEHICLE, CURRENT

MQ-9 REAPER

Although development of unmanned combat vehicles continues, some successful designs are already in production. These include the MQ-9 Reaper, the weaponized version of the RQ-9 high-altitude reconnaissance aircraft, and a larger, deadlier version of the USA's mainstay MQ-1 Predator UAV (Unmanned Aerial Vehicle).

ABOVE AND RIGHT:
At top is a military-spec MQ-9, while to the right is the machine from which it was developed, the MQ-1 Predator, equipped here with Hellfire missiles.

RQ-8 FIRE SCOUT

Not every unpiloted aerial vehicle is based on a fixed-wing concept. The RQ-8 Fire Scout is the biggest unmanned helicopter flying today. The fact that it beats everything else in stature is hardly surprising: It is based on a real manned helicopter, the Schweizer Model 333.

ABOVE AND RIGHT: Comparison with an army Humvee vehicle demonstrates the size of the RQ-8—it's definitely no toy helicopter. Cameras are prominently mounted at the front.

With so many fixed-wing drones either in use or being developed, it was inevitable that a true helicopter equivalent would eventually appear. Northrop Grumman Corporation was the company that took this step, by converting an existing make of American helicopter into a completely robotic craft.

Rocket power

The RQ-8 Fire Scout is still in the testing phase at the moment, but if, and when, it goes into service, its role will be for surveillance, communications, and designating targets. Future models may even carry weapons for an offensive role. In fact, some flights, and some trials, have been undertaken in which an RQ-8 fired rockets. The US Navy has shown the most interest in the RQ-8, as an unmanned helicopter poses fewer logistical and technical difficulties than attempting to land an unmanned fixed-wing plane on a sea vessel.

Such is the degree of technology packed into the Fire Scout that it has a level of autonomy—the ability to fly itself. This was impressively demonstrated in early 2006. For the first time ever, an example managed to land aboard a moving ship entirely unmanned.

The RQ-8 is capable of staying aloft for up to eight hours, although its useful working time is around five hours in total. In addition, it is capable of working up to 126 miles (203km) away from its base.

SPECIFICATIONS

Country: USA
Year built from: 2002
Dimensions: 23ft (7m) long (folded); 27ft 6in (8.5m) rotor diameter
Weight: 1.5 tons (1429kg)
Maximum speed: 144mph (232km/h) plus
Power: 250hp (186kW)
Cost: Approximately $8 million

THE LARGEST CARRIER-BASED AIRCRAFT

DOUGLAS A-3D SKYWARRIOR

The A-3D Skywarrior was the biggest, heaviest aircraft ever intended to land and take off from another aircraft as part of its routine duties. Such was its size and cumbersome nature that it was christened "The Whale" by aircrew, and landing one on a carrier was considerably more difficult than landing a smaller plane.

SPECIFICATIONS

Country: USA
Year built: 1952–61
Dimensions:
76ft 6in (23.5m) long;
23ft (7m) wingspan
Weight (loaded): 35 tons (31,750kg)
Maximum speed: 520mph (980km/h)
Power: 21,000lbf (93.4kW) from two engines
Cost: N/A

Commissioning such a big plane as the Skywarrior in the late 1940s, when jet technology was still in it infancy, and expecting it to be able to land on a moving aircraft carrier as well must have seemed like a foolhardy idea. However, the US Navy wanted a bomber aircraft with nuclear capabilities that was able to operate from a sea platform, and the A-3D was the result.

Original career shortlived

Needless to say, the development process was beset by problems, and although the first prototype was built in 1952, it wasn't until 1956 that the Skywarrior was actually accepted into the Navy fleet. But by that time, submarine-based nuclear systems were in development, and the Skywarrior's role as a bomber was shortlived. From 1960 onward, it moved over to reconnaissance, electronic warfare, and refueling roles, the latter being particularly useful at sea because it enabled strike forces to extend their range; it was also useful for rescuing returning aircraft that were low on fuel. Retirement came in 1991, although some examples are still flying privately.

The standard crew compliment was three. In order to keep the weight down for carrier landings, certain items that were standard on similar aircraft were omitted on the A-3D. Among the more significant were ejector seats, leading some personnel to comment that A-3D actually stood for "All three dead."

BELOW: Landing anything on an aircraft carrier is dangerous and tricky, but all the more so when it's as large as a Skywarrior.

THE LARGEST BALLISTIC MISSILE

R-36 ICBM

During the Cold War, a continual game of oneupmanship was played out between the Soviet Union and the USA and Western Europe. If one side built something big, then the other side had to have its equivalent as well, only just a little larger. However, it was the USSR that eventually ended up with the largest missile in the world. Its nuclear R-36 was such a threatening weapon that it was dubbed the "City Buster" by America.

Conceived during the peak of the Cold War in April 1962, the R-36 family were massive missiles that could also be used as space launchers. They were of such size and destructive force that they were regarded as one of the USSR's most serious threats. Thus, when the Soviet Union broke up in 1991, the R-36s were one of the targets the US sought to reduce by arms treaty.

Catastrophic consequences

The two-stage R-36s could carry a range of potent nuclear weaponry from a five-megaton nuclear device up to a highly destructive 20-megaton warhead. Of even more concern to the West were the versions that could carry up to 10 smaller warheads and, at one point, an upgrade was considered that would have allowed the R-36 to yield 38 nuclear devices. Just one of these versions could have had catastrophic consequences if launched in a strike.

In 1991, it was discovered that 308 R-36 silos were operational—ready to fire at short notice. Around 85 remain, and by 2009, it should go down to 40, these should continue serving until 2014 at least. The R-36 menace has not yet gone away even though the Cold War has.

ABOVE AND BELOW: The traditional Soviet May Day Parade was one of the few times the public got to see an R-36 ICBM.

SPECIFICATIONS

Country: Russia (USSR)

Year built: 1965–91

Dimensions:
105ft 6in (32m) long;
10ft (3m) diameter

Weight: 201 tons
(183,000kg)

Maximum speed: 5
miles/sec (8km/sec)

Liftoff thrust:
531,965lbf (2366kW)

Cost: 8–10 billion
Roubles (research,
development, and
testing)

THE LARGEST FLYING "OFFICE"

AIR FORCE ONE

ABOVE: Air Force One always comes to a standstill with its left side facing onlookers, to protect the President's quarters, on the right side, from potential attack.

The American Presidential Boeing 747-200B can justifiably be called the largest flying office in the world, or perhaps even the largest flying government building in the world. It has all the facilities needed to continue the running of the USA while the President is on board.

SPECIFICATIONS

Country: USA
Year built: 1990
Dimensions:
232ft (71m) long; 195ft 6in (60m) wingspan
Weight: (Estimated, loaded) 413 tons (375,000kg)
Maximum speed:
630mph (Mach 0.92/1014km/h)
Power: 226,800lbf (1000kN) from four engines
Cost: N/A

Air Force One has been the callsign used for any USAF aircraft carrying the President of the United States since 1953. However, the term is generally recognized by the public as being the designation of the Boeing 747-200B in the distinctive "United States of America" design. There are actually two—identical—747s, which were introduced in 1990. Both take off almost simultaneously to foil any possible terrorist attack, by creating confusion as to which one the President is actually aboard.

Flying White House

Heavily modified from a standard Boeing 747, Air Force One's features and furnishings include enough storage for 2000 meals, two galleys that can cater for up to 100 people at a time, medical facilities (a doctor is always on board), guest and staff sleeping quarters, and extensive offices, with 85 telephones and 19 televisions, plus all other essential communications equipment. The President himself has a suite and a private dressing room, workout room, bathroom, shower and private office. Effectively, Air Force One is almost the White House with wings.

In the event of a national crisis or threat, Air Force One can keep flying indefinitely, thanks to its aerial refueling capability. It is also fitted with antiattack systems—many of which are classified—although at all times, the plane flies with fighter escorts as well.

6 SPACE VEHICLES

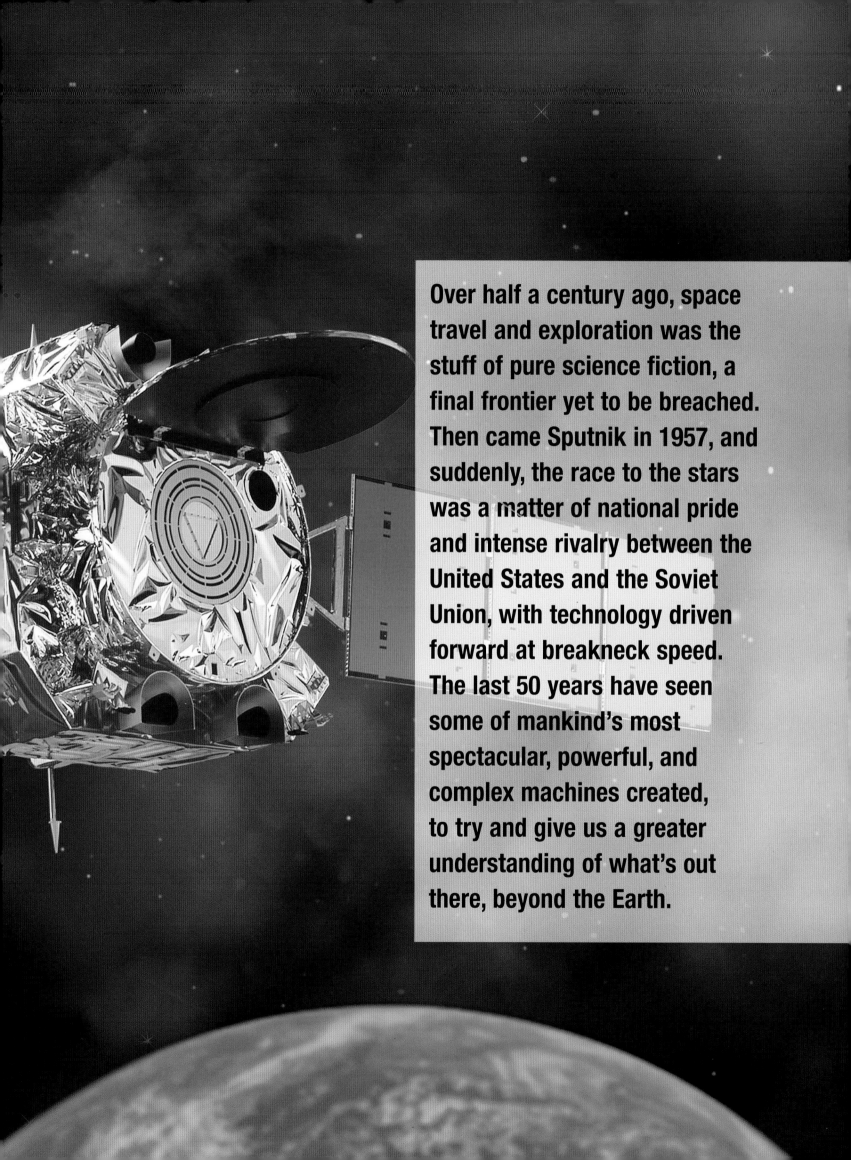

Over half a century ago, space travel and exploration was the stuff of pure science fiction, a final frontier yet to be breached. Then came Sputnik in 1957, and suddenly, the race to the stars was a matter of national pride and intense rivalry between the United States and the Soviet Union, with technology driven forward at breakneck speed. The last 50 years have seen some of mankind's most spectacular, powerful, and complex machines created, to try and give us a greater understanding of what's out there, beyond the Earth.

Spaceflight, of a type, has been around longer than most people realize. It was in 1942 that the first manmade vehicle achieved suborbital flight, in the form of a prototype German V-2 rocket. After World War II, the scientists and engineers from this program were snatched by the USA and the USSR to work on making travel beyond the Earth's atmosphere a reality. The Space Race had begun.

LEFT: Space shuttles are such specialized machines that an enormous infrastructure is also needed to maintain them.

Russia took an early lead with Sputnik 1, the first artificial satellite, which was launched on October 4, 1957. Compared to the satellites of today, it was a very simple creation, sending back basic information in the form of beeps. But it marked a new era for the human race, beyond the confines of our home planet. The following month, Sputnik 2 took the first living animal—Laika the dog—into orbit.

The contest between the two great superpowers intensified even more. Russia was again first with the getting a human being into space. Vostok 1, with Yuri Gagarin aboard, achieved an orbital trip "around" the world in April 1961. It lasted just 108 minutes and almost ended in disaster, but it made an international hero of Gagarin as the world's first astronaut.

By the end of the decade, America had seized the initiative, having successfully landed a man on the moon. Space travel was starting to become less a scientific wonder and more just an everyday fact of modern life, although the march of technological progress continued to promote astounding new achievements. Humans were able to live in space, long term, with the advent of Mir. This pioneering space station was the first consistently manned facility in space, and survived from 1986 to 2001. It also fostered international collaboration between the two former rivals of America and Russia. Supplies were carried up by

LEFT: Voyager I has traveled further than any other machine, carrying Earth and mankind information, should it ever encounter another civilization.

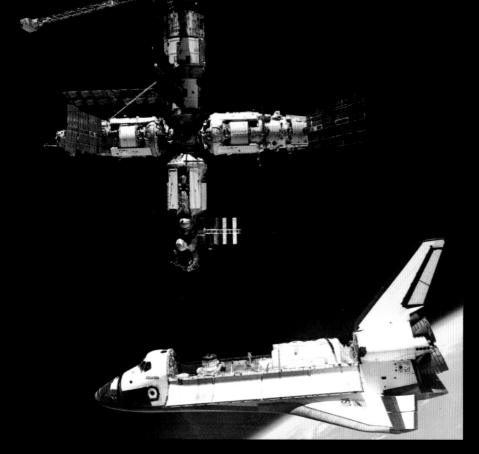

space shuttle, and while that was docked, the two craft combined to form the largest spacecraft in history.

NASA's revolutionary space shuttle had its first launch in 1981, after an exhaustive program that had seen the construction of a test glider during the 1970s named *Enterprise*—and, yes, it really was christened after the starship of *Star Trek* TV fame. Unlike its later sisters, or its fictional namesake, it never traveled into space. The same year, 1977, that *Enterprise* was pioneering the future of reusable space transport, NASA also launched the Voyager 1 deep space probe. It is still operational today, making it the longest space mission of all time, as well as the furthest-traveled manmade item. Signals now take at least 13 hours to reach Earth, and it is believed Voyager 1 will continue transmitting until 2020.

The exploration of space has also resulted in some impressive machinery on Earth as well, with the huge tracking and observation radar dishes, such as that at Jodrell Bank in England (for years the largest fully steerable radar dish on the planet), the most visible and awe-inspiring symbols of high technology used to support our thirst for further knowledge. The future, however, is bound to bring many more, both above and around us.

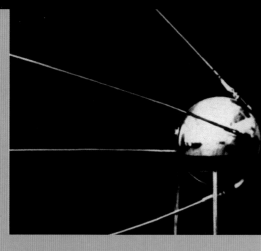

THE LARGEST SPACE ROCKET

SATURN V

The largest, most powerful, and most successful space rocket of all time remains the Saturn V launcher. It was responsible for taking man to the moon and for putting the first US space station in orbit.

RIGHT: The roar from the first launch of Saturn V could be heard miles away.

I n 1961, President John F. Kennedy announced that the USA would try to land a man on the moon before the end of the 1960s. One major barrier to this goal was that there were no rockets powerful enough at the time to carry a human being all the way to the lunar surface.

Under Wernher von Braun, the director of NASA, scientists at the Marshall Space Flight Center in Huntsville, Alabama, gradually developed a series of Saturn launchers to achieve Kennedy's dream. The culmination was the enormous Saturn V. This three-stage rocket was huge compared not just to other existing launchers, but also to other manmade structures. For example, at 364ft (111m) tall, it measured only 12in (30cm) shorter than St Paul's Cathedral in London.

SPECIFICATIONS

Country: USA
Year built from: 1967
Dimensions: 190ft (58m) long; 38ft (11.5m) diameter
Payload: 130 tons (118,000kg)
Liftoff thrust: 1400 tons (12,494kN)
Cost: $200m

First flight

The first Saturn V launch was in 1967, carrying the unmanned Apollo 4 spacecraft. A year later, the first Saturn V manned mission was undertaken, with Apollo 8.

But the rocket's greatest moment came on July 16, 1969, when it blasted off for the moon with the Apollo 11 capsule. The mission to land was a success, and the Saturn V, as well as the crew of Apollo 11, became the stuff of space legend.

Further landings followed, until the cancellation of the Apollo program, after which Saturn V was used to help launch the Skylab space station in 1973. It was to be the culmination of the monster rocket's career, during which no payload was ever lost. With thoughts turning to cheaper and easier ways to fly to the stars, the Saturn V fell away in favor of what was to become the Space Shuttle. Three examples remain on display, however, as a testament to this most powerful of engines ever created by man.

LEFT: And this is what it was all about—the command module once atop the Saturn V, after all the rocket stages had been shed.

RIGHT: The Russian Space Shuttle, which used the Energia to launch it. The Buran shuttle flew only once, and Energia only twice.

THE LARGEST RUSSIAN SPACE ROCKET

ENERGIA

When the USA announced its plans for a reusable spacecraft— the Space Shuttle—it was predictable that the Soviet Union would start working toward the same goal. At that time, the USA and the USSR were locked in the Space Race—a competition to outdo each other in space.

In the end, the Buran Shuttle, which was the name of the Russian attempt to build a version of the US Space Shuttle, was aborted. The launch system for the failed Buran was a rocket called the Energia. It flew only twice, yet its size and power made it significant because it was the only rocket ever to come close to the USA's mighty Saturn V.

Development on the Energia, which was also intended to serve as an expendable heavy-duty booster for conventional flights, started in 1976. The plan was to have three different variants for different payloads: The larger the weight being carried, the more supplementary booster rockets could be attached to the main body. The ultimate Energia—which never actually flew—would have had eight strap-on boosters. This would have given it enough power to carry 192 tons (175,200kg) into space, a much greater amount than the 132 tons (120,000kg) the Saturn V model could carry. Fittingly, the name for this version of the Energia was Hercules (though it was christened Vulcan as well).

Doomed by politics

But political, not technical, issues spelt doom for the Energia. The first one flew in 1987, carrying a military satellite. A year later, the Buran Shuttle successfully lifted off on the back of an Energia. Then came the fall of the Soviet Union. The Energia and Buran Shuttle programs were canceled, and the equipment was put into mothballs.

Parts of the Energia system live on in current rockets. But in the same way that the USA now has nothing to compare to its old Saturn V, so current Russian launch systems are mere shadows of the mighty Energia.

SPECIFICATIONS

Country: Russia (USSR)
Year built: 1987
Dimensions: 318ft (97m) long; 25ft (7.75m) diameter
Payload: Up to 192 tons (175,200kg)
Liftoff thrust: 7,897,516lbf (35,129.900kN)
Cost: $764 million

LEFT: An Apollo space capsule is recovered from the ocean. The damage to the outer surface is caused by the heat of re-entry.

THE LARGEST MANNED SPACE CAPSULE

APOLLO MANNED SPACE CAPSULE

Prior to the Space Shuttle, manned capsules had to be quite small so that early rockets could lift them into space. Being small also made it easier for a space capsule to parachute back to Earth safely. But the Apollo crafts were bigger than most.

The US Apollo Program was the name given to the project designed to land astronauts on the moon. The launch system they used consisted of manned capsules mounted at the top of huge rockets, such as the Saturn V. With previous manned spaceflights, all the crew really had to do was orbit the Earth, and then land successfully. For Apollo though, there was an extra, rather important aspect. The goal was to launch a vehicle to the moon and return it to Earth safely.

Larger than earlier craft

This meant that the Apollo capsules were much larger than earlier craft. They consisted of three different sections: The Command Module (CM) at the top; the Service Module (SM) in the middle; and the Lunar Module (LM) at the bottom. The Command Module was, as its name suggests,

the control center of the spacecraft, as well as the crew's main living quarters. Mounted on to this was the service module, which contained essential equipment vital to the mission, such as fuel cells, batteries, water, and oxygen, plus the rocket engine that was used to get Apollo in and out of lunar orbit. And underneath this was the Lunar Module: The moonlanding vehicle itself. All this was enclosed by what was known as an SLA, which stands for the Spacecraft Lunar Module Adapter. The SLA was simply four long aluminum panels that made the whole capsule streamlined when taking off. Once the capsule was safely launched into space, the SLA was detonated away.

By the time the Apollo spacecraft returned to Earth, it was considerably smaller, having shed its other attachments. The reduced size enabled the capsule to float down into the ocean.

THE LARGEST PLANETARY VEHICLE

LUNAR ROVER

On Earth, a Lunar Rover wouldn't be a mega machine at all. In reality, it is little bigger than a very basic beach buggy with a few high-tech gizmos attached. On the moon, however, such a vehicle allowed astronauts far greater freedom than before.

Only four Lunar Rovers were ever built in total (one each for Apollo 15, 16, and 17, plus another for spare parts after the Apollo program was canceled) but their importance to the exploration of the moon was significant. No longer were astronauts confined to staying around the Lunar Module, and instead could travel some distance away from the landing zone. On the Apollo 17, the final mission to the moon, the Lunar Rover traveled almost 5 miles (7.6km) away from the Lunar Module. That may not sound like much, but it was by far the longest distance any machine has been driven on the surface of Earth's natural satellite.

A sportscar on the moon

With a top speed of about 8mph (13km/h) and only 1hp (744kW) total power (thanks to the lack of gravity, this was all that was needed), the Lunar Rovers were far from fast. However, they did have a chassis similar to that of a sportscar, made up of aluminum alloy tubing and featuring double wishbone suspension. This made them maneuverable and rugged. But they were also lightweight, an essential factor allowing them to be carried in the Apollo Lunar Module. One thing that did distinguish the Rovers from conventional Earth vehicles was the large antenna dish mounted on the front of the vehicle. Other bits of equipment included film and TV cameras, and a toolkit, just in case.

Despite their light weight, the Lunar Rovers could not be brought back to Earth from the moon, so that's where the three of them remain to this day, joined by two of the Soviet Union's two unmanned Rovers, Lunokhod 1 and Lunokhod 2. With no definite plans for people to land on the moon in the foreseeable future, they're all likely to be parked there for quite some time to come.

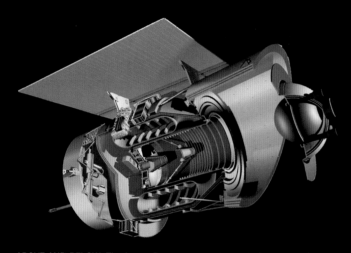

ABOVE AND BELOW: The Lunar Rovers gave astronauts far greater freedom on the moon than they had before. And they're all still up there.

SPECIFICATIONS

Country: USA
Year built: 1971
Dimensions: 10ft (3.1m) long; 4ft (1.14m) high
Payload: 1,080lb (490kg)
Power: 1hp (744kW) from four 0.25hp (186kW) motors on each wheel
Cost: Approximately $38 million

THE LARGEST EARTH TELESCOPES
KECK OBSERVATORY TELESCOPES

No optical telescope on Earth is bigger than that to be found at the Keck Observatory in Mauna Kea, Hawaii.

But the laboratory doesn't just have one telescope. It has two, both of which are identical in size.

SPECIFICATIONS

Country: USA

Year built: 1993 and 1996

Dimensions: 81ftx33ft (24.6mx10m)

Weight: 270 tons (245,000kg)

Resolution: 279ft (85m)

Cost: Approximately $140 million

TOP AND ABOVE: Perched high atop a mountain, the twin Keck observatories have an exceptionally clear view of space.

The summit of Mauna Kea, which rises to 13,800ft (4206m), usually well above the cloud layer, is regarded as one of the most significant astronomical sites in the world. Due to its height and location, it allows exceptionally clear views through telescopes, and enables observers to see both the southern and northern skies.

Small wonder then that it has become a popular place for mounting telescopes. But none can compare with the two optical/near infrared telescopes, known as Keck I and Keck II, of the W. M. Keck Observatory. Equal in height to an eight-storey building, they are by far the largest of their types in the world.

Two domes close together

Two large domes on top of the mountain shelter the two precision telescopes. The first was built in 1993, and the second in 1996. Both measure 32ft 10in (10m) in diameter. To counteract the forces of gravity at this height, the system must make minute but vital adjustments to the positions of the telescopes twice every second. However, thanks to this computer-controlled adjustment, the telescopes give an incredibly accurate, fine image.

Because Keck I and Keck II are sited so close together, in addition to working independently, they can also be linked together as one huge "hyper-telescope" (or interferometer). This ability makes them an important part of NASA's ongoing search for planets and possibly even life beyond our own solar system.

NATIONAL SCIENCE FOUNDATION VLA

SPECIFICATIONS

Country: USA
Year built: 1972–80
Number of dishes: 27, plus 8 more soon to be added
Size of each arm: 13 miles (21km) long
Weight of each dish: 230 ton (s208,650kg)
Cost: $78.5 millon

BELOW: All the dishes can be moved using a motorized crane, which operates on this railroad track running alongside the array. At one point, it even crosses a major highway.

VLA are the three letters that provide the name for the radio astronomy observatory on the Plains of San Augustin in New Mexico, USA. However, this enormous site houses 27 radio antennae, making it the largest establishment of this type in operation.

VLA stands for Very Large Array, but even that description is something of an understatement for the enormous radio observatory between the towns of Magdalena and Datil in New Mexico. This research center consists of a Y-shaped network of 27 radio dishes, with each arm of the "Y" measuring 13 miles (21km) in length.

Railroad dishes

Each of these antennae is impressive enough in its own right, weighing 230 tons (208,650kg), with a dish diameter of 82ft (25m). Together, however, they act as an extraordinarily powerful astronomical instrument, capable of seeing far into space. One of the more amazing aspects of the VLA is the way that the dishes can be moved around, using a lifting locomotive that operates on the railroad tracks that shadow the shape of the "Y." There is even a level crossing across on Highway 60, which must be quite a sight when the dishes are passing across it. Four different shape configurations are used, with the positions being changed every three to four months. This means that it takes 16 months for the VLA to go through all its different patterns.

The VLA is about to become larger still. Soon, it will become the Expanded Very Large Array (EVLA), thanks to the addition of a further eight dishes elsewhere in New Mexico. With advances in technology, the other dishes don't need to be physically located at the San Augustin location, but will be connected to it by fiber-optic links. At the same time, existing equipment at the VLA is due to be upgraded.

THE LARGEST RADAR DISH

ARECIBO OBSERVATORY

If this huge radio telescope looks familiar, it may be because it served as a villain's lair in the James Bond 007 movie *GoldenEye*. But the real-life task of the Arecibo Observatory, serving as the source of data in the Search for Extra-Terrestrial Intelligence (SETI), is almost as fantastic as the movie.

ABOVE AND BELOW: The distinctively designed Arecibo observatory has featured in several movies, but its chief claim to fame is that it has led the search for extra-terrestrial intelligence for several decades.

SPECIFICATIONS

Country: USA, located in Puerto Rico
Year built: 1958–63
Dish diameter: 1000ft (305m)
Weight: 300 tons (270,000 kg)
Focal length: 435ft (132.5m)
Cost: $9.3 million (plus $9 million and $25 million respectively for upgrades)

The Arecibo Observatory telescope in Puerto Rico takes some beating when it comes to sheer size. Built inside a natural sinkhole, the installation is the biggest single-aperture telescope on the planet. Its 1000ft (305m) plate, the largest curved focusing dish on Earth, is made up of aluminum panels supported by a network of steel wires. In total, there are 38,778 of these plates, each of them 3 x 6ft (1 x 2m) in size.

All-seeing

The actual dish itself is fixed, but the telescope can be "aimed" using a receiver strung out on cables 450ft (137m) above it. This allows the observatory, sited very close to the equator, to "see" every planet in the solar system.

Despite looking futuristic, the telescope is actually close to its fiftieth birthday, having been proposed in 1958 and opened in 1963. Twice during its existence it has been significantly upgraded. The three main purposes of Arecibo are radio astronomy, aeronomy (the study of the Earth's atmosphere), and observing the solar system. It has also been used for military purposes but has become best known as the collection point for incoming SETI data. In 1974, a message was sent out from the observatory in an attempt to communicate with aliens. Nobody has replied yet.

THE LARGEST FULLY STEERABLE RADAR DISH (SPACE)

GREEN BANK TELESCOPE

The huge equipment at Green Bank, West Virginia, looks like everybody's idea of a radio telescope. However, this moveable dish has one very significant claim to fame: It is the world's largest fully steerable space-radio telescope.

The full name of this gigantic dish is the Robert C. Byrd Green Bank Telescope. A hefty label for a hefty piece of machinery, it was named after the longest-serving US senator of West Virginia, the state in which the Green Bank telescope stands. Fortunately for those with a bad memory for long names, it's more commonly known as the GBT.

A surface of 2004 panels

The considerable size of the radio telescope dish makes it quite a local landmark. The GBT monitors space using an enormous 328 x 361ft (100 x 110m) dish. These immense measurements make it quite unusual among such equipment because it is not completely symmetrical. The GBT has a parabolic design so that the receiver, which is mounted on a large gantry sprouting from the top of the dish, doesn't interfere with the view of the sky.

The surface of the dish alone was also made to very precise specifications, consisting of up of 2004 aluminum panels, machined to an accuracy of just 0.0003in (76.2 micrometers). The GBT also has laser rangefinders, which allows the telescope's motors to compensate for weather conditions, for example, when moving.

The usefulness and efficiency of the GBT are enhanced by its location in the middle of the US National Radio Quiet Zone. An area 13,000 miles^2 (33,670km^2) in size, all other radio transmissions are either banned here or limited by arrangement. These circumstances enable the sensitive GBT to pick up signals from space that, ordinarily, would be lost amid normal radio chatter.

SPECIFICATIONS

Country: USA
Year built: 1990–2000
Dish diameter:
328ftx361ft
(100mx110m)
Weight: N/A
Focal length: 197ft
(60m)
Cost: $74.5 million

LEFT: Despite its size and complicated structure, the steerable Green Bank telescope can be moved to very precise positions.

THE LARGEST FULLY STEERABLE RADAR DISH (METEOROLOGICAL)

CHILBOLTON ADVANCED METEOROLOGICAL RADAR

BELOW AND BOTTOM: These two pictures demonstrate some of the angles achievable by CAMRa—"looking" straight upward is no problem, despite the size and weight of the dish.

The largest radar dishes are used to explore space. However, antennas used for atmospheric research of planet Earth are also sizeable machines, and the most impressive can be found at the Chilbolton Observatory in the UK.

SPECIFICATIONS

Country: UK
Year built: 1963–67
Dish diameter: 82ft (25m)
Dish weight: 420 tons (381,000kg)
Concrete base weight: 2300 tons (2,086,524kg)
Frequency band: 3 GHz
Cost: £325,000

The Chilbolton Observatory, in Hampshire, in southern England, is dedicated to the studies of radiowave propagation and meteorology, and it contains many items of high-tech equipment used for these causes. The centerpiece of the site, however, is a Doppler radar. At 82ft (25m) in diameter, it is the largest fully steerable meteorological dish in the world.

Construction on the Chilbolton Advanced Meteorological Radar, (known as CAMRa) started in 1963. A site on the isolated Salisbury Plains was chosen because it was remote from any major roads, the traffic of which could affect signals. This position also gave CAMRa an excellent view of the horizon, which was essential for accurate meteorological readings.

Early problems

This enormous aluminum dish, weighing 420 tons (381,000kg), was so heavy that shortly after the observatory opened, its azimuth bearing failed. This vital component, responsible for rotating the dish through 360 degrees, was buried deep within the concrete, which meant that mounting a repair was a very complicated affair. It didn't put the radar completely out of action, but it did mean that, for a few months, the dish was unable to move.

The dish has been a lot better behaved (and mobile) ever since, monitoring weather systems and providing vital data for meteorological projects. The main task of CAMRa these days is to monitor rain, snow, and ice passing over the observatory. Over the years, while it isn't in operation, CAMRa has been gradually upgraded to increase its sensitivity and usefulness.

PALOMAR OBSERVATORY'S SAMUEL OSCHIN TELESCOPE

BELOW: Although it looks like a conventional telescope, QUEST records the images of space it 'sees' in the same way as a digital camera does.

Digital cameras are a relatively recent invention, certainly as far as most private users are concerned. And the trend is for ever smaller personal cameras. However, this isn't the case with the telescope at San Diego's Palomar Observatory, currently the biggest digital camera in existence.

SPECIFICATIONS

Country: USA
Year built: 1949
Number of sensors: 112
Resolution: 161 megapixels
Aperture: 4ft (1.2m)
Cost: N/A

The telescope at Palomar Observatory didn't start life as a digital camera, because when the 48in (122cm) Schmidt telescope was first set up in 1949, such equipment didn't exist. The telescope simply recorded its images onto glass plates. However, by the early part of the twenty-first century, storage and cataloging was becoming a problem, with over 19,000 images accumulating in 500 boxes. The solution was to covert the telescope to digital technology.

Finding the tenth planet

The camera itself is known as the Quasar Equatorial Survey Team (QUEST) and was designed by astrophysicists at Yale and Indiana Universities. It uses image sensors, known as charge coupled devices (CCDs), to scan the sky. Before the Oschin installation, the largest number of CCDs in an astronomical camera was 30. However, the Palomar telescope has 112, making it far more sensitive to light than ordinary film, and able to deliver data immediately. All this high-tech development paid off in 2005 when the Oschin installation was credited with discovering and photographing (as early as 2003) the tenth planet in our Solar System, currently given the less than glamorous name of 2003 UB313.

You can forget about looking through a conventional viewfinder to use this camera because it doesn't work that way. Once guided by hand, using a smaller telescope mounted by its side, the QUEST camera is now controlled robotically from a site in Pasadena, California. All data is wirelessly transmitted there, so the only person needed on site is the employee who opens and closes the dome.

THE LIVERPOOL TELESCOPE,
CANARY ISLANDS

SPECIFICATIONS

Country: UK, located in Spain

Year built: 1999–2003

Dimensions: 21ft (6.5m) wide; 28ft (8.5m) long

Diameter: 6ft 6in (2m)

Weight: 26.5 tons (24,000kg)

Cost: N/A

Size and innovation make the Liverpool Telescope highly impressive. Situated in the Canary Islands, the instrument is completely controlled by remote from a site several hundred feet below its mountaintop site.

The telescope is named after the city in the UK that is the home of the John Moore University, which owns the telescope. But the Liverpool Telescope is sited far away from its "home," at the Observatorio del Roque de Los Muchachos in the Canary islands. It's one of several telescopes there, but what makes the Liverpool telescope so special is that it is fully robotic and, at 6ft 6in (2m) in diameter, it is the largest of its type to be used primarily for astronomy.

Internet speed

Thanks to increasingly clever technology, many telescopes are operated by remote control these days. The Liverpool Telescope can accept a list of observations to make, which it can run through without any need for human involvement. This enables the telescope to quickly view many objects for several different projects during one night and, if something significant is spotted, it can obtain images quickly. Observations from the Liverpool Telescope can be viewed on the Internet just 15 minutes after they have taken place.

Constructed using a complicated system of yokes and trusses, the telescope is able to move through 360 degrees and can be positioned as accurately as just 20 microns, which is about the thickness of a human hair. Its location on top of a 8,200ft (2500m) high extinct volcano can get blustery, so the construction is also designed to stand up to winds of 50mph (8km/h) without losing any of its efficiency.

ABOVE AND TOP: The Liverpool Telescope is sheltered by the folding roof of its building when not in use, to protect it from the elements.

LEFT: This illustration is of Hubble, way out beyond the Earth's atmosphere.

THE LARGEST SPACE TELESCOPE

HUBBLE SPACE TELESCOPE

The best images of space come from outside the interference of Earth's atmosphere. And that's exactly what the Hubble Space Telescope (HST), in orbit around our planet, is able to provide. It's not just the largest telescope in space, but one of the most significant telescopes ever built.

The idea of Hubble (named after a leading American Astronomer Edwin Powell Hubble) was first mooted in 1946, well before humanity had ever launched anything into space. But it took until 1990, after a difficult and protracted development, for Hubble to be sent into space. Unfortunately, the difficulties didn't end once it was up there. Problems were found with its main mirror, meaning the HST's abilities to view were seriously compromised. Thanks to the Space Shuttle, repairs were successfully undertaken, and Hubble reached its full potential in 1993. Since then it has become an incredibly useful astronomical tool.

Hubble contains five scientific instruments of varying types, including cameras, spectrographs, and photometers. It's made some spectacular discoveries and recorded amazing images, including the formation of new stars, supernovae, and a comet collision with Jupiter (something that only happens once every few centuries). The HST has even helped scientists work out how old the universe actually is.

Despite its usefulness, Hubble's life span is limited, and it is due to be replaced by an even larger item—the James Webb Space Telescope—in 2013. However, by that time Hubble might not be around to witness the change. Unless adjustments are made to Hubble's gyroscopes, its current orbit will result in it burning up in Earth's atmosphere sometime from 2010 onward. As yet, no definite decision has been made as to whether or not these adjustments will be made.

THE LARGEST X-RAY SPACE TELESCOPE

NASA'S CHANDRA X-RAY TELESCOPE

The Earth's atmosphere absorbs most X-rays from space. This meant that an orbiting telescope was needed to observe this space phenomenon, so NASA launched the Chandra space telescope—the heaviest item ever to be launched—in 1999.

Named after the Indian-American physicist Subrahmanyan Chandraskhar, the Chandra Telescope is one of NASA's four "Great Observatories" in orbit around Earth. Its purpose lies in the field of X-ray astronomy, something that can't easily be carried out from the planet itself because of atmospheric interference.

RIGHT AND BELOW: The Chandra X-ray telescope, filling practically the entire loading bay of the Space Shuttle *Columbia* shortly before its launch. When in orbit, its solar panels unfolded to provide power, as shown below.

Heavy load

First proposed in 1976, work started on the instrument the following year. Progress was slow, and it was only in the 1990s, after the telescope was redesigned to cut costs, that its construction accelerated. When the Space Shuttle *Columbia* took it into space in 1999, it was the heaviest item ever to be carried by the craft, the extra weight being the booster rocket system needed to take it into an orbit beyond the reach of the shuttle.

It currently circumnavigates the globe at a distance approximately one-third of the way towards the moon. This means that, should Chandra ever go wrong, it won't be possible to repair it, but it also puts it above the planet's radiation belt, ensuring that its delicate instruments are out of harm's way. Despite this, its imaging spectrometer has already suffered minor damage from radiation particles. Luckily, this hasn't compromised the telescope's effectiveness or the data it has transmitted back to its base at the Chandra X-ray Center in Cambridge, Massachusetts.

SPECIFICATIONS

Country: USA

Year built: 1976–199

Dimensions: 57ft (17.5m) long

Weight: 26.5 tons (24,000kg)

Orbit height: 87,000 miles (140,000km)

Cost: $1.5 billion; $2.8 billion to operate

THE LARGEST GAMMA-RAY SPACE TELESCOPE

COMPTON GAMMA RAY OBSERVATORY

At the time it was launched in 1991, the Compton Gamma Ray telescope was the heaviest astrophysical tool ever launched into space. It observed the universe's electromagnetic spectrum to a degree that had never been achieved before.

SPECIFICATIONS

Country: USA

Year launched: 1991

Dimensions: 29.80ft (9.10m) long; 69.8ft (21.3m) wide

Weight: 17 tons (17,000kg)

Orbit height: 280 miles (450km)

Cost: $500 million

BELOW: The Compton Gamma Ray observatory is delicately maneuvered into space from the loading bay of the Space Shuttle *Atlantis*.

The second of NASA's "Great Observatories" to go into space after the Hubble Space Telescope, the Compton Gamma Ray Observatory (CGRO for short) is the only one of the four no longer in operation. After a failure of one of its gyroscopes (used to keep it in a low orbit a mere 280 miles [450km] above the planet, beneath the Van Allen radiation belt) it was allowed to crash down to Earth in 2000. Although it was still functional at the time, it was decided that letting the telescope fall into the Atlantic Ocean would be preferable to allowing it to come down uncontrolled if another gyroscope failed.

Black hole births

However, in the nine years of its operation, this largest of space gamma-ray telescopes proved itself of immense use to scientists. Gamma rays are an electromagnetic radiation, emanating from significant cosmic events, such as the birth of black holes. If black holes occurred close to Earth, they could wipe out all life. The four instruments on board the CGRO allowed it to observe the full range of these emissions, and it was able to discover 271 sources of rays from space, 170 of which were completely unknown before. On average, one gamma ray was being detected every day, resulting in over 2000 monitored before the CGRO's mission ended. It also completed the most comprehensive survey ever of the galactic center, and in the process discovered an antimatter cloud there. Antimatter on Earth only exists in laboratories.

The CGRO also observed atmospheric effects around our own planet, and found that thunderstorms also emit gamma rays—something that wasn't known before.

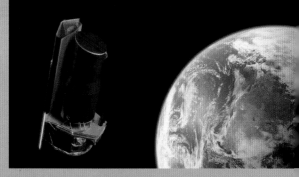

LEFT AND RIGHT: The Spitzer launches on a Delta II 7920H ELV rocket, and an illustration of how it looks in orbit above the Earth.

THE LARGEST INFRARED SPACE TELESCOPE

NASA'S SPITZER SPACE TELESCOPE

Great by size and definition, the Spitzer Space Telescope was the fourth—and final—of NASA's "Great Observatories" to go into orbit. Its task is to monitor infrared rays in the cosmos.

Named after Dr Lyman Spitzer Junior, the scientist who originally came up with the idea of putting telescopes into space back in the 1940s, the Spitzer was launched in August 2003. It was the only one of the four not to be carried by the Space Shuttle (due to the *Challenger* disaster), and was taken up into space by a conventional rocket instead.

Big Bang answers

Three very sensitive instruments on board Spitzer allow it to observe the infrared spectrum, something that Earth-based telescopes are handicapped in doing because of interference from the planet's atmosphere. Spitzer is probably second only to Hubble in terms of scientific significance, and public recognition, thanks to some of the spectacular images it has sent back. Among the pictures it has captured are dust clouds in the process of forming a planet, distant galaxies and even planets in other solar systems. Astronomers also believe that it has captured the light of the first stars ever formed after the Big Bang gave birth to the universe.

Although Spitzer is in orbit around the Earth, it is gradually drifting away from the planet. Eventually, it will become so distant that all contact will be lost. Spitzer was designed to have had a minimum active timeframe of 2.5 years. It has now achieved this, with an extra five years or so now envisaged before its useful life is over.

SPECIFICATIONS

Country: USA
Year launched: 2003
Weight: 2090lb (950kg)
Distance from Earth (current): 26 million miles (42 million km)
Telescope size: 2ft 7in (0.85m)
Cost: $800 million

THE BIGGEST SPACE STATION

INTERNATIONAL SPACE STATION

The International Space Station truly lives up to its name as a cooperative effort between many countries to maintain a continuous human presence in space. Although fully functioning at the moment, it is still being built. This means the largest manmade object in space will gradually get bigger still.

Space stations are usually the stuff of science fiction. But they've also been science fact since 1971, when Russia launched its Salyut 1 station. The International Space Station is currently the only manned station in orbit around the Earth, and therefore the largest human space machine. This US-conceived project is a genuine global effort with involvement from Russia, Japan, Canada, and Brazil, plus the countries of the European Space Agency.

Space jigsaw

Because of its modular construction, different components can gradually be added on to the ISS. The first piece of the jigsaw—a cargo module—was launched in 1998, two other sections having to be added before the first crew could join. This happened in 2000.

The ISS was due to be completed by 2005, but the grounding of Space Shuttle upset this schedule. It is now conceived that the station will be complete by 2010, by which time it will hold a crew of six (current capacity is three). Extra laboratories will allow the ISS to expand its research potential as well. The most noticeable features of the station are its huge solar panels, which provide all the power for its various functions, including life support.

Famous just for being itself, the ISS also made the headlines when it became the venue for the first space wedding. A cosmonaut on the station, Yuri Malenchenko, married Ekaterina Dmitriev in 2003. His bride, though, was in Texas at the time. The ISS has also been the "holiday" location for three space tourists.

SPECIFICATIONS

Country: Multinational
Year built: 1998–2010 (projected)
Dimensions (current): 146ft (44.5m) long; 239ft 6in (73m) wide
Weight (current): 202 tons (183,300kg)
Distance from Earth (current): 26 million miles (42 million km)
Cost: $100 billion (projected)

LEFT: The modular construction of the International Space Station can clearly be seen in this illustration from above. There's still more to be added.

THE LARGEST COMMUNICATIONS SATELLITE

IPSTAR-1

Modern communication—the ability to transmit anything anywhere in the world almost instantly—would be impossible without the network of communications satellites that now surround the Earth. First and foremost of these now is iPSTAR-1, the heaviest commercial satellite ever.

At 14,340lb (6505kg) the iPSTAR-1 communications satellite, also known as Thaicom 4, weighed more than any previous commercial satellite when launched by the European Space Agency's Ariane rocket in 2005 and, as yet, nothing else has been put in orbit that matches it.

Twenty times greater capacity

This geostationary satellite, which sits over Indonesia, was designed for voice, video, and broadband communications, under the auspices of Shin Satellite plc for 14 countries in Asia, Australia, and India. With seven onboard antennas and a transmit/receive capacity about 20 times greater than a conventional communications satellite, iPSTAR-1's stated purpose was to bring broadband technology (high-speed Internet services) to areas where it was either too expensive or too difficult to provide them before.

Its advanced technology meant it was able to provide Internet services operating at twice the speed of any of its competitors.

To make full use of iPSTAR's advanced capabilities, it requires 18 Earth station "gateways." These alone cost $20 million, just a small portion of the $400 million that was required to build iPSTAR. They are located in a variety of different world locations too, including Delhi and Bombay in India, Beijing and Shanghai in China, Cambodia, Tokyo, Taipei, Bangkok, Seoul, the Philippines, Jakarta, Hanoi, and Kuala Lumpur, along with Auckland, in New Zealand. The most remote locations are at Broken Hill and Kalgoorlie in Australia.

It is planned that iPSTAR-1 will stay in service until around 2017, by which time new advances in technology should have rendered it obsolete anyway.

SPECIFICATIONS

Country: Thailand
Year launched: 2005
Dimensions: 33ft (10m) long; 85ft 6in (26m) wide
Weight: 14,340lb (6505kg)
Distance from Earth: 22 miles (36km)
Cost: $400 million

BELOW: Large dishes mounted on iPSTAR-1 provide communications between the satellite and the ground stations, while power for everything comes from the sun via the even bigger solar panels.

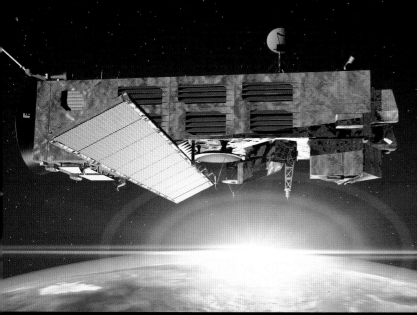

ABOVE AND RIGHT: ENVISAT pictured during its painstaking construction on Earth, mounted on a moveable platform, and an illustration of how it looks in space with solar panels unfolded.

THE LARGEST EARTH OBSERVATION SATELLITE

ENVISAT
(ENVIRONMENTAL SATELLITE)

One of the best places to observe Earth's environment is from outside it. The European Space Agency's ENVISAT satellite does just that, monitoring the planet using an array of 10 different instruments.

Put into orbit in early 2002, ENVISAT looks down upon the Earth from a distance of 491 miles (790km). It takes a 101-minute journey around the globe at an inclination of 90 degrees to the equator, and encompassing both poles. This is the optimum path for "planet watching," giving the satellite the best viewpoint of both the globe and its environment.

Packed with technology

ENVISAT is the largest Earth-observation satellite ever built, and it is unlikely anything comparable of this size will ever be launched again. Its impressive size partly comes from the number of instruments it carries. Because its role is such a multifaceted one, involving looking at land, water, ice, and atmosphere, it is equipped with 10 different

monitoring tools. These include a radar that can detect variances in height down to a submillimeter, devices for measuring the temperature of the sea's surface as well as the amount of ice on it, a radiometer for measuring atmospheric water vapor, and, perhaps most significant of all in these days of environmental concern, an ozone monitor. It's also capable of capturing some pretty stunning photographs.

One of its more recent—and more amazing—uses was to monitor a huge crack that appeared in the Earth's surface in Ethiopia over three weeks in 2005. ENVISAT was able to measure the fissure, which was 26ft (8m) wide and determine that it stretched for over 37.3 miles (60km), something it would have taken far longer to realize without the use of the environmental satellite.

THE LARGEST REUSABLE SPACECRAFT

SPACE SHUTTLE

NASA's Space Shuttle is by far the most famous (real) spacecraft of all time, a technical tour de force that goes into space like a conventional rocket, but lands like an aircraft. However, despite its practicality, the shuttle program hasn't been without its problems.

As space mega machines go, the American Space Shuttle takes some beating. It was the first orbital vehicle to be reusable, and the only winged vehicle capable of going into space and returning again. It can carry up to eight astronauts, take extremely large payloads in its cargo bay and also recover items from space. Nothing else comes close to the sheer versatility of the Space Shuttle.

Conceived during the 1970s, there have been six shuttles in total, although the first (named *Enterprise* after a campaign by *Star Trek* fans) was simply a test vehicle and never went into space. The other five (*Challenger*, *Columbia*, *Discovery*, *Atlantis*, and *Endeavor*) have all been launched beyond Earth's atmosphere. The first takeoff was on April 12, 1981, by *Columbia*, an event that was witnessed on TV by millions.

To obtain orbit, the Space Shuttle launches on top of an external fuel tank with booster rockets on either side. Once the boosters have fallen away, the fuel tank then supplies the Space Shuttle's own engines until it, too, is detached. That leaves the shuttle alone once it reaches space. Upon re-entry into Earth's atmosphere, the craft just glides back to base, using no power whatsoever.

The shuttle has revolutionized space travel, but it has also highlighted just how dangerous it still is too. Two vehicles, *Columbia* and *Challenger*, have been destroyed in service, resulting in the loss of all crew.

SPECIFICATIONS

Country: USA	
Year launched: 1981	
Dimensions: 122ft (37m) long; 78ft (24m) wide	
Weight (empty): 151,205lb (68,586kg)	
Payload: 55,250lb (25,061kg)	
Liftoff thrust: 3.076 million kgf	
Cost: $174 billion (projected, by 2010)	

LEFT AND ABOVE: As familiar and famous as the Space Shuttle is now, its reusable nature—taking off the same way an ordinary spacecraft does, but then landing like a conventional aircraft (albeit a non-powered glider) was radical when it was introduced.

SPACE SHUTTLE CRAWLER

The Space Shuttle is extraordinary in its own right. However, mention must be made of the way it gets to the launch site. It travels there on the Crawler-Transporter, the largest nonengineering tracked vehicle around.

SPECIFICATIONS

Country: USA
Year built: 1967
Dimensions: 131ft (40m) long; 114ft (35m) wide
Weight: 2,976 tons (2,700,000kg)
Power: 2750bhp (2050kW)
Maximum speed: 2mph (3km/h)
Cost: $14 million

LEFT: Fast as the shuttle may be, the first part of any space shuttle trip requires one of these with a top speed of 1mph (1.6km/h).

Only the German Bagger 288 excavator has bigger tracks than the two Crawler-Transporters (nicknamed Hans and Fritz) used to carry the Space Shuttle (and its ancestor rockets) from its Vehicle Assembly Building at the Kennedy Space Center in Florida out to the launchpad. The distance is 3.5 miles (5.6km) but with a top speed of 1mph (1.6km/h) when laden—and only 2mph (3km/h) when returning unburdened—a crawler is hardly quick. Typically, a Space Shuttle will take between three and five hours to reach the pad. Any faster, and the craft would be in danger of toppling over, although the crawlers have a tilting platform to help prevent this. Because such vast vehicles can't be easily turned around, they have a cab on each end.

Slow 'n' thirsty

Despite the snail-like speed, the crawlers are immensely powerful. Two 2750hp (2050kW) engines drive the four generators and 16 traction motors that power the eight tracked sections (each pair the size of a Greyhound bus), two of which are in each corner of the crawler. However, it's a thirsty machine with the average fuel consumption being 150 gallons per mile (350 liters/km). To accommodate this, the tank on a crawler holds 5000 gallons (19,000 liters) of fuel.

The Crawler-Transporters have been in operation since the Saturn V days, and will outlast the Space Shuttle and used for the next generation of NASA spacecraft.

THE LARGEST COMMERCIAL SPACECRAFT

SPACESHIPONE

Prior to the twenty-first century, space was the preserve only of the richest nations that could afford the immense costs associated with travel into space. But by 2004 this was no longer the case, when SpaceShipOne (SS1) became the first privately funded spacecraft.

On October 4, 2004 (coincidentally the forty-seventh anniversary of the Sputnik launch) the space plane SS1 scooped the coveted Ansari X prize by becoming the first nongovernment funded reusable manned spacecraft to go into space twice within two weeks.

Undoubtedly, the $10-million award money was welcome, although SS1 had cost $25 million to develop (a minuscule amount compared to most programs). But no doubt of far more significance to the Tier One team who built SS1 was that they had managed to go where nobody else in a private craft had gone before.

Piggyback into space

SS1 may only have entered the lower reaches of designated space, 62 miles (100km) up, but that was still enough to officially make it a spacecraft, albeit one actually registered as a glider, since most of its flight was not powered. The SS1 wasn't launched like the Space Shuttle, but instead "piggybacked" up to 8.7 miles (14km) using a White Knight aircraft. The SS1 then detached and used its own rocket to reach space, achieving a speed of Mach 3 in the process. It came back down to Earth simply by gliding, albeit with its wings folded up, operating like a huge shuttlecock.

SS1 has retired now, and can be found on display at the Smithsonian Air and Space Museum in Washington, D.C. However, its successor (which flies in the same manner) is currently in development, with finance by Sir Richard's Branson's Virgin Group. Its aim is to start space flights carrying passengers from 2008.

SPECIFICATIONS

Country: USA
Year built: 2003
Dimensions: 16ft 6in (5m) long; 16ft 6 in (5m) wide
Weight (loaded): 7937 lb (3600kg)
Speed: 2186mph (Mach 3.09/3518 km/h)
Rocket burn time: 87 seconds
Cost: $25 million

ABOVE AND BELOW: SpaceShipOne started its journey into space slung underneath a White Night aircraft, and only used its own rocket once it has detached at a height of 8.7 miles (14km).

LEFT AND BELOW: In orbit around the red planet, the MRO's current mission is to gather information on Mars, but it will eventually change role to become a control and communications point for future spacecraft from Earth.

THE LARGEST MARS PROBE

MARS RECONNAISSANCE ORBITER

The Mars Reconnaissance Orbiter (MRO) is the largest and latest of probes to be sent out to orbit the fourth planet from the Sun. Its aim is to collect data and smooth the way for any future missions to the Red Planet.

When the Mars Reconnaissance Orbiter achieved orbit around Mars in March 2006, after eight months of travel, it brought the number of spacecraft studying Mars to six, the largest for any planet ever before. However, the MRO is so advanced it could almost render the other probes redundant. In fact, its systems will be able to pass more data back to Earth than all the other Mars missions combined.

Martian mapmaking

Beginning operations at the end of 2006, one of the MRO's primary objectives is to map the Martian landscape in unprecedented detail using a high-definition camera, to aid scientists in finding suitable landing sites for future land vehicles. In addition, it will study the climate, weather, atmosphere and geology of the planet, using the array of eight scientific and engineering instruments on board. It is envisaged that this should take two years.

However, once these operations are over, the MRO will switch roles to become a communication and navigation hub for other craft visiting Mars. Its most prominent piece of equipment is the 10ft (3m) antenna mounted above its large solar panels. This is the most sophisticated telecommunications device ever sent into deep space, and should ensure that future Mars explorers are able to send and transmit messages to and from Earth easily and quickly.

SPECIFICATIONS

Country: USA
Year launched: 2005
Dimensions: 22ft (7m) long; 44ft (13m) wide
Weight: 4806lb (2180kg)
Distance above Mars: Approximately 160–200 miles (255–320km)
Cost: $720 million

THE LARGEST MOBILE VEHICLE TO LAND ON MARS

MARS EXPLORATION ROVERS

Long-distance telescopes and satellites aren't the only devices carrying out the exploration of Mars. Although a manned visit to the Red Planet is some way off, robot vehicles have made landfall and continue to investigate its surface.

TOP AND ABOVE: The MERs face a tough life, as Mars is inhospitable in terrain and environment. The two vehicles have already lasted much longer than expected.

It is fantastical to realize that human-designed robotic vehicles haven't just landed on Mars, but are still traveling around on it under human control. Even just getting to the far distant planet is more happenstance than design, as the loss of several past probes has proved. Yet the two NASA Mars Exploration Rovers (MERs) are currently millions of miles from home, and are operated by "drivers" back on Earth. They have been incredibly successful in their research and survival, so much so that their working lives have been extended.

MERs on Mars

The two MERs are known as *Spirit* and *Opportunity*. Although small in Earth terms, these rugged, six-wheeled vehicles are still the largest mobile craft to traverse the Martian landscape. They landed in January 2005 (on different sides of the globe to each other) with their primary brief to collect geology data for the next 90 days. So harsh is the Martian environment that the MERs were not expected to last long past this. However, they were both still "alive" well into 2006, thanks to their robust design.

The solar-powered Rovers have motors on all six of their wheels, with the front and rear pairs responsible for steering. Unusually, the wheels can spin independently to dig into the terrain as well. There are 18 cameras deployed between the two craft, which have sent back some fascinating images. For example, the images have helped prove that water once flowed on Mars, something that was only suspected before.

THE LARGEST "GUN" EVER USED FOR LAUNCHING SPACECRAFT

HIGH ALTITUDE RESEARCH PROJECT

The High Altitude Research Project (HARP for short) was a fascinating "what might have been" idea for launching items into orbit using a big gun. In fact, this space cannon did actually manage to reach space with one of its projectiles.

BELOW: Will a HARP successor launch a satellite into space? The original proved its potential by shooting a small object beyond Earth's atmosphere.

A space cannon is the stuff of Jules Verne. It was he who popularized the idea of getting objects beyond the Earth's atmosphere by firing them from a gun, in his 1865 book *From the Earth to the Moon*. However, during the early days of space travel, Canadian scientist Gerald Bull seriously took up his concept and established the High Altitude Research Project on the island of Barbados in the 1960s to try and do just this.

Supergun

With finance from both the Canadian and American governments, Bull used a 16in (41cm) old battleship gun (at the time the largest artillery item in the US arsenal) to fire small missile-shaped objects known as Marlets into the sky. The ultimate aim of the project was to develop a system for launching satellites without the need for rockets. By the time the Martlet left the 16m (52.5ft) long barrel, it would be traveling at a speed of around 0.9 miles (1.5km) per second, carrying a payload of chaff, chemical smoke, or meteorological balloons fitted with a tracking system.

Testing

There were over 200 tests between 1962 and 1965, and each one resulted in a huge explosion that could be heard all over Barbados. Most launches managed to achieve a height of around 50 miles (80km). In 1966, however, 111 miles (179km) was reached, which was well beyond the officially recognized "space boundary" of 62 miles (100km).

HARP came to an end in 1967, but tests continue today with other space cannons.

SPECIFICATIONS

Country: USA and Canada
Year built: 1962
Dimensions: 52ft 6in (16m) long; 16in (0.41m) wide
Weight: N/A
Maximum distance reached: 111 miles (179km)
Cost: Approximately $3 million funding for 1964

7 OTHER MEGA MACHINES

We live in a world full of machines. We have done for centuries of course. But over the last 50 years or so, the march of mechanization has been relentless. Take a look around you, at life today. The majority of the modern things we now take for granted would have been totally alien to our grandparents. This final chapter looks at some of the greater ones—and some of the more offbeat examples—from the past, present, and, just maybe, the future.

It was the steam engine that started it all. Using steam for power had been understood since the first century, but it wasn't until the 1700s that the first practical ones were built, which actually worked rather than exploded. Machines of all types started to become more complex and powerful than those that operated by human, animal, wind, or water force alone, and with this development came an increase in size and imagination.

By the beginning of the nineteenth century, the groundwork for the modern age was set—a powered road vehicle had been built, as had a steamboat and a railroad locomotive. However, the greatest machines of this era were those static steam engines used to

LEFT: Some steam engines were epic: This Prescott pump is 62ft (18.9m) tall and weighs over 800 tons (813,000kg).

ABOVE: It may not seem a conventional machine but beneath the stonework, London's Tower Bridge is just a huge lifting device.

provide motive effort for other devices. Unhindered by the need to be mobile, and thus unconfined by the dimensions of anything to pull or push around, some towered as high as a multistorey building. Thankfully, a few are preserved today in operational state. The world's largest working steam engine, a triple expansion water pumping design by Sir William Prescott, can be found in London besides the River Thames. It's a monumental and awe-inspiring piece of work, especially when it is in motion, oozing steam and atmosphere.

Machinery went everywhere. It formed the basis for major structures, one of the best known of which is Tower Bridge in London, opened in 1894. Maybe it's difficult to think of a building—and a much-loved one at that—as one giant machine. But that's exactly what this London landmark is, a bascule (lifting) bridge where size and design were dictated by the mechanisms inside.

Whatever the nineteenth century pioneered, the twentieth century refined. One of the largest pre-World War II engineering projects was the 1930s Hoover Dam on the Colorado River in the Western United States. A machine though? Well, yes. For, effectively, a dam is a giant electrical generating device, converting the might of the water behind it into a more usable form of power. The Hoover Dam was construction of an epic scale for its time, and rightly remains world famous despite being since surpassed in size.

The future promises bold new inventions. In California, 2008 will see the world's largest laser at the National Ignition Facility. Built for research purposes, it will have 192 beams, and produce an estimated 500 trillion watts of power, about a thousand times the electrical generating power of the USA. Cost so far is about $2.25 billion and the laser, plus associated components, will be the size of a sport stadium. Its target, however, is the size of a pencil eraser. Now that's quite some mega machine…

Slightly further away—in all senses—is the space elevator. And yes, it is as it sounds, a 62,000 mile (100,000km) physical link lift between the Earth and a satellite. Theoretical maybe, but it is seriously being looked at. Impossible? Perhaps … but that's probably what our ancestors would have said about the machines we take for granted today.

ABOVE AND RIGHT: Still magnificent today, the Hoover Dam generates a massive amount of electricity from the Colorado River.

THE LARGEST SUPERCOMPUTER

NASA "COLUMBIA" SYSTEM

There are several different machines competing for the title of "The world's largest supercomputer," their claims being measured in sheer size, processing power, or other factors. However, one of the most impressive, and biggest, is definitely NASA's recent "Columbia" system.

SPECIFICATIONS

Country: USA
Year built: 2004
Operating system: LINUX
Processing power: 10,240 processors of 1.5ghz each
Storage: 440 terabytes with 10 petabytes for archive
Cost: Approximately $45 million

BELOW: Pictures of NASA's Columbia computer system are less exciting than the operations the machine can do!

N amed in honor of the crew of the Space Shuttle *Columbia*, destroyed in service the year before its electronic namesake was constructed, NASA's "Columbia" supercomputer was installed at the administration's Advanced Supercomputing Facility near Mountain View, California, in 2004.

Definitely no home computer

Built in just four months by Silicon Graphics, Columbia is capable of a bewildering 51.87 billion "floating point" calculations per second. To put that into perspective, an average home computer can manage about 2 million calculations per second. But that will only have one processor. Columbia has 20 nodes, each one of which contains 512 Intel processors, making a total of 10,240. Put far too simply, it is effectively 10,240 "ordinary" computers all linked together to do the same job. However, each node can be separated to work on different projects if required, as even a single one is extremely powerful in its own right.

The introduction of Columbia gave NASA 10 times more computing power than it had ever had before, and all in one place as well. Some of the projects that the supercomputer has been involved in include space exploration, global-warming research, and aerospace engineering. In fact, pretty much anything complicated that NASA scientists and engineers need an answer to tends to go to Columbia these days, with projects that would have once taken weeks now being done in a fraction of the time.

However, amazing as Columbia may be in what it does, it's not exactly fascinating to look at. That is, unless you get excited by lots of big grey boxes in a very sterile large room, deep within a government research facility!

THE LARGEST REVOLVING CRANE

YANTAI RAFFLES SHIPYARD CRANE, CHINA

It's rather difficult to miss a structure that is over 443ft (135m) high, can lift 2204 tons (2,000,000kg), and is painted bright red and white. This is why the world's largest land-based revolving pedestal crane at the Yantai Raffles shipyard in China has become something of a local landmark, visible from miles around.

The Yantai Raffles shipyard is the only shipyard to be owned and managed by a foreign concern. One of its specialties is in the construction of oil and gas equipment such as offshore drilling rigs—some of the tallest structures to be found at sea. Such huge construction projects call for big equipment to help build them, and when it comes to revolving pedestal cranes, nothing comes larger than the mega machine that Yantai Raffles uses to build other mega machines.

Two in one

Usually just referred to as the "2000 ton crane," due to its lifting abilities, the Raffles crane's main tower is made of concrete and rises to 131ft (40m) high, with the steel gantry mounted on top. And it's actually two lifting devices in one. The main hooks have a 2204 ton (2,000,000kg) potential but mounted above this is a smaller mechanism capable of managing a huge 220 tons (200,000kg). The crane can reach out as far as 279ft (85m) and has a maximum lifting height of 443ft (135m). These are impressive figures for any piece of heavy lifting equipment

The crane's size means that it towers convincingly above the biggest rig the yard has ever built, with the high-level operator's station around 44ft (13m) higher than the deck of any semisubmersible drilling platform currently in operation. It is large enough for practically any heavy-lifting job.

SPECIFICATIONS	
Country: China	
Year built: 2001	
Height: main tower: 131ft (40m); gantry: approximately 443ft (135m)	
Reach: 279ft (85m)	
Maximum capacity: 42204 tons (2,000,000kg)	
Cost: N/A	

ABOVE AND BELOW: Even if it wasn't bright red and white, the Yantai Raffles crane—seen here lifting a ship—would stand out due to its size.

THE LARGEST GAS TURBINE JET

GENERAL ELECTRIC GE90-115B GAS TURBINE JET ENGINE

A jet engine as a work of art? Yes, if it's General Electric's GE90. In 2004, a fan blade from one was acquired by New York's Museum of Modern Art to put on display because it was regarded as such a beautiful piece of design work. The rest of the engine is pretty special, too, through being the largest and most powerful gas turbine in existence.

ABOVE: Comparison with a man illustrates just how big and complicated the GE90-115B jet is. Just one of the black-finished, curved blades of the front fan was deemed an art form by NYC's Museum of Modern Art.

Even if they've never visited NYC's Museum of Modern Art, many people will already be familiar with the GE90-115B turbine, even if they don't realize it. For the GE90 is the main engine choice for the Boeing 777 civil airliner, in service all over the world.

Guinness record holder

Introduced in 1995, and only available on 777s, the latest 115-B variant of the GE90 has its own entry in *The Guinness Book of Records* because it is so large and powerful, with a front fan diameter of 128in (325cm). The curved design is unique, and the black blades —one of its most distinctive features—come from its composite material. The carbon-fiber polymeric construction is far lighter than the traditional titanium used on jet fans, and is able to help deliver a tremendous amount of thrust. For comparison purposes, one jet engine of a Boeing 747 can put out 65,000lbf (289kN) of thrust. The GE90 115-B has managed 127,900lbf (569kN).

Physically, the whole engine is so huge that it's bigger than the fuselage on a Boeing 737 (11ft/3.4m). And if a replacement engine has to be flown anywhere, it requires an ultra-large plane, like an Antonov An-124 (see page 176), to carry it.

SPECIFICATIONS

Country: USA	
Year built from: 1995	
Dimensions: 24ft (7.3m) long; 11ft (3.43m) diameter	
Weight: 9 tons (8282.6kg)	
Maximum thrust: 127,900lbf (569kN)	
Number of fan blades: 22	
Cost: N/A	

THE LARGEST AND MOST POWERFUL DIESEL ENGINE

WARTSILA -SULZER RTA96-C DIESEL ENGINES

Forget about using this diesel engine in a car, truck, or train. The world's largest and most powerful diesel engine is about the size of a house and weighs over 2535 tons (2,300,000kg). It is used primarily for powering the biggest container ships in the world.

SPECIFICATIONS

Country: Japan

Year built from: 1994

Dimensions:
85ft (26m) long;
44ft (13.5m) high

Weight: 2535 tons
(2,300,000kg)

Power: 108,920hp
(81,221.6kW)

Number of cylinders:
Up to 14

Cost: N/A

ABOVE: An RTA96-C during construction; the gigantic crankshaft moves the pistons up and down.

Not many diesel engines have flights of steps installed so that mechanics and engineers can reach their parts. But at almost 85ft (26m) in length and 43ft (13m) tall, not many diesel engines are like Wartsila-Sulzer's RTA96-C series. Available in 6- through to 14-cylinder versions, these turbocharged, very tough mechanical monsters are the biggest reciprocating engines in the world, with the ultimate 14-cylinder version putting out a whopping 108,920hp (81,221.6kW). However, with container ships growing ever greater in size, what powers them also has to grow to meet these increasing requirements, especially as many companies prefer the simplicity of a single engine/single propeller setup within their vessels.

The power of 3747 Rolls-Royces!

To compare the 14-cylinder model to an "ordinary" engine is like contrasting a skyscraper with an outhouse. The current Rolls-Royce Phantom motorcar has what is regarded as a quite substantial powerplant of $415in^3$ (6.8 liters). The capacity of the RTA96-C is $1,556,002in^3$ (25,480 liters), which represents 3747 Phantoms all working together! All the RTA96-C types are built to run on cheap, low-grade fuel but, despite this, they're still far from cheap to run, with fuel consumption at around 1660 gallons (7,546 liters) of diesel fuel per hour on the 14-cylinder example. And that's at its most efficient setting!

THE LARGEST TELEVISION

SONY POWER TRON TV

Televisions are just getting bigger and bigger. Recent innovations in liquid crystal display (LCD) technology have meant larger and flatter screens in our homes than ever before. But the home system of the future will still have some way to go to beat the world's most substantial TV screen, set up near Tokyo, Japan.

ABOVE: With a screen this big, it's difficult not to get a good view. However, the equivalent remote control must be difficult to handle.

There are two main players in the contest to be called the world's largest TV. One is the Diamond Vision display, built by Mitsubishi at the Hong Kong Jockey Club, which is as long as a Jumbo Jet—widescreen TV indeed. It measures 70.4m (231ft) across, and is used to show three different views of a race at once. However, in height, it is only 26ft (8m) tall, which means it can't quite compare to the Sony Power Tron installation in Japan, that was as tall as an eight-storey building.

International showcase

Although giant Power Tron screens have seen much use at major events—one at which they usually feature is New Year in Times Square, New York City—none has surpassed the one that was unveiled in March 1985 in Tsukuba near Tokyo in Japan. Erected as part of the International Exposition that was being held there, it measured 80ft (24.3m) high by 150ft (46m) across and showed specially made videos and artworks.

Because it stood outside and needed to be seen against daylight, Sony used large fluorescent tubes—like office lights—to boost the picture. However, its pixel resolution, of 378 vertical by 400 horizontal, left a little to be desired in picture clarity. By contrast, the newer, more advanced Mitsubishi Diamond Vision LCD rival has a pixel count of 400 x 3520.

SMIT DEEP-SEA SAW

In December 2002, the Norwegian MV *Tricolor* vehicle carrier capsized on its side in shallow water in the English Channel after a collision. The next night, another ship struck the wreck, and in subsequent weeks, more vessels came to grief. It was obvious the 22,046 ton (20,000,000kg) *Tricolor* needed to be salvaged, but how?

ABOVE AND BELOW: A similar saw was used in 2000 to recover the sunken Russian submarine *Kursk*, by cutting away its damaged bow.

The answer was to bring in the world's largest and toughest saw, which was the only way possible way of shifting the 600ft (183m) by 100ft (30.5m) obstacle, plus its cargo of 2871 cars.

In July 2003, Netherlands salvage firm Smit International started work on cutting up the wreck using a grit-encrusted hard-steel cutting wire strung out at high tension between two specially erected self-elevating platforms either side of the ship. Winches on each platform moved the abrasive wire back and forth—the same way a handsaw works—to cut the ship into pieces that could be more easily moved.

Starting from below the *Tricolor*, the wire simply oscillated, as the jacks on the platforms pushed both of them upward simultaneously until a 105ft (32m) deep section of the ship—and the vehicles inside—was completely severed. It was actually that simple, although each slice did take around 50 hours.

Cut and carry

Eventually, the entire ship was sawn into nine 3306 ton (3,000,000kg) pieces, with one wire used for each cut. The chunk was then lifted onto a huge semisubmersible barge by floating cranes and removed. This part of the salvage operation was actually the more involved, and it wasn't until almost September 2004—a year and nine months after the *Tricolor* sunk—that the wreckage was finally cleared. The cost of removing the ship ran into millions of dollars and 2871 premium new cars were destroyed in the process.

SPECIFICATIONS

Country: Netherlands
Year: 2003–04
Saw wire length: 230ft (70m), plus 131ft (40m) each end wound around winch drums
Leg length of jacks for platforms: 189ft (57.5m)
Maximum jacking speed: 39ft (12m)
Power: 1102.3hp (822kW) from two engines
Cost: N/A

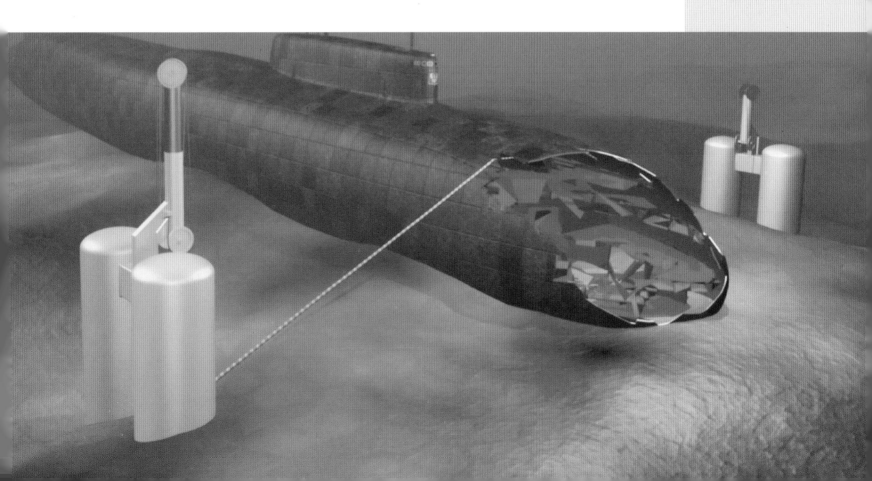

THE LARGEST MAGNET

NATIONAL HIGH MAGNETIC FIELD LABORATORY

As its name suggests, the NHMFL in Tallahassee, Florida, is rather interested in magnets. Especially very big, very powerful ones. In 2005, it unveiled the largest one on Earth, which just happens to be 420,000 times stronger than the pull of our own planet.

Get too close to the latest super magnet to be installed at Florida's State University institution, and you could lose anything metal you're carrying. The biggest magnet ever built is capable of pulling objects out of people's hands, or at least it would if anybody was allowed near enough for this to happen.

Magnetic camera

The magnet, which weighs 15 tons (13,608kg), rises to more than 16ft (5m) tall, and had been 13 years in development, is used for worthy purposes such as biotechnology, chemical, and scientific research. Applications include looking at why and how earthquakes occur, and how flu attacks the human body. It can also be used to take high-definition pictures of molecules and cells. But despite the mass of the magnet itself, the chamber into which objects are placed to be exposed to the magnetic field is a mere 4in (10.2cm) wide. Exposed to such a concentrated high magnetic force, some objects can start to morph or transform their shape and atomic makeup, which is fascinating for scientists.

An older device, built in 1999, has a pull of one million times the Earth's magnetic field and the total system weighs 35 tons (31,751.4kg) and stands 22ft (7m) tall. However, it is actually formed of two enormous magnets working together, neither of which is as large individually as the 2005 installation.

RIGHT: Magnets of this size and power don't look anything like a conventional version and you won't come across many household magnets that can also take high-definition pictures of molecules and cells!

SPECIFICATIONS
Country: USA
Year: 2005
Dimensions: 16ft (5m) tall
Weight: 15 tons (13,608kg)
Magnetic power: 19 tesla (420,000 times Earth's pull)
Cost: $16.5 million

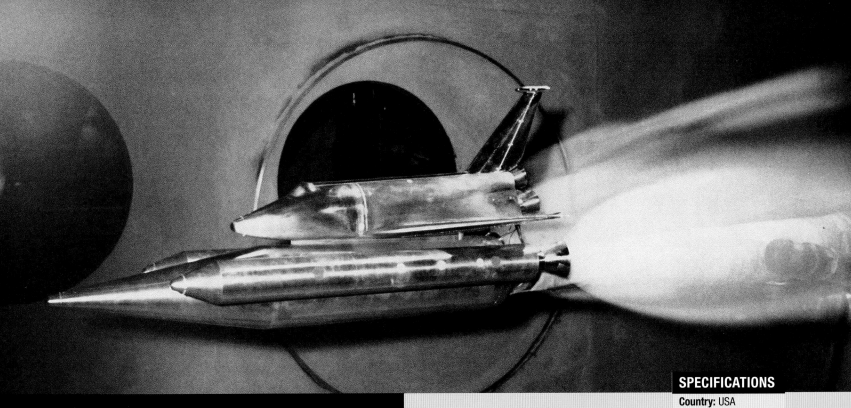

NASA/USAF NATIONAL FULL-SCALE AERODYNAMICS COMPLEX WIND TUNNEL

The Ames Research Center in California, operated by NASA, has 12 major wind tunnels, but the most famous of them is its ultralarge subsonic facility known as the National Full-Scale Aerodynamics Complex. As its name suggests, it is capable of testing real-size aircraft.

A s aircraft became more sophisticated and complex, from the 1940s onward, so wind tunnels started to proliferate as a way of allowing engineers to simulate flight parameters without having to build actual planes. One of the premier testing facilities to open around this time was the Ames Research Center. The center was founded in 1939, and by 1944—to support research in aerodynamics, structural dynamics, and acoustics—possessed the world's largest wind tunnel.

Superstructure

Known as the National Full-Scale Aerodynamics Complex, this enormous structure, characterized by its vast double doors, looks from the outside more like a conventional aircraft hanger than a high-tech engineering laboratory. The full tunnel measures over 1400ft (427m) long and 180ft (55m) tall, and can accommodate aircraft with wing spans of 100ft (30.5m) across. However, the area is split into two sections for test purposes. One is 80ft (24m) high and 120ft (37m) across. The other is slightly smaller at 40ft (12m) high and 80ft (24.3m) wide.

Its size calls for immense force to be created and pushed through the building. Six 22,500hp (16 778kW) engines do this, with each motor connected to a 15-bladed fan approximately the size of a four-storey building. Together these can create a wind velocity of up to 350mph (563km/h). Both the Apollo and Space Shuttle programs had some of their development programs at NFAC. The tunnel was closed by NASA in 2003, due to budgetary pressures, but the United States Air Force announced plans to take it over and reopen it in 2006.

ABOVE: An early space shuttle model with external tank pointed nose during testing in the wind tunnel.

SPECIFICATIONS

Country: USA	
Year built: 1944	
Dimensions: 1400ft (427m) long; 180ft (55m) high	
Power: 135,000hp (100,669kW) from six engines	
Maximum speed: 304 knots/350mph (563km/h)	
Cost: N/A	

THE LARGEST WIND TUNNEL, SKYDIVING TRAINING

BODYFLIGHT BEDFORD VERTICAL WIND TUNNEL

Fancy going skydiving without actually having to do anything as vaguely dangerous as jumping out of an aircraft with only a bit of fabric attached to you? No problem! For the world's largest vertical wind tunnel allows people to do just that, by creating such an amount of wind that those inside can float.

What would you do with a redundant, ex-military, 1950s wind tunnel 16ft (5m) in width and 26ft (8m) high? Well, British company Bodyflight Bedford decided to turn the one that they bought into a skydiving simulator, with the main fan mounted at the bottom of the chamber so that occupants of the chamber can effectively "fly" in midair, in what is known as "body flight."

Skydiving without a parachute

Body flight is a safe and easy way of learning the techniques of skydiving, such as rolls, turns, and other aerodynamics, as well as how to fly close to other skydivers. It's suitable for both beginners and professionals, with the latter often nicknamed "tunnel rats" if they visit a wind tunnel a lot.

The facility at Bedford in England can create wind speeds of over 160mph (257.5km/h) from its 16ft (5m) propeller, which is obviously protected by a safety grille to prevent any potentially unpleasant fan/customer interactions. The prop is so wide that the "air" fills the entire chamber with no calm pockets. One distinctive feature of the tunnel is that its walls are painted blue, which means that skydiving action sequences can be filmed there, with a realistic background added at a later style using a "blue-screen" technique.

BELOW: The huge propeller mounted at the bottom of the wind tunnel allows those inside to "fly," experiencing all the effects of genuine skydiving.

SPECIFICATIONS

Country: UK
Year built: 1950s, modified 2005
Dimensions: 16ft (5m) wide; 26ft (8m) high
Fan blade: 16ft (5m)
Speed: 160mph (257.5km/h) plus
Power: 4000hp (2983kW)
Cost: N/A

REPOWER 5M WIND TURBINE

Wind farms are becoming a common sight throughout the world as mankind searches for alternative ways of generating power without harming the environment or further diminishing dwindling fossil-fuel supplies. The largest and most powerful generator currently in production is the 5M, made by German company REpower.

RIGHT: The 5M during construction and towering above the landscape.

Suitable for mounting onshore or off (in the sea) the huge 5M turbine has become the new standard in wind-farm technology. While generating electricity from an air stream isn't a new idea, it is only in recent decades that large-scale sites, with dozens of towers, have started to appear around the world.

Superpower

Much less environmentally damaging than a conventional power station and, in the eyes of many, very graceful and beautiful to look at, one of the criticisms against wind farms is that the amount of power they produce isn't all that great compared to how much of a "footprint" they have. But that isn't the case with the 5M. Its maker, REpower, estimates that a farm with turbines of this size can easily rival the output of a traditional powerplant, with a single tower capable of generating 6705hp (5mW)—enough electricity to power around 4500 households. It was in 2004 that the first 5M was experimentally erected in Germany, but the success of the machine has now led to orders from all over the world.

Just the rotor on a 5M measures 413ft (126m) across, and weighs 132 tons (120,000kg), with the turbine nacelle 193ft (59m) tall. The diameter of the rotor is actually greater than the height of the tubular tower on the first 5M to be constructed, which rose 426ft 6in (120m) into the air.

SPECIFICATIONS

Country: Germany
Year built from: 2004
Tower size: 329/426ft 6in (100/120m) high onshore; 295ft (90m) tall offshore
Rotor diameter: 413ft (126m)
Speed: 6.9 to 12.1 revolutions per minute
Power generated: 6705hp (5000kW)
Cost: Varies on installation

THE LARGEST DAM

THREE GORGES DAM, CHINA

The largest hydroelectric plant in the world bridges the Yangtze River in China and, when complete, will be able to generate 24,406,602hp (18,200mW) of power, approximately three percent of the power that the nation consumes every year. The structure is more than five times the size of the Hoover Dam in the USA.

ABOVE: Seen here still under construction, the 1.4 mile (2309m) length of the Three Gorges dam makes it an amazing feat of engineering.

It might be made mainly of concrete, but the Three Gorges Dam in the Hubei province of China is still a machine because of what it does: Effectively, it's the biggest electricity generator on the planet. And as mega machines go, it's one of the more visually impressive, with a height of 607ft (185m) and a total length of 1.4 miles (2309m). The reservoir that has been created behind it stretches for 370 miles (600km). Although the dam itself was completed in 2006, all the equipment needed for it to realize its full power potential has yet to be installed, and it is envisaged that the plant won't be fully operational until 2009. However, when that happens, the Three Gorges will contain 26 turbines, and produce almost 8,046,132hp

(6000mW) more than the next largest hydroelectric plant, at Itaipu in Brazil/Paraguay.

LA times four

In total, the electricity created will be enough to power a city four times the size of Los Angeles, something it would take 18 typical coal power stations to do.

It was in 1993 that work got underway on the project, with the diversion of the Yangtze River, with the first generators online by 2003. But although the dam has brought some environmental benefits, critics have also pointed out that, to build it, 1200 towns and villages were submerged, with over a million people displaced.

SPECIFICATIONS

Country: China
Year built: 1993–2006
Tower size: 1.4 miles (2309m) long; 607ft (185m) high
Power generated: 24,406,602hp (18,200mW)
Annual generation: 315 PJ (84.7 TWh)
Cost: $25 billion (unofficially estimated at $100-billion)

THE LARGEST DOUBLE SWING BRIDGE

GEORGE P. COLEMAN BRIDGE, USA

When the world's largest double-swing span bridge (with two decks that revolve in the center) was constructed in 1952, it was intended to carry a maximum of 15,000 vehicles a day. By 1995, 27,000 were using it. So, a project was devised to make the George P. Coleman Bridge in Yorktown, Virginia, even bigger still.

Because it spans the York River, which allows access to several military installations around Yorktown, the Coleman Bridge, as it is known locally, was built with its roadways 90ft (27.5m) above the river. But that wasn't enough for some naval vessels, so it also had two central deck sections that could revolve around their supports to allow these bigger craft through.

Floating bridge

By 1995, though, with congestion caused by the ageing machinery and the US Highway 17 having to go from four lanes to two across the 3750ft (1143m) bridge, a decision was made to rebuild the structure, albeit wider. However, because blocking a major road was impractical for the length of time it would have taken to demolish the old bridge, then construct a new one, the new Coleman Bridge was built offsite, then floated downstream in six sections and mounted on the existing foundations. This was the first time such an engineering feat was attempted. Everything was accomplished in nine days, and now three times wider than it was before, up to 50,000 vehicles a day can be carried by the bridge.

One unusual feature of the Coleman Bridge is that its swing mechanisms also slightly lift and lower their spans, so that when they rotate, they don't end up hitting each other.

SPECIFICATIONS	
Country: USA	
Year built: 1952, rebuilt 1995	
Dimensions: 3750ft (1143m) long; 77ft (23.5m) wide	
Longest span: 500ft (152.4m)	
Weight: 5000 tons (4,535,923kg)	
Cost: $9 million originally; $76.8 million reconstruction	

BELOW:
The Coleman Bridge in swinging action, its two mammoth swiveling decks allowing a large Naval vessel to pass through unimpeded.

NEWPORT TRANSPORTER BRIDGE

Only eight transporter bridges exist worldwide, with the one near Newport in Wales, the largest example.

Because the banks of the River Usk here are so low but major ships still need to pass, two towers were built on either side, connected by a high-level platform that carries gondolas containing traffic and passengers across.

BELOW: As river crossings go, there can be few more unusual ways than the Newport Transporter Bridge, with its underslung car and passenger carrying gondola shuttling back and forth between banks.

Newport's transporter bridge is an anachronism, a relic from the early part of the twentieth century that rapidly became obsolete as car usage grew. However, it also a fascinating example of engineering eccentricity and, fortunately, is still in operation today as a tourist attraction and local landmark.

Ingenious arrangement

Built from 1902–06 by French engineer Ferdinand Arnodin, each tower of the bridge rises to 242ft (74m), with the beam in between them covering 592ft (181m). From the "railroad line" on this, a gondola is suspended that shuttles back and forth between each side of the river at a rate of 10ft (3m) per second. A cable connected to a motor house on the east bank electrically operates the system. It's an amazingly ingenious arrangement, but a lot of effort for something that is only able to carry six cars and 120 passengers in one go and takes five minutes for the trip, including loading and unloading.

Born again

Inefficiency was partly the reason for the closure of the bridge in 1985, but good sense, and financing, prevailed and in 1995 it reopened after renovation. A conventional bridge was built nearby in 2005, but the transporter bridge remains in operation for those who appreciate crossing rivers in a more interesting and novel way.

SPECIFICATIONS

Country:	UK
Year built:	1902–06
Dimensions:	645ft (196.6m) long; 108ft (33m) wide
Longest span:	594ft (181m)
Tower weight:	627 tons (568,986kg)
Gondolier speed:	7mph (11km/h)
Cost:	£98,124

ABOVE AND LEFT: Although the particle accelerator ring itself is small in circumference, the outer concrete tunnel housing is much more substantial.

SPECIFICATIONS

Country: European multinational
Year built: 1983–89
Main tunnel dimensions: 43.5 miles (26.67km) circumference; 12ft 6in (3.8m) diameter
Number of magnets: 4600
Detector size: 33–39ft (10–12m) high
Cost: Approximately £100 million

ABOVE AND LEFT: Although the particle accelerator ring itself is small in circumference, the outer concrete tunnel housing is much more substantial.

THE LARGEST PARTICLE ACCELERATOR

CERN'S LEP PARTICLE ACCELERATOR

A particle accelerator is a device that propels electrically charged subatomic particles to immense speeds using magnetic or electric fields, for the purposes of high-energy physics research. The largest one ever built was the Large Electron-Positron Collider (LEP) at the European research laboratory CERN.

The Large-Electron Positron Collider (LEP) certainly lived up to its name. Built as a giant ring, it had a circumference of 43.5 miles (27km) meaning it actually occupied two countries—France and Switzerland—due to the geographical location of the CERN multinational research facility that housed it. In size, it was similar to the Circle Line on the London Underground.

Engineering and science

CERN (European Organization for Nuclear Research) was established in the mid-1950s, but it wasn't until 1989 that the LEP was finished, after the biggest civil-engineering project in European history, to bore out the main ring plus other associated caverns. Such a huge continuous vacuum tunnel was needed so particles could reach almost the speed of light before colliding with other particles (either static or coming the other way), allowing scientists to study the results.

The ring was fitted with magnets throughout to keep particles in the center of the ring while being accelerated, together with four detectors —each the size of a large house—to measure energy, momentum, and charge, and other results when the electron and positron collide.

LEP was closed in 2000, but under construction in its place and using the same ring is the even more powerful Large Hadron Collider (LHC). This will take over as the world's largest particle accelerator and be able to create conditions similar to the Big Bang creation of the universe.

THE LARGEST LIFT BRIDGE

AERIAL BRIDGE, DULUTH

Originally built as a transporter bridge in 1905, the Aerial Bridge in Duluth, Minnesota, was converted into a vertical lift bridge 25 years after traffic outgrew its capabilities. Today, it is still the world's largest of the type, as well as the fastest.

BELOW: The Duluth Aerial Bridge, with its lower deck lifted to allow a passenger ship to travel underneath.

In 1870, a small canal was created near the port city of Duluth. One of the side-effects of this was the creation of an inhabited island, whose residents had no way of crossing the water, with both ferries and a swinging footbridge affected by the weather.

From transporter to lift

The solution was to build a transporter bridge. This was fine for a few years until it simply became unable to cope with the rapid growth around Duluth. A solution had to be found, but one that was able to still allow tall ships to use the canal.

Thus, in 1930, the transporter structure was reworked into a lifting bridge, with a deck that could be moved up and down as required. A new deck was fitted, with counterweights installed into the original towers to balance it. This is the setup that still remains in operation, lifting between 25 to 30 times a day during busy periods. When the main deck is lowered, it sits a mere 15ft (4.6m) above the water. After 55 seconds though (the time it takes to raise fully), the deck can be at 138ft (42m). Although obviously without any cars or people on it.

The bridge has become Duluth's main tourist attraction and it was listed as a national historic monument in 1973.

THE LARGEST BASCULE (LIFTING) BRIDGE

BROADWAY BRIDGE, PORTLAND

When it opened in 1913, Portland's imposing Broadway Bridge was the largest bascule (lifting) bridge on the planet. Others have since superseded it, but it still holds the record as the longest Rall-type bridge (where the counterweights and machinery are suspended in sheds above the main deck). And its complicated construction makes it visually fascinating too.

Portland drivers and pedestrians complain about how long it takes for the Broadway Bridge to lift itself. Other, newer bridges nearby can manage the task in about five to eight minutes, the Broadway Bridge takes about 20 minutes, or even longer.

ABOVE: The shade of red paint used on the Broadway Bridge is a common one on older steel—it helps disguise signs of rust!

Getting on, getting up

What they don't appreciate is that the bridge is heading toward its one-hudredth birthday, and is also a complex piece of machinery. While other bascule bridges have their counterweights (which balance out the raising spans) hidden in their piers, the Broadway has its sitting atop the steel framework that surrounds the roadway. These counterweights, made out of concrete, weigh 1,250 tons (1,133,981kg) each, and have to cope with "leaves" (the name for the very heavy lifting sections) that are 140ft (43m) in length and weight over 2000 tons each. That's a lot to ask of an old bridge! Especially one equipped with two motors of just 75hp (56kW) at each end (although this small amount of power is explained away by the gearing the power goes through, in addition to how effective those massive counterweights are). The Broadway Bridge operates about 25 times a month, and carries approximately 27,000 vehicles a day.

243

RIGHT: An operator sits in the "cab" on top of Robotsaurus's head, and this whole machine can be folded away into something the size of a truck trailer, for towing.

SPECIFICATIONS

Country: USA
Year built: 1988–89
Dimensions: 40ft (12m) high, but can extend up to 57ft (17.5m)
Weight: 29 tons (26,399kg)
Power: 500hp (373kW) from one twin-turbocharged diesel engine
Number of hydraulic pumps: 100
Cost: $2.2 million

THE LARGEST ROBOT

ROBOTSAURUS

It crushes cars. It bites airplanes. It breathes fire. And it's a very big robot with a very bad attitude. Fortunately though, Robotsaurus is purely for fun, a mechanized monster that tours the United States and Canada giving shows for entertainment.

Robotsaurus was inspired by the *Transformers* cartoon series of the 1980s, about robots that could transform from ordinary objects into fighting machines. Built at a cost of $2.2 million in 1988 and 1989, Robotsaurus travels like an ordinary truck trailer between shows, but once there, metamorphoses into the armored appliance that has enthralled so many over the years.

Fly-by-wire claws and teeth

The 40ft (12m) tall diesel-powered creation is "driven" by a pilot inside the head section, and has 10 tons (9072kg) of force behind his jaws, equipped with 12in (30.5cm) stainless-steel teeth, plus a flamethrower to soften things up a bit. Each claw has the force of 0.5 ton (443kg) too.

To perform its "act," Robotsaurus uses an electro-hydromechanical system, with the operator strapped inside linked to controls that mirror his own limb, hand, and feet motions. Thus if the pilot spreads his hand in a certain way, so does Robotsaurus. Without this fly-by-wire system, which carries electrical inputs to the hydraulic system, the human inside the machine would have had to operate up to 18 hydraulic levers simultaneously.

In addition to the more destructive components, such as the hot-air balloon burner that projects flame 20ft (6m) from Robotsaurus's mouth, there's also a great sound system too. Installed in the chest are six 18in (46cm) speakers powered by 10 car batteries, so Robotsaurus can roar, howl, and scream. Or even burp.

THE LARGEST ROLLERCOASTER

STEEL DRAGON 2000

BELOW: If you suffer from vertigo or simply don't like fast thrill rides, Steel Dragon definitely isn't the funfair attraction for you!

The enormous Steel Dragon 2000 rollercoaster in Japan is so big, it's actually been dubbed a "gigacoaster."

Taller than any of its rivals, it has the world's longest track as well. Just building it cost more than $50,000,000,

a massive investment that puts it on a financial par with many of the more "serious" machines in this book.

You have to feel a little sorry for the owners of the Millennium Force rollercoaster, completed in Ohio in May 2000. When it opened, it was the largest complete rollercoaster in the world. But it was only a few months before Steel Dragon 2000 popped up in August of the same year to steal its title.

Steel in more than name

With 2000 being the year of the Dragon in Japan, the naming of the amusement ride was entirely appropriate, especially as it also contained far more steel than any other previous 'coaster, as it needs to withstand earthquakes.

Because of the size of the first "lift hill," a complete train is pulled by two chains, one attached to the first half, the other to the bottom half. Having crested the summit, the train has a drop of 307ft (93.5m), which allows it to reach a maximum speed of 95mph (153km/h) before it encounters the rest of the ride's peaks and troughs.

Although Steel Dragon 2000 lost its crown as the world's tallest complete rollercoaster in 2003 to the Top Thrill Dragster in the USA, it is still the longest around, and holds the record for the tallest where the trains are pulled up its lift hill by the traditional chain system.

SPECIFICATIONS

Country: Japan
Year built: 2000
Dimensions:
318ft (97m) highest point; 8133ft/1.54 miles (2479m /2.5km) long
Maximum speed:
95mph (153km/h)
Number of cars in train: 6
Train capacity:
36 people
Cost: Over $50 million

LONDON EYE

The British Airways London Eye, also known as the Millennium Wheel, is one of the UK capital's newest landmarks, standing on the bank of the River Thames close to the Houses of Parliament. As the largest ferris wheel ever built, it gives tourists amazing views over the city and its many other familiar sights.

The end of the twentieth century saw many new projects instigated to mark the passing of the millennium. Probably the most high-profile and successful in the United Kingdom was the London Eye observation wheel. It took seven years to come to fruition, being officially opened by the British prime minister on New Year's Eve, 1999. With a height of 443ft (135m) it can be seen from all over the capital, and can let those riding in its cars see all over the capital, too.

Keep on going

When loading passengers—800 can ride at any one time—the wheel never stops revolving. But as it only travels at 0.6mph (0.9km/h), it's easy enough for passengers to walk on and off at the wide platforms at the bottom of the structure. A complete revolution takes around 30 minutes. However, because the Eye keeps turning, its cars notch up a huge 2,107,749 miles (3,392,000km) over the course of an average year. That's the equivalent of going to the moon and back 4.4 times! The pods turn within circular mounting rings fixed to the outside of the main frame, ensuring a 360-degree view.

Like that other great European "temporary" structure, Paris's Eiffel Tower, the Millennium Wheel was never intended to be permanent. It only had planning permission for five years originally, but such was its popularity—it carries 3.5 million people a year—that it has now become permanent.

LEFT: The tall London Eye can be glimpsed from all over the city, especially when illuminated at night. It's a mesmerizing sight.

SPECIFICATIONS

Country: UK

Year: 1998–99

Dimensions: 443ft (135m) high; wheel circumference 1392ft (424m)

Weight: 2314 tons (2,100,000kg)

Number of cars: 32

Passenger capacity: 800

Speed: 0.6mph (0.9km/h)

Cost: £75 million

ABOVE AND LEFT: Ride the London Eye on a clear day, and the view from the top can stretch for 25 miles (40km).

SPECIFICATIONS

Country: Canada (built), USA (operated)

Year built: 2006

Dimensions: 118ft (36m) long; 27ft 6in (8.4m) wide

Overall height with platform extended: 33ft (10m)

Weight: 110 tons (100,000kg)

Maximum speed: 10mph (16km/h)

Cost: N/A

THE LARGEST AIRCRAFT LOADER

BOEING 747 LCF CARGO LOADER

Used exclusively for transporting components for its 787 "Dreamliner" aircraft, the Boeing 747 Large Cargo Freighter is an astonishing machine in its own right, as its entire rear section, including the tail, is hinged to swing open sideways. However, what actually loads a 747 LCF is almost as incredible too.

Problem: You're the largest aircraft manufacturer around, and you've just converted three Jumbo Jets to be able to hold gigantic parts for a new type of big aircraft you're building. But how do you actually get the items into these oversized planes? Answer: You simply just build the world's largest cargo loader. In fact, why not make six?

Long and flat

Forget about all about the luggage and freight machines you might have seen being used at commercial airports. The 747 LCF loader makes these look like toys. This flatbed vehicle stretches for 118ft (36m) in length, and has 16 axles, all of which are steerable.

It is exclusively for use with the 747 LCF, having been built with the dimensions of the aircraft in mind. Driven by an operator in a cab mounted at the front righthand side of the machine, it can be aligned perfectly with a 747 LCF using electronic sensors, and has been constructed to be able to withstand—and lift to a height of 25ft 6in (7.7m)—787 parts, such as an entire section of fuselage or whole wings. Maximum capacity is 75 tons (68,000kg).

Thanks to its extreme length, this mega machine, with its 32 tires in total, is far from maneuverable, so it's probably somewhat fortunate that it only has a top speed of 10mph (16km/h)!

ABOVE AND LEFT: With a plane the size of a 747 LCF, it takes a "jumbo"-sized vehicle to load it with aviation equipment.

THE LARGEST GLOBE CLOCK

COLGATE CLOCK

If you're ever in the west side of Manhattan, New York, discover you've left your watch behind, and want to know the time, no need to ask someone. Just look across the Hudson River to New Jersey, where you should easily be able to make out the world's largest clock, on the former site of Colgate-Palmolive's headquarters.

SPECIFICATIONS

Country: USA
Year built: 1924
Dimensions: 54ft (16.5m) diameter; 1963.5ft² (598.5m²) surface area
Weight: N/A
Cost: N/A

At over 50ft (15.24m) in diameter, the Colgate Clock is twice the size of its more famous counterpart on the Big Ben tower at the Houses of Parliament in London. Looking out across the river and brightly illuminated at night, it was originally built as a novel promotional tool for the Colgate Company—the view from Manhattan ensuring it maximum publicity. Completion was in 1924, when it replaced another clock at the same spot that had been built for the firm's centenary in 1906. That timepiece had been the largest in the world, up to its removal and preservation in Indiana.

Electric timekeeper

The clock is operated by 28 high-voltage batteries, with the hour hand measuring 20ft (6m) long and the minute one 26ft (7.8m). When the Colgate factory and office was in operation on the site, the clock was kept accurate to one minute by checking it against the time from the US Naval Observatory in Washington.

Colgate-Palmolive left New Jersey in 1985. All its premises were demolished except for the clock, which had become a much-loved local landmark. Sitting in the middle of a vacant lot of prime real estate, its future is uncertain but hopefully it will be saved because of its novelty value.

RIGHT: Fully illuminated at night (unlike the real thing!), Eartha makes a fascinating sight inside its glass-walled building as it slowly turns. But the view gets a lot better inside.

SPECIFICATIONS

Country: USA
Year built: 1998
Dimensions:
41ft 6in (13m) diameter; 131ft (40m) circumference
Surface area: 2727.5ft² (831.4m²)
Weight: 6000lb (2721.5kg)
Cost: N/A

THE LARGEST REVOLVING GLOBE

EARTHA

The world's largest rotating globe is, of course, the world itself. But there's a smaller version of it, called Eartha, in Yarmouth, Maine, which is a 1:1,000,000 scale representation. Using satellite imagery, it gives the largest accurate representation of the globe as it currently is.

The vast majority of us will never have the opportunity to go into space. So the closest we're likely to get to seeing what Earth looks like from way up there is the highly detailed rotating model of the planet to be found at the headquarters of the Delorme mapping company on America's northeast coast. Built in 1998, Eartha entered *The Guinness Book of Records* the following year, after it was confirmed that it had surpassed the previous largest globe in Italy, which is 8ft (2.4m) smaller in diameter.

A light from within

Kept in an illuminated steel and glass building at the corporation's headquarters, and open to the public, Eartha's surface is fully 3D, complete with mountains and landforms. It is tilted at a 23.5-degree axis, like the Earth, and revolves every two minutes on a cantilevered arm in the same way as the real world, but, at 41ft 6in (12.7m) in diameter, is just a little bit tinier.

To showcase its mapping abilities, Delorme created an intricate database compiled from satellites, ocean data, relief information, and terrestrial sources such as roads and towns to make Eartha as correct as possible. Compiling everything took a whole year. The scale works out that 1in (2.54cm) on the model globe equates to 16 miles (25.7km) on the actual globe.

Another significant model globe in America is the 1935 Mapparium in Boston, Massachusetts, which is 30ft (9m) in diameter, and can be walked through and viewed from inside.

WHEATON STATION ESCALATOR, WASHINGTON

Escalators were invented at the end of the Victorian area, and have found widespread use everywhere in the intervening 100 years. However, it's in underground metro stations— where their ability to move a great number of travelers up and down levels very quickly— where they have become most widespread. And it's also where the world's longest examples can be found.

BELOW: The deep Washington metro system has some of the longest escalators around. It takes almost three minutes to ride this Wheaton Station one.

The five longest escalators in the Western hemisphere can all be found on subway (underground) transit systems in the USA. The fifth ranked is at Porter Square Station in Boston, but all the rest can be found on the Washington system, with the most impressive of them all at Wheaton Station.

Continuous span

Measuring 230ft (70m) long in a single uninterrupted span, it takes almost three minutes for a rider to travel the escalator in its entirety. However, despite this, the station, which was opened in 1990, is not the deepest on the Washington system. Those laurels go to Forest Glen, the next station down the line, which is so deep, 230ft (70m), that high-speed lifts have to be employed. Wheaton is a mere 196ft (60m) underground.

One of the problems that staff at Wheaton Station have to deal with every day is people ringing up to ask if the escalator really is as long as they've heard, just to satisfy their own curiosity!

The Ocean Park entertainment complex in Hong Kong also claims the longest escalator in the world, but although it stretches 745ft (224m) as it rises 377ft (115m), it isn't in a single continuous belt as the Wheaton one is.

SPECIFICATIONS

Country: USA
Year built: 1990
Dimensions: 230ft (70m) long
Cost: N/A

THE LEGACY PROJECT CAMERA

The Legacy Project was started in 2002 to document the transformation, in photographs, video, and recorded/written accounts, of the El Toro Marine Corps Air Station in Southern California into a large Metropolitan Park. One of its more unusual offshoots was the creation of the world's largest camera.

The Great Picture, as the plan to create the largest photograph ever was christened, was unveiled on July 12, 2006 inside (yes, that's right, actually inside) the world's biggest camera. However, the photographic equipment in question happened to be an old helicopter hangar on the El Toro Air Station, in Orange County, California, which was converted over a two-month period into a giant pinhole camera by Legacy Project photographers Jerry Burchfield, Mark Chamberlain, Jacques Garnier, Robert Johnson, Douglas McCulloh, and Clayton Spada.

The big image

Black paint, tape, foam gap filler, and 24,000ft² (7315m²) of black viscine material was used to make the 45ft (14m) high by 80ft (24.3m) long and 160ft (49m) wide "camera" completely lightproof, save for a 0.25in (6mm) pinhole mounted at 15ft (4.6m). The huge muslin-based photographic fabric inside was exposed for 35 minutes during the middle of a bright July day and captured a black and white image of the control tower and twin runways with the San Joaquin Hills in the background. The image itself was the equivalent size of a building three stories high by 11 stories across.

At the time of writing, the photograph was in storage awaiting a place big enough to display it, and it's unlikely the camera will ever be used for any more "snap shots," leading the team to joke that they also created the world's largest disposable camera too.

ABOVE: And this is what the world's largest camera produced, a gigantic image of the El Toro Air Station on a sunny day.

252

THE LARGEST MOTORIZED MOBILE SOFA

CASUAL LOFA— THE MOTORIZED SOFA

This has to be the ultimate vehicle for couch potatoes who love the comfort of their sofa far too much to spoil things by leaving it for a drive in an uncomfortable old "real" vehicle. The "Casual Lofa" is fully street legal and capable of 87mph (140km/h) and the functioning television on the table means that occupants won't miss their favorite program either. Although it's probably best not to watch while doing 70mph (110km/h).

The British Cummfy Banana Company has been behind some of the more bizarre vehicles of recent years. It specializes in creating weird and wacky creations for publicity, promotions, and special events. Among the mobile curiosities it has unleashed on the world are sport balls that can be driven, a four-posted bed propelled by Volkswagen Beetle power, and even a motorized toilet and bathtub, although using either while out during rush hour probably isn't advisable.

The fast seat

However, its most famous invention is the Casual Lofa, a rather nippy article of soft furnishing that has gone down in *The Guinness Book of Records* as the fastest piece of furniture around. Built in 1998, it uses components from a Rover Mini and Reliant Rialto, and is totally legal to drive on the road.

It takes a little bit of examination to work out where everything is on the Casual Lofa. The steering wheel is a pizza pan, the hand-operated brakes are a drinks can, and a chocolate bar operates the gears. The coffee table at the front is the front fender, the clock has a speedometer in it, and the TV, well actually, that is a real TV!

It is absolutely perfect if you get stuck in a big traffic jam and fancy a bit of a rest.

TOP: If you've got a very big house, this could be the ideal way to get around it!

SPECIFICATIONS

Country:	UK
Year built:	1998
Dimensions:	7ft (2.2m) long; 6ft (1.8m) wide
Weight:	1763.7lb (800kg)
Acceleration:	60mph (0–96.5 km/h) in 22 seconds
Power:	65hp (48.5kW) from a 1275cc engine
Capacity:	3
Cost:	N/A

INDEX

PICTURE CREDITS

6(a): Corbis (Keren Su), 6(b): Rex Features, 7(a): Liebherr, 7(b): US DOD/USAF, 7(c): NASA, 7(d): Corbis (Sandro Vannini), 8(a): NASA, 8(b): US DOD, 8(c): Al Jon Inc., 9(a): Gino Kloster, 9(b): Richard Dredge, 9(c): Royal Caribbean, 10/11: Liebherr, 12(a): Gomaco, 12(b): The Robbins Company, 13(a): Terex, 13(b): Gomaco, 13(c): Bucyrus International Inc., 14: MAN TAKRAF Fördertechnik GmbH, 15: Liebherr, 16(a): Amber Books (Mark Franklin), 16(b): Caterpillar, 17: Bell, 18: Ron Smith, 19: RHAM Equipment, 20: Caterpillar, 21-2: Komatsu, 23(a): Amber Books (Mark Franklin), 23(b): LeTourneau, 24-5: Caterpillar, 26(a): Bucyrus International Inc., 26(b): Marshall Cavendish, 27: Bucyrus International Inc./Indresco-Marion, 28: Bucyrus International Inc., 29(a): Amber Books (Mark Franklin), 29(b): Caterpillar, 30: Caterpillar, 31(a): Gomaco, 31(b): Amber Books (Mark Franklin), 32: Roadtec, 33: P&H Mining Equipment, 34: O&K, 35-6: Trencor/Astec Underground, 37: Caterpillar, 38: Herrenknecht, 39: Major Drilling Group International Inc, 40: Tower Cranes of America Inc., 41: Mammoet, 42/3: John Deere/ASM Public Relations Ltd., 44(a): Jensen Photo Collection, 44(b): Kern County Museum, 45(a): Michael Williams, 45(b): Jensen Photo Collection, 46: Keith Richardson, 47-8: Michael Williams, 49-50: John Deere/ASM Public Relations Ltd, 51: Claas Lexion, 52: Komatsu, 53: Spearhead, 54: Caterpillar, 55: John Deere/ASM Public Relations Ltd, 56: Kalmar Industries AB, 57: Trans-Gesco, 58: John Deere/ASM Public Relations Ltd, 59: Liebherr, 60: Michael Williams, 61: Al Jon Inc., 62/3: Richard Dredge, 64(a): Richard Dredge, 64(b): Giles Chapman: 64(c): Art-Tech/Aerospace, 65(a): Private Collection, 65(b): Corbis (Hulton-Deutsch Collection), 65(c): Cody Images, 66: Andy Graves/andrewgraves.biz/ssc.htm, 67(a): Corbis (Reuters), 67 (b): Richard Dredge, 68: Getty Images (Orlando/Stringer), 69(a): Giles Chapman, 69(b): Getty Images (Jeff Haynes) 70: Koenig, 71: Richard Dredge, 72(a): Giles Chapman, 72(b): Rex Features (Peter Brooker), 73: Rex Features (Robert Knight), 74: Rex Features, 75: Richard Dredge, 76: April Martinez, 77: Tim Page (Webshots), 78-9: Volvo, 80: UPPA/Photoshot, 81: Gregory Dunham, 82: Smokey/anacondalimo.com, 83(a): Corbis (Hulton-Deutsch Collection), 83(b): Giles Chapman, 84(a): Alamy, 84(b): Richard Field, 85: The Mack Trucks Historical Museum, 86: Bronto Skylift, 87: Klein Products Inc, 88: International Truck & Engine Corporation, 89(a), Getty Images, 89(b): International Truck & Engine Corporation, 90: Corbis (Neville Elder), 91: Richard Dredge, 92(a): Mack Trucks Australia Pty Ltd, 92(b): Corbis (Christine Osborne), 93: Milepost 92½, 94(a): Milepost 92½, 94(b): Brian Solomon, 95: Brian Solomon, 96: BHP Billiton Iron Ore, 97(a): BAE Systems, 97(b): US DOD/US Army, 98: Amtrak, 99: Bombardier, 100: Corbis (James Leynse), 101(a): BAE Systems, 101(b): Cody Images, 102: General Dynamics Land Systems, 103: Cody Images, 104: The Tank Museum, 105: Cody images, 106(a): Cody Images, 106(b): Art-Tech/Aerospace, 107-8: Cody Images, 109: Laboch Technologies, 110/1: Getty Images (David McNew), 112(a): Art-Tech/Aerospace, 112(b): Corbis (Philip Spruyt), 112(c): Cody Images, 113(a): Art-Tech/MARS, 113(b): Cody Images, 113(c): Freedom International Inc., 114: AKG Images, 115(a): Getty Images (Hulton Archive), 115(b): Art-Tech/Aerospace, 116: Delta Queen Steam Boat Company, 117(a): Corbis (Hulton-Deutsch Collection), 117(b): Getty Images (James Valentine), 118(a): Art-Tech/Aerospace, 118(b): Corbis (Hulton-Deutsch Collection), 119(a): Art-Tech/Aerospace, 119(b): Hagley Museum and Library, 120: Cody Images, 121(a): Getty Images (Roger Viollet), 121(b): Corbis (Swim Ink 2), 122: Topfoto, 123(a): Cody Images, 123(b): Art-Tech/Aerospace, 124-5: Cody Images, 126(a): Getty Images (Oleg Nikishin), 126(b): Getty Images (Laski Diffusion), 127: Cody Images, 128: US DOD/US Navy, 129: Irish Ferries, 130: First Olsen AS, 131(a), Bergesen Worldwide Gas ASA, 131(b), Art-Tech/Aerospace, 132: Maersk Line, 133(a): US DOD/US Navy, 133(b): Corbis (Reuters), 134: Allseas Group, 135: US DOD/US Navy, 136: Rex Features (Action Press), 137(a): Corbis (Layne Kennedy), 137(b): TransOcean, 138(a): Corbis (Bettmann), 138(b): Corbis (Bettmann), 138(c): Corbis (Dan Guravich), 139: Corbis (Dan Guravich), 140: picture-newsletter.com, 141: Thomas McConville (AP), 142: Getty Images (Mario Tama), 143: Getty Images (Frank Perry), 144: Royal Caribbean, 145: Yacht-Images.com (Benoit Donne), 146: Corbis (Reuters), 147: Yacht-Images.com, 148: Art-Tech/Aerospace, 149(a): Getty Images (Sam Shere), 149(b): Corbis (Bettmann), 150: Chevron, 151: Hibernia, 152: InCat, 153: Ship Building Research Centre of Japan, 154/5: Cody Images, 156(a): Cody Images, 156(b): Corbis, 156(c): Getty Images (Hulton Archive), 157: Philip Jarrett, 158(a): Rex Features (News (UK) Ltd), 158(b): Rex Features (Sipa Press), 159: Aerostar, 160(a): MARS, 160(b): Philip Jarrett, 161: ZT, 162: Getty Images, 163(a): Getty Images (Peter McBride), 163(b): Philip Jarrett, 164(both): Art-Tech/Aerospace, 165-7: Philip Jarrett, 168: Art-Tech/Aerospace, 169(a): Cody Images, 169(b): Art-Tech/Aerospace, 170(a): Philip Jarrett, 170(b): US DOD/USAF, 171-2: Art-Tech/Aerospace, 173(a): Cody Images, 173(b): Airbus, 174: Airbus, 175: US DOD/USAF, 176(a): Corbis (George Hall), 176(b): Getty Images (Sean Gallup), 177(a): Philip Jarrett, 177(b): Art-Tech/Aerospace, 178: Philip Jarrett, 179: US DOD/USAF, 180: NASA/Dryden Flight Research Center, 181: US DOD/USAF, 182: US DOD/USAF, 183: Philip Jarrett, 184: US DOD/USAF, 185(a): Philip Jarrett, 185(b): Art-Tech/Aerospace, 186(a): Art-Tech/Aerospace, 186(b): US DOD/USAF, 187: US DOD/USAF, 188(a): Art-Tech/Aerospace, 188(b): BAE Systems, 189: Philip Jarrett, 190: Getty Images (Pierre Verdy), 191(a): General Atomics and Aeronautical Systems, Inc., 191(b): US DOD/USAF, 192: Northrup Grumman, 193: US DOD/USAF, 194(a): Corbis (Peter Turnley), 194(b): Corbis (Stringer/epa), 195: US DOD, 196/7: Chandra/Harvard, 198(a): NASA, 198(b): Getty Images (Time & Life Pictures), 199(a): NASA, 199(b): Getty Images (Hulton Archive), 199(c): Novosti, 200(a) Corbis, 200(b): Amber Books, 201: Corbis (Roger Ressmeyer), 202: NASA, 203(a): Art-Tech/Aerospace, 203(b): NASA, 204(a): Dreamstime (Annedave), 204(b): Corbis (Roger Ressmeyer), 205: Dreamstime (Gregait), 206(a): NAIC, Arecibo Observatory – A Facility of the NSF (David Parker), 206(b): NAIC, Arecibo Observatory – A Facility of the NSF (Tony Acevedo), 207: iStockphoto, 208: CCLRC Rutherford Appleton Laboratory, 209: CalTech, 210: Liverpool John Moores University (Dr. Robert Smith), 211: Art-Tech/Aerospace, 212(a): NASA, 212(b): Chandra/Harvard, 213: Corbis, 214: NASA/JPL-CalTech, 215: Art-Tech/Aerospace, 216: Shin Satellite Plc., 217: ESA, 218-9: NASA, 220(a): Corbis (Jim Sugar), 220(b): Corbis (Gene Blevins), 221-2: NASA/JPL-CalTech, 223(a): McGill University (Canada Wide Photo), 223(b): McGill University, 223(c): McGill University (W.E.Alleyne), 224/5: Corbis (Angelo Hornak), 226(a): Kempton Great Engines (Peter Matthews), 226(b): Photoshot/World Pictures, 227(a): John MacNeill, 227(b-c): Bureau of Reclamation, 228: NASA Ames Research Center, 229: Yantai-Raffles Shipyard Limited, 230: General Electric Company, 231: Wärtsila Switzerland Ltd., 232: Sony, 233: SMIT, 234: NHMFL (Walther Thorner), 235: Art-Tech/Aerospace, 236: Bodyflight Ltd/bodyflight.co.uk, 237: REpower Systems AG, 238: Getty Images (Goh Chai Hin), 239: VDOT/Public Affairs (Tom Saunders), 240: Getty Images (Reg Speller), 241: CERN, 242: Duluth Seaway Authority, 243: Oregon Department of Transport (James Norman), 244: Corbis (John H. Clark), 245: coastergallery.com, 246: Corbis (Alex Steedman), 247(a): Corbis (Ben Wood), 247(b): Corbis (Dave Bartruff), 248(a): Martin Fenner, 248(b): Boeing, 249: Rex Features (Stuart Atkins), 250: Delorme, 251: WMATA (Larry Levine), 252(a): The Legacy Project (Robert Jackson), 252(b): The Legacy Project (Jacques Garnier), 253: Rex Features (Patrick Barth).
Cover Images: Front: Corbis (Lester Lefkorvitz); Back: US DOD/US Navy (left), Richard Dredge (middle), General Electric Company (right).